MY
SPEED
KING

MY SPEED KING

LIFE WITH DONALD CAMPBELL

TONIA BERN-CAMPBELL

FOREWORD BY SIR ANTHONY HOPKINS

SUTTON PUBLISHING

First published in 2002 by
Sutton Publishing · Phoenix Mill
Thrupp · Stroud · Gloucestershire · GL5 2BU

British Library Cataloguing in Publication Data
A Catalogue record for this book is available from the British Library.

ISBN 0 7509 2931 6

Typeset in 11/16 pt Photina.
Typesetting and origination by
Sutton Publishing Limited.
Printed and bound in England
by J.H. Haynes & Co. Ltd, Sparkford.

Donald Campbell – more than a hero

The amazing Mr Campbell.
A true Jonathan Livingstone.
An unpredictable giant.
A mischievous daredevil.
I loved him.
I hated him.
But I always admired him.
And his power lingers on . . .

Tonia Bern-Campbell

I dedicate this book to ANTOINE BEUN,
my wonderful father, who through his love and wisdom
showed me how to celebrate life instead of just living it.

He promised me that if I faced the world with a smile it
would eventually smile back at me. To this day his
promise has been kept.

CONTENTS

FOREWORD

by Sir Anthony Hopkins

I remember, as do many people in Britain, the photographs and television newsreels of the *Bluebird* rising out of Coniston Water that day when the life of Donald Campbell came to a tragic end.

I didn't know Campbell personally, but in early 1987 I played him in a BBC television docu-drama titled *Across the Lake*. Tony Maylam was the director and he had given me the script to read two months earlier. In the months before filming started, the BBC generously supplied me with videotapes, including interviews with and early footage of Sir Malcolm Campbell (Donald's father), who had set his own waterspeed record in the 1930s. The BBC further supplied me with a filmed documentary of Donald himself as well as several of his written biographies. I was especially fascinated by the filmed interviews with him that took place just a few months prior to his death. I was intrigued by the man's vulnerability, by his anger with the British tabloid press, and by his acidic and biting responses to some of their inane and meaningless questions. I so admired his belligerent honesty. He was a man possessed of supreme courage and tenacity who had overcome many obstacles in his lifetime. According to biographies, he had tried to emulate his stern and demanding father, and had succeeded in battling early health problems.

I was particularly impressed with one interview during which Donald was standing near his workshop in Coniston. A television journalist asked, in that peculiarly strangled, snide vocal trick of so many British television journalists, 'Are you ever afraid, Donald?' Donald turned with contempt and replied, 'Of course I'm afraid every time I get into the *Bluebird*. Courage is not being fearless. Courage is overcoming and smashing through fear.' And then, with his usual Donald Campbell grin, 'Still it's better than sitting on your damn backside watching television day in and day out, isn't it?' That's what I admired about Donald: his gall, his feisty courage, and his vulnerability and pain when facing the media's typical needling criticism.

David Benson, a journalist from *The Times* and a close friend of Campbell's, was present during our filming and during the morning of the tragedy. Before Campbell stepped into the *Bluebird*, Benson asked him what he'd had for breakfast and Campbell said quite cheerfully, 'Cornflakes,' adding, as a joke, 'and a slug of brandy. See you later old boy!' Then he closed the hatch on the *Bluebird* and went to meet his destiny. He reminded me of those young Battle of Britain pilots who took off in their Spitfires to fight the mighty German Luftwaffe – with dauntless unassailable courage.

When we started filming in Coniston in February of 1987 I hadn't realised that we would be filming in the same location at which Donald went down. Nor did I realise that I would be staying at the Sun Hotel where he spent most of his evenings talking to the locals. Being there was heady stuff. Campbell's spirit seemed to haunt the place and the whole town of Coniston.

Campbell was a great soul and hero of his time!

Anthony Hopkins
February 2002

PREFACE

O n 8 March 2001 the *Bluebird*, and sometime later Donald's remains, were raised from Coniston Water. This was done without consulting me first. Indeed, the diving work and production of a BBC TV documentary had begun months before, and without my knowledge. I will never be reconciled with these events. I wanted Donald, the man who was the love of my life, to remain alive in the eyes of his countrymen and women – a dashing daredevil surrounded by mystery. The only consolation about this sad affair is that maybe now he will be left in peace.

Some parts of this book were written during Donald's lifetime when I kept a diary. Less than a year after the fatal crash, while re-establishing my career in America, I decided to put some of my memories down on paper. I did this to help ease the pain but also because I did not want time to erase those sometimes flamboyant, sometimes sentimental conversations between us. Before his death I had already begun to record in my diary the things we said to each other. After the crash it was good therapy and today it is wonderful to be able to relive those conversations so clearly.

Eventually, as Donald used to say, I bounced back. My career took over, my finances went from non-existent to healthy and, although I still treasured my memories, they were no longer painful. Except, that is, for the nightmare of 4 January 1967 when Donald crashed his jet boat and his body could not be found. At that time, and even today, I sensed that a mysterious force had willed it to be that way and that Donald and his boat should be left in peace. They were for thirty-four years.

During those years it was rumoured that Donald had committed suicide. This was a ridiculous suggestion because he was excited about his new project – a pleasure inboard boat he called 'Jet-Star' – and plans for a new marina in England or Belgium with a Campbell museum. A successful record attempt would easily have financed this and he spoke of it with enormous enthusiasm. Suicide? No way!

Another rumour was that he had been seen alive and well in Rio de Janeiro. When the press called me with this nonsense I answered, 'Oh yes, he's probably staying with Elvis Presley'. Then there were the romantic affairs that the media claimed Donald enjoyed and which would have made him quite a superman in that department. It would make him hoot with laughter if he knew! As for me, I was supposed to have had liaisons with men I had never even met, which would have been quite a trick on my part.

Now, at last *I* can tell our story. When I was asked who should write the foreword for this book, my mind immediately went to Sir Anthony Hopkins. I wanted opinions and impressions of Donald from a man who, although they never met, had studied Donald's character in depth. Hopkins got to know Donald's personality when he portrayed him in the BBC's *Across the Lake*. He actually became Donald in that film; he understood that Donald was very much a man's man. Tony, as he calls himself, had a long conversation with me at the premier for *Across the Lake* and I was amazed at the similarity between the two men. I am very grateful that he immediately agreed to write the foreword for this book and his words prove that I was right to approach him. He knows Donald Campbell better than some of my husband's close friends did.

By allowing this book to be published I hope to set the record straight on behalf of Donald and myself. And in so doing I hope to bring him back to life – dashing and exciting, although at times infuriating. This is the true story of Donald and Tonia, soulmates who lived a volcanic life and a beautiful love affair.

IN LONDON'S
TRAFALGAR SQUARE

Thursday 23 February 1967. The weather in England should be cold, rainy or at least cloudy. But no, today it's bright and sunny. The only clouds are the clouds within me. Today I publicly admit that my man must be dead after all. I've agreed to this memorial service and yet I still refuse to call him dead. No one saw him die; he simply disappeared. And, like everything else he did, that too was spectacular. Today I kneel in this church, together with his daughter Gina, his relatives, business associates and the people who admired him. What was he to them? I wouldn't know. And to me? He was the sun, the moon, the stars, my whole world.

* * * *

I mustn't think of Donald, not now. I mustn't cry, not here. It's going to be murder when the music starts. His mother, his daughter, everyone here will sing his favourite hymn, but this time I won't sing. Will I ever sing again? God knows. Where is God now? Can he see my pain? *God, why don't you let me die too?* So many here in this church are in pain. So many tears in St Martin-in-the-Fields. Today, this beautiful, old, famous church is full of spring flowers, yellow and blue. I asked for those colours, the racing colours of the Campbells. But no chrysanthemums. He didn't like chrysanthemums. *Donald . . . can you see it all?*

Hey, you've stopped the traffic in Trafalgar Square! Hundreds of people are standing outside. They couldn't all get in. It's a full house, Donald, and they all love you. Even your first wife, Daphne, is here. I know you didn't like her much, but I also know you once loved her, and I like her for being here. I'm glad you got divorced from her. I wasn't around at the time, but you were free when I came along.

What's that? Someone just said my name. Dare I listen? I might cry. There it goes again. 'Tonia, the lady who was nicknamed "Fred" by the Bluebird team.' I didn't want to listen any more to Victor Mishcon, Donald's solicitor and friend, who was speaking. I had chosen him to give the eulogy. Funny to see him, a Jew, standing up there in the pulpit of a Christian church. I'm glad it's him. I wonder what it was he said about me? But I still mustn't listen. I mustn't feel sorry for myself. Victor didn't approve of me at first, but he learned to like me, I am sure of that. He also knew my love for Donald was beautiful. No one told him. A man like him sees through people.

He's coming down from the pulpit now and everyone's starting to sing. *Quick, I've got to think of something else. Vegetables? Yes, that's good! I'll eat some endives. I'll cook them myself. What other food can I think of?* Suddenly, Victor was by my side. As if in a dream, I heard him. His voice was soft. 'It's all over, Tonia. I'll lead you out of the church.' I managed a faint smile and started walking down the aisle towards the open portals. I looked around me but saw no one. I held my head high, with no trace of tears. I must have looked tired, but certainly not pathetic. I thought this walk would never end before finally I reached the doors. Vaguely I heard Victor introducing me to two gentlemen. They looked very dignified and traditional. The first represented the Duke of Edinburgh, the other the prime minister. I smiled at their sympathetic phrases and heard a strange voice, which was supposed to be mine, thanking them. It seemed as if somebody else was doing all of this. As I walked on, the cold winter air hit me and shook me out of my dream-like state.

Finally I reached the car, and just as I was about to climb in through the open door a strong hand touched my arm. I turned around to face four young men dressed in black leather jackets, holding crash helmets in their hands. Slightly embarrassed, but determined, the first one spoke.

'Mrs Campbell, we want you to know that, for us, he'll never die.' Tears broke loose now, but it didn't matter. It was great to feel them running down my cheeks. I took the young man's hand in both of mine.

'Thank you. What's your name?'

'George, George Amsley, Mrs Campbell.'

'Thank you, thank you, George. I hope Donald knows you loved him.' I turned away, got into the car, leaned back, and closed my eyes. By now the tears were falling freely down my cheeks. It felt so good to release them. The car's comfortable seats felt good, too, and leaning back I remembered how it all began.

Chapter 1

A MEETING WITH DESTINY

Memory isn't always the trusted family servant you expect it to be. You send it to fetch an hour long past and it returns to you a tangled mesh of days and weeks which you don't want at all. And yet somewhere in the fabric that hour is caught, and you say to yourself, 'Do I really want to remember all that?' But the little voice inside tells you that you will never forget it anyway.

The hour and the day I had reached for began on a clear and sparkling English morning in early December 1958. The week that preceded it had been glorious. For the moment Tonia Bern owned London! Well, a particular place in it called the Savoy. I graciously ceded Buckingham Palace to the Queen, but the Savoy was mine, right from the moment I made my entrance at a press reception to celebrate my gala debut the following week.

I barely remember who I was talking to, or what facet of the 'Chic Belgique' (as I was called) was on display, but I glanced across the room into a pair of piercing blue eyes. Their message drowned out every sound in the room. 'I want you.' Neither a command, nor a petition, but a simple statement of fact. I felt naked and desired. Nearby, I overheard a woman's voice saying, 'Isn't that Donald Campbell? I thought he was in Austria.' And a man responded, 'He's going next week. Would you like to meet him?' I never knew if she replied because Donald was walking towards me and we were the only two people who were really alive in that crowded room. Who introduced us? Does it matter? He was kissing my hand and smiling.

'Miss Bern, your smile lights up this entire room.' My smile indeed! The fire between us could have kindled another Great Fire of London, but fortunately I was whisked away for photos and interviews.

I was known to be a highly paid singer so perhaps it was inevitable that one of the reporters should ask me how much I was getting for my season at the Savoy. None the less, I was still taken aback and paused for reflection before speaking.

'I can't answer that question. You see, I've always felt that money is like sex – delicious to have but vulgar to discuss.' Everyone laughed including Donald, who was within earshot. I turned around and looked at him. He winked and gave a thumbs-up sign that I would get to know and love. As the crowd thinned he reappeared at my side and asked if I would care to dine with him. I didn't hesitate and said that I'd love to. He seemed surprised at how quickly I agreed. Did he expect me to play games? There was no time for that. From the first moment we met I sensed there would never be enough time and that we would never be completely alone. I was anxious to be with him and needed to know him – now.

Leaving the Savoy, we were on our way to Donald's car when we heard a man and woman arguing, her voice frightened, his abusive and drunk. We looked up the street to where a burly figure was man-handling a less-than-young lady of the night. Donald quickly ushered me into his car, and with a brief 'Excuse me' walked up to them. I could barely hear the conversation. Donald good-naturedly apologised to the woman for keeping her waiting and joked with the man for trying to queue-jump his 'booking' with the 'lady'. The drunk was totally flabbergasted by the stream of humour that Donald poured out and the woman looked as though she thought she was dealing with two complete lunatics. Nevertheless, Donald sent the man on his way without argument and then, taking the woman's arm, brought her towards the car whereupon he handed her a £20 note. She eyed him suspiciously.

'What's that for?' she snapped.

'To take a cab home and rest,' said Donald, smiling. 'Wouldn't that be a nicer way to spend this evening?' She looked up at him, tears welling in her eyes. 'Thank you, thank you.'

Donald hailed a passing cab. The woman suddenly noticed me and before climbing into her waiting taxi she turned back. 'You be good to him, d'you hear?' she instructed. 'You be very good to him!' And with that she disappeared inside the cab and was driven off into the London night. As Donald got into the car I casually enquired of him whether she was an old business acquaintance. 'Never saw her before in my life! But one night in my salad days I had a bit too much to drink, took a nasty fall, and my so-called friends left me to it. I woke up next morning in the room of a lady of the night. She'd found me, dragged me to her bed-sitter and let me sleep it off.'

'For which you paid her twenty pounds?' I asked.

'Not a bit of it. She wouldn't take a sou, cooked me breakfast, pressed my clothes and sent me away with the advice to watch out where and with whom I went out. I've never forgotten her kindness. She actually made me porridge. I guess I had "Scot" written all over me. Since then, I've tried to repay the kindness whenever I can. Girls like this don't have an easy time, but they all have their own reasons.'

It was my first glimpse of Donald's attitude to women. He had an appetite for sex, but would probably not sleep with a woman for whom he didn't feel something. And he would never take advantage, be she duchess or tart.

We drove to Rules, that wonderful old restaurant near Covent Garden, replete with medieval grandeur. It had been a favourite of Donald's famous father, Sir Malcolm Campbell, and I sensed it had a special aura for his son. He selected our dinner without consulting me. I was too intrigued to demur, and was to regret it almost immediately. The waiter brought us steak and kidney pudding and a vintage bottle of Châteauneuf-du-Pape. How could I tell him that I loathed and detested steak and kidney pudding? As for the wine . . . any red wine, however vintage, led me straight to indigestion. But I really didn't give a hoot at that moment. I nibbled at the food and pushed it from one side of my plate to the other. Donald finally caught on.

'You don't like my choice?'

I smiled at him. 'How can I eat anything when the conversation and the company are so interesting?' And it was true. I was also very much aware of the attention we had attracted. The management and the other patrons were eyeing us discreetly. I was used to being looked at as a performer and as a woman, but this was altogether different. Donald was a national hero. Where he went and with whom fascinated people, as I was to understand much later by conversations I overheard – 'Oh yes, I saw him once with Tonia. I wonder if she thinks he could get killed.' It seems that gambling with your life holds a morbid interest for even the best of people.

Watching him that evening as he laughed and joked with me before dropping into some intense story of his work was like watching a mystery. I knew almost nothing about his career except that he was the best. It was the man himself I was drawn to. I've always been a good listener. My dad always said that listening is the key to really getting to know someone. Donald was a wonderful raconteur when he chose to be, and this evening he certainly exercised this talent to the full. I remember startling the quiet dining room by laughing out loud at his stories. He grinned back at me, clearly enjoying every moment.

'You laugh from the bottom of your heart. It's almost like a song.'

I told him that I didn't often laugh like that.

'So beautiful, talented and successful. What happened to the laughter?' With that I don't know what possessed me to spill out my real feelings. I told him how my brother Daniel had died and that nothing, indeed no one, had ever really brought the laughter back.

'You really did love him, didn't you?' said Donald.

'More than life,' I answered. 'He was my life and when he left, he took my whole reason for being with him. Oh, there have been love affairs since, but the empathy, the warmth, the laughter . . .' I stopped suddenly, embarrassed by my own frankness and wondering if I'd already said too much. The Scots have a certain reserve. Had I overstepped the mark? I quickly put on a social smile and nonchalantly quipped, 'I didn't mean to pull "hearts and flowers" on you. I'm sorry. It's the red wine.' Those piercing blue eyes were looking unblinkingly into mine and I saw that he'd responded to the pain in my voice.

'Darling girl, we'll find the laughter again together, I promise you.' Reaching across the table he took my hand. 'I've never really believed in

friendship, pure friendship between a man and woman.' With Donald I felt
as if I'd found a friend to whom I could say anything and who would
never turn it to his own advantage. I could be myself and he would be
himself and it would be the best of both of us. All this within two hours
of meeting!

Dinner over, we got back into his car and he suggested a nightclub he
knew where the music and the lights were soft. I had a feeling it was as
familiar to him as Rules, and that a long procession of lovelies had
accompanied him there. *Not for Tonia*, I thought. I suggested a far more
intimate club where the lights were just as soft and the music too – my
apartment. He grinned and said, 'What a refreshing offer. I accept.'

'You do like brandy, don't you? I haven't any red wine.'

'Brandy it is!' he laughed. 'Now, you're not going to seduce me, are
you?' I smiled and with a feigned look of resignation calmly told him that
seduction was a worn-out word and that if either of us had to be seduced,
then something was missing. It was neither a yes nor a no. The drive
home was fast, very fast.

I put on some music, poured the brandy and we talked, but not so
feverishly. He mentioned his obsession with speed and where it might end,
and suddenly he was a different man. The poise diminished, a
vulnerability, almost boyish, came into his voice. He didn't do it for
himself, he confided, it wasn't an ego trip. It was for the prestige of his
country. But he doubted if anyone believed that. I looked at him and said,
'I do, I really do.'

'I know you do,' he answered, and taking my hand he led me towards
the bedroom. No questions. No games. I smiled and snuggled into his
arms like I belonged there.

The ritual of love that grew between us after our first meeting moved
from one high to another. Our bodies fitted together as if made for each
other and it seemed as if there had never been another man for me before,
or a woman for him. What is the magic fire of mating that consumes two
strangers, burning them together in one tremendous moment of ecstasy
that leaves them both satisfied, yet still craving more? Well, we had it.
When he left the following morning to fly to Austria for the boat show I
knew I had met my Waterloo.

A few days later on the morning that Donald was to return I was woken by a ringing telephone. Sleepily, I picked up the receiver hoping it would be Donald. 'Your wake-up call, Miss Bern, it's 10 o'clock.' Disappointed, I thanked the operator and went to draw back the curtains to greet another glorious day, something that I thought kind of rare in England. Smiling to myself, I made a pot of tea, grabbed the morning newspaper from the letterbox, and settled cosily in the bay window seat to read. There on the front page was a picture of Donald staring me in the face, his arm around a beautiful blonde. She looked adoringly at Donald while he was smiling at the camera, giving a thumbs-up sign with his free hand. Curiosity overcame my shock and I read the caption: 'Speed king Donald Campbell returning from a three-day visit to the Austria boat show with current girlfriend, model Dory Swan.'

Every word struck me like a blow. This was the first I had heard of an existing girlfriend. He had never mentioned her name during the time we had spent together. Since he left, I had received numerous phone calls from Austria. Two-dozen roses had been delivered, the card reading: 'To a most enchanting Vixen, with all my love. Fondly – Donald.' The roses, complete with card, were still on the coffee table. The newspaper in my hand practically burned my fingers. Was this his girlfriend or were the press just jumping to conclusions? Having lived among men most of my life experience told me not to be taken for a ride, but at the same time I was certain that the feelings we had shared could not have been faked. Maybe it had all happened too fast. My thoughts were interrupted by the ringing of the doorbell. Again it rang, this time persistently. I went to the door, opened it and looked right into those blue eyes.

'Hello, Vixen. Missed me?' Amused at my surprised expression, he continued, 'Unless you're hiding someone under the bed, you could kiss me.' He walked into the apartment. I closed the door leaning against it to steady myself. 'And now young lady,' he smiled, 'how about a kiss then?' Although every inch of me wanted to do so, I remained steadfastly by the door. Donald looked at me.

'How stunning you look. Do you know how important you've become to me? So much so that I feel like doing something I promised myself I would never do again. I'm going to ask you a crazy wonderful thing. Miss Tonia Bern, will you please make an honest man of me and be my wife?'

My voice just managed a feeble 'Do you mean it?'

Donald came over, took my hand in his and kissed me gently on the lips. Then looking deep into my eyes he said, 'Yes, dear girl, I mean it. We already belong to each other – you know that don't you?'

More sad than angry I asked, 'What about Miss Swan?'

For a split second he lost his composure, then noticing the paper, smiled. 'Ah, ah, I see. The press have been at it again.'

He walked to the window, took out a cigarette and lit it. 'Dory Swan has been living in my apartment as my social secretary for the last two years.'

'Do you sleep with her, Donald?'

'She has her own room here but not so in Austria. I'm a Scot remember, and separate hotel rooms are a plain extravagance!'

'It's not really the price of a room we are discussing here, are we, Donald?'

'No, it's not,' he answered. His voice became soft and serious. 'Sex with her was like a lovely liqueur after dinner served in the nicest possible way and much nicer than self-service. I like Dory and wanted to give her this last trip. You have the right to know what you're taking on, and I do want you to be my wife.' Part of me wanted to run to him, but what remained was confused and indignant. I told him I loved him but needed some time to find out if I was the kind of woman who could cope with this sort of infidelity.

'Donald,' I said finally, 'if you can cheat on me now at the height of our romance, you'll always do it. I need some time to think about this.'

'All right, my love,' he added. 'I need to go to the little boy's room. That'll give you all the time you need, won't it?' And winking at me he disappeared into the bathroom.

A few minutes later he returned, looking at me with that little boy charm I would get to know so well, and my resistance melted. I told him, determined now, that I was the woman who could love him just as he was. He came towards me and settled on the arm of my chair.

'And, my lovely Vixen, I can take you as you are, and that's a promise.'

I laughed and thought to myself, *Well, I'm not perfect either you know!* 'I can't cook, don't like kids, I live out of a suitcase and I'm very fickle.

Come to think of it, I'll make a rotten wife!' But my frank admission of human fallibility didn't put him off.

'I married two who claimed they would be good wives and that didn't work. I'd like to try a rotten one!' Then suddenly his mood changed. Very serious now, he added, 'I think, Tonia, we both have a strong wild streak hidden beneath the surface. Maybe that's why we fell in love so fast, and we are in love – deeply. Now let's learn to love each other as we are. I don't want you to change – ever – and promise you won't try to change me like the others did.' His hand was on my shoulder. I covered it with mine, then whispered, 'I promise.' And for the eight exciting years that followed we kept our promise to each other.

My three-week season at the Savoy flew by and I floated on cloud nine. The reviews had been great and I sang to a packed house at each show. Donald came almost every evening and always with several friends in tow. Although the gossip columns had been at work, we had still been able to keep our romance a secret, but when Donald told Victor Mishcon, his friend and confidant as well as legal adviser, of our plans, he told us we needed to make an announcement.

We first decided to get married on my return from New York in the spring and on the *Queen Mary*, but Donald soon changed his mind. He was worried he might lose me to America and wanted us to be married on Christmas Eve before I went to New York.

The day after closing night at the Savoy we travelled to Brighton where Donald had a meeting to attend. We booked into a hotel and gave a press conference the following morning to announce the news. And so the front page headlines appeared: 'Speed king to marry singer.' Of course, in a decision typical of the press, photographs of me in my most daring bikini appeared with the story – what else is new?

Chapter 2

MRS DONALD CAMPBELL

Our wedding ceremony was eventually held on 24 December 1958 at London's historic Caxton Hall in Westminster, a thirty-minute drive from my South Kensington apartment. I quickly learnt that Donald was invariably late. He was due to pick me up at 10.30. It was 10.45 when the doorbell rang and I'd been ready for hours. As I opened the door there he stood, handsome in a dark blue suit, cream silk shirt and grey satin tie, the whole ensemble set off by a red carnation. He looked at me for a moment and was silent. Then taking my chin in his hands he said, 'Woman, you look positively devastating.' He noticed the bluebirds in my hair and smiled, adding 'And lovable!'

'How do you feel, Donald?'

'Scared out of my mind, and as excited as a schoolboy, but now that I see you, proud and happy. Come on darling, we mustn't keep Caxton Hall waiting!'

I shouted nervously to my friend Wendy, who had come to help me, that I would see her later at the Savoy, picked up my gloves and mink stole, and walked out of number 5 Ashburn Place and into Donald Campbell's life.

The ceremony was very dignified and cool. I was not over-impressed by it; the only glowing moment was when Donald put the wedding ring on my finger. The look he gave me when he did so went right to my soul. He didn't believe in wedding rings for men so I had therefore given him an initialled signet ring. Suddenly it was all over and we were being congratulated.

Donald whispered to me, winking, 'Do you think, Mrs Campbell, that we should now depart?' I nodded, smiling. I was thrilled he was the first to call me by that name, and felt a great pride creeping over me.

Outside Caxton Hall it was sheer pandemonium. A big crowd had gathered and the eager press photographers were having a field day. Donald led me to the car but I sensed he wanted to get away quickly, so I hurried on and got into the waiting Rolls. As I slid into the far corner a photographer opened the door on the other side to get some close-up shots. I reached out to shut it at the same time as a police officer, who pulled the photographer away and slammed the door. In the process he caught one of my fingers. Realising at once what he'd done he quickly reopened the door. I'd made no sound but saw a thousand stars. I put my bouquet over my hand and managed a smile at the policeman to reassure him. We drove away.

'Well, darling, that's it. Went quite well, didn't it?' I nodded but couldn't yet speak. My hand was throbbing. Donald noticed something was wrong. 'What is it dear? You've gone very pale.' When I took my hand from behind the flowers my forefinger had swollen horribly and acquired a red-blue tinge. 'Dear God, Tonia, what happened?'

I explained in a few painful words. Donald put a protective hand around me, then called to the chauffeur to drive us to the London Clinic where we were received immediately by a doctor. After taking an x-ray he bandaged my ailing finger but not before putting some balm on it to kill the pain. He told me it would hurt later because the bone was bruised but, thankfully, not broken. On the way to the Savoy Donald asked me how it felt.

'Fine,' I smiled. 'I think the good Lord was just giving me a signal that this wasn't going to be a sleigh ride!' Donald's laughter was young and loud.

'Hey, Tonia, that's the understatement of the year! I'm murder and I know it. You were so brave not showing your pain.'

'It had nothing to do with bravery,' I answered. 'When I'm photographed I'm going to smile, even if it kills me, and after all it's only a "bobo" as my dad used to say when I got hurt.'

Donald took my hand, kissed the ugly finger and declared, 'Well, from now on you are my Bobo and it doesn't hurt a bit!'

The reception at the Savoy was a splendid affair and it finally ended at about four in the afternoon. Donald explained to me that he had to go into town to organise some Christmas presents for the Bluebird team and his family, so after the excitement of the day I retired alone to the suite he had booked for our honeymoon night. It had a fabulous view across the River Thames and the Christmas decorations strung out along the South Bank made the whole scene look like a fairy tale. I was completely exhausted and glad to be alone for a moment.

We had decided to stay in England for the holidays and would leave for the French Alps via Belgium for a belated honeymoon a week later. My father had been ill in bed for a few weeks suffering from a liver complaint and sadly had not been able to travel to London for our wedding. When I had telephoned to tell him of my marriage he had been most surprised and asked if I was marrying Jacques, to whom I was engaged at the time. When I told him that it wasn't Jacques and that I'd fallen in love with someone else, he was somewhat taken aback – even more so when I told him that we were getting married on Christmas Eve. He wanted to know who this new man in my life was.

'His name is Donald Campbell,' I told him.

'Donald Campbell? The record breaker?'

'That's right, Daddy.'

'What a shame. He's such a nice chap!'

'Daddy, you're terrible. Am I not a nice girl?'

'The nicest in the world, my darling, but I dread to think what kind of wife you'll make. Oh well, if he can control the high-speed *Bluebird*, he should be able to handle my high-speed daughter!'

I smiled, remembering this conversation with my father and once again felt his warmth. It didn't really matter what I did because my father's love was always there for me. I also smiled when I remembered the problem that Donald and I had had in deciding where to honeymoon. We wanted to go somewhere neither of us had ever been before. This was not easy as I had done film and TV work on most continents. Donald was a world traveller too, but neither of us had ever gone winter sporting because of our work and the danger of breaking something while skiing. So the decision was taken. We would go to a highly recommended new resort in the French Alps, Courchevel 1850. We would stay with my father in Knokke for two days, then drive through France to our skiing honeymoon. Knokke-le-Zoute on the Belgian coast close to the border with Holland was my home town. It was a lovely seaside resort filled with pastel-coloured villas fringing beautiful sandy beaches and it had an elegant gambling casino. Among the many properties my father owned was the highly successful five-star Hotel Le Carlton with its popular bar, nightclub and restaurant. It would be fun introducing Donald to it all.

For about a year I had been dating Jacques Nellens, the son of the casino owner. This fact had been known to the press and unfortunately they had been the first to break the news to him of my speedy marriage to Donald. Although Jacques had been shocked to learn of this he remained the perfect gentleman and had simply told reporters that I must be madly in love with Campbell because despite his (Jacques') younger age and greater wealth, I had chosen Donald. I was thinking of all this while relaxing on the beautiful king-sized bed in my very special black negligee. I looked around me at the flowers, the champagne, and luxuriated in the almost palpable aura of happiness. The view of London from the windows was so romantic that I didn't want to close the curtains. By now it was 6 o'clock and already dark. Hundreds of lights were flickering outside and I wondered if anyone out there was as happy as me. I did hope so.

A knock on the door brought me swiftly back to reality. I got up and opened it. Donald's voice came from behind a mountain of parcels. 'Sorry to disturb you, Vixen, but just couldn't manage to open the door.'

'Good heavens, Donald, have you bought presents for the whole world?'

'With the mood I'm in, frankly I felt just like doing that. Most of them are for you anyway.' We laughed and joked, unwrapping the presents and in the glow of this moment I made a promise to Donald.

'Every single night I'm going to thank whoever up there is responsible for what I'm feeling. I'm going to pray like I've never prayed before so that I may keep this and be worthy of it.' Donald looked at me, very seriously now. He kissed my cheek then walked to the window and with his back to me he spoke.

'Bobo, this is something very rare. We must treasure it. I only wish my father had known this kind of happiness.' He turned to face me, hands in his pockets. 'I can honestly say that for you, Tonia, I would give up record breaking, and what's more, I'm delighted and thrilled that someone finally means that much to me.' I realised the importance of this moment and could hardly believe what I had heard, but I will remember it until my last breath because at that second Donald Campbell offered me his life.

We returned to his home in Dolphin Square and the hustle-bustle of the Christmas holidays, but Donald was in a sad mood. This was the anniversary of his father's death and we all felt the gloom. On top of all this Maxie, his beloved dog (a labradoodle, as he called him, half-labrador, half-poodle), was suffering heart attacks on a daily basis. He was eleven years old and although he was quite sweet, I didn't truly enjoy his nightly presence in our bedroom. But the dog had become used to this routine and, knowing he could not last much longer, I made no comment. The worst was yet to come. On New Year's Eve Maxie became more ill and Donald decided we could not go away. We had to postpone our honeymoon. At first I was stunned, but slowly I gathered indignation. I could not, and would not, put a dog before my father's feelings, so I approached Donald at once.

'Do you realise how disappointed my father will be? They'll all be ready to receive us. The whole town has been alerted to your impending arrival.'

'That's too bad, Bobo. I'm not leaving Maxie and we're only postponing our trip.'

'I know, but what about all the arrangements?'

'Arrangements, my darling, are details of life and very unimportant.'

Now, quite fed up with all of this, I hit back. 'And so are dogs.' I knew at once I had said too much. The look in his eyes became icy cold, his voice hard.

'My dear girl, this dog has given me more warmth and companionship than any woman. I can hardly consider that a detail.'

We postponed our honeymoon, of course. What's more, I devoted myself to Maxie's care. I even tried to love him. But I never had the courage to tell my father the true reason for the change of plans.

I simply said that Donald had been unavoidably detained. Maxie died on 7 January.

Our honeymoon started as a complete fiasco after our fleeting visit to my father in Knokke. We drove to Geneva to stay at one of Donald's favourite places and arrived very late. We decided to eat dinner in our room so I asked Donald to choose from the menu and order while I took a bath. By the time I came out of the bathroom the food had arrived and the room was filled with the most disgusting, fishy odour.

'What in heaven's name is the stink?' I demanded.

'I ordered trout,' replied Donald defensively. 'This hotel is renowned for its fine fish dishes, you know, but I'm not so sure it should smell like this.' I uncovered the serving dish and nearly passed out. Donald had ordered *truite au bleu*, which is indeed a smelly way of preparing the fish, and I suspected at once what had happened.

'Did you order in French?' I asked.

'Yes, of course I did, but I certainly didn't order this bloody thing.' I didn't explain to Donald that the waiter, just like me, did not understand the kind of French which, like most Englishmen, Donald insisted on using. We eventually ended up in the downstairs restaurant where I had a heavenly dinner, but by then Donald was in a thunderous mood. To crown it all, the next day we had another disagreeable surprise in store.

The drive to Courchevel had started well, except for the fact that we had not seen any snow and had spent a fortune on ski attire. We were getting quite worried about this but then we began to notice some patches of white and suddenly there it was, more and more snow. Donald started to enjoy the drive. The roads became icy and difficult. He had a challenge and he was happy. Then it happened. We had passed Courchevel 1500, the last resort before the top of the mountain where we would find Courchevel 1850. There was a sharp corner which made the car slide dangerously. Donald's handling of the vehicle was very good but immediately after the corner we came to a halt, although the wheels continued to turn. The more he accelerated, the worse it became. Because we were on an incline Donald let the car roll back half a dozen times and tried again, but each time we reached that particular spot the infuriating performance was repeated. He tried every possible line of approach but the wheels simply refused to grip the ice. When the inhabitants of the village heard the awful racket and came out in droves to advise Donald, it made him even more furious.

'Bloody French morons,' he cursed. 'They keep telling me to stay in fourth gear when I get to the icy patch. How can I bloody well stay in fourth when the car is an automatic? At this slow speed it'll naturally be in second and there's fuck-all I can do about it!' We ended up phoning a garage for assistance and that's how the great British speed king made his entrance into Courchevel – fuming with anger, sitting behind the wheel of his Jaguar, being towed in by a snow truck.

We arrived at the Hotel Rondpoint-des-Pistes by eleven but when we were shown to our room we were confronted by two single beds. Donald asked me to complain at once at the reception desk. He wanted a double. I was told there was only one double bed in the entire hotel, but was advised not to take it if this was our first time skiing. Not understanding quite what they meant I insisted on the double. We were led down to a room with a view overlooking the ski-lift, but very little else. Donald remarked that the bed was now fine, but he didn't want to be woken by the screeching of the ski-lift. I went to deal with reception again, but I did become quite irritable at the thought that he was always anxious to speak French except when there was a complaint to be made. I admired the hotel owner, who by then had joined us. A handsome Frenchman, Monsieur Toussaint patiently ordered that the double bed be placed in the first room we had seen in place of the two singles. While this removal went on, Donald, now very charming, invited Monsieur Toussaint for a drink in the hotel's Discotheque St Nicolas.

The hotel's great attraction was its mountainside location. Even the cellar that contained the discotheque offered a fantastic Christmas view over the illuminated panorama of white mountains. In no time at all Donald was inviting everyone for drinks. It was at this point that we met Pierre Grunberg who was to be our ski instructor.

Pierre was the picture of a bronzed, healthy, strong sportsman. Intelligent and well educated, he had a degree in physiotherapy and spoke four languages fluently. After Donald's impossible moods I couldn't help having a good look at Pierre and for a very small moment I wished I'd met him during my single days. Donald caught the sparkle in my eyes. Realising this, I quickly changed my expression, but not soon enough. My man smiled as he bent over me and whispered, 'Bobo, you naughty girl! Still, I must admit you've got good taste!'

We finally retired to our bedroom, but the events of the night weren't over yet. Donald was now in a terrifically good mood and threw himself headlong on to our newly installed double bed, whereupon the two front legs collapsed with an almighty crash. For a moment we were dumbstruck, but then quickly dissolved into hysterical laughter. After all the drama of the day, we finally spent the night on the original single beds in the room facing the ski-lift, much to the amusement of the reception staff. The story was soon the joke of the hotel and we became known as the English honeymooners who had broken the hotel's one and only double bed.

A few days later we discovered why single beds were advised for those learning to ski: making love when covered in painful bruises was pretty well impossible. Our ski instructor told us that the French had not yet come up with a love-making position that took skiing injuries into account! The other customers certainly thought of Donald as madly passionate: they would never have believed the same man had brought the memoirs of General Montgomery to read on his honeymoon.

During our stay in Courchevel Donald had really taken to skiing and was very irritated when one morning a reporter came up to speak to him. He asked Donald if it were true that we had been towed in some days before and could we repeat the performance for him so he could take a picture for his paper. Needless to say Donald, furious at having missed half an hour on the piste, spoke to him in no uncertain terms and sent him on his way.

One night in the St Nicolas discotheque my patience with Donald was severely tested. He had started a hot flirtation with a very pretty Parisian girl, but it was getting so obvious that everyone in the club was embarrassed for my sake. Monsieur Toussaint was constantly trying to divert my attention so I would not see what was going on. I stayed for as long as I could bear, but eventually had to leave. Donald had been drinking heavily and when he approached the bar where I was sitting I said softly, 'Darling, you stay and have fun, but do you mind if I go and nurse my bruises? I'm a little tired.'

He looked at me and smiled. 'You don't mind if I stay?'

I kept smiling, drawing on the experience of my acting lessons. 'Darling, as long as you enjoy yourself, I'm happy too. We only live once so make the most of it.'

I kissed him on the cheek and to keep things light I did the same to Monsieur Toussaint. Then I walked away. I had hardly reached the top of the nightclub stairs when I heard footsteps behind me. Unseen hands suddenly grabbed me by the waist and then I heard Donald's voice.

'You silly little bitch, don't you know you're the only girl I want to go home with?' And this silly little bitch smiled. She had just won the first round.

At Courchevel we enjoyed three weeks of beginners' skiing and put up with lots of mood swings on both sides, but at least we got to know each other. On our journey home we decided to drive back through Belgium and visit my father properly this time. We called to tell him of our plan and went on our way. It was a fun drive but then everything was fun if Donald wanted it to be. He had loved Courchevel and Pierre Grunberg had been a great companion to us. Before leaving the resort we promised to return the following year, but of course this all depended on the next record attempt scheduled for the spring.

Donald never talked much while driving, so I jumped a little when, out of the blue, he said, 'You're not really jealous, are you Bobo?'

'Oh yes I am, but that's my problem, not yours.'

'Well, you're to be congratulated. I never noticed.'

'I know you didn't. Remember, I'm an actress.'

Donald became very serious and shook his head slightly. 'I'm a bastard, aren't I? Flirting on our honeymoon. You should hate me.'

'No, Donald, I don't. You'll always chase girls. I knew that when I found out you took Dory to Austria.'

'Is there anything you wouldn't accept?' he asked.

'Oh yes, I have my rules,' I replied. I thought for a while, then more to myself than to him I said, 'I have no respect for a man who makes passes at a friend's wife. It makes him a louse in my eyes. That's one rule. The other: if my man wants a change that's one thing, but I would never accept it if he brought the woman back to his own home.'

'Don't worry, Bobo, those rules are mine too. There must be loyalty among friends and one doesn't shit on one's own doorstep. You know something, I think we'll make it.'

I looked at him and smiled. 'Tell me, Donald, would you be jealous?'

With boyish charm he winked at me. 'Have I got any right to be? Anyway, Bobo, if I was you'd never know it – two can play the same game you know.'

Our first visit to Belgium had been a very rapid affair and incognito, but this time it had been properly announced and Donald was received like a king. Most people in Belgium speak fluent English. They loved and admired him, and nothing was too much trouble for my friends and family. This included my former boyfriend, Jacques Nellens, who graciously conceded that I had definitely landed the better man. It actually became slightly ridiculous because Donald and Jacques got along famously and were constantly out driving together in Jacques' Mercedes-Benz, leaving me at home, much to the amusement of my father. I also had to correct my stepmother Annie's admiring glances when she saw all my bruises. I had to explain to her that it wasn't my husband's passionate love-making that had caused them, but rather my novice efforts at skiing.

During our visit my father asked Donald how he was coping with me. In his beautiful, very British accent, Donald replied, 'Oh, quite well sir. I can take your daughter anywhere twice – the second time to apologise.'

Chapter 3

NEW YORK, HERE I COME!

Back in London Donald was greeted with the news that his favourite house in Surrey was up for sale. Roundwood Manor was in the leafy countryside four miles outside the charming town of Reigate. As soon as he heard the news I had to drop everything and off we went. Even before we reached the house I knew it would be our next home. It was March and the greenery and spring flowers were beginning to show as we drove through Reigate and on to what seemed like miles of narrow, winding country lanes. I began to get a little worried because I couldn't see any houses, only more and more trees.

'Donald, are you sure they build houses around here?'

'Sure, Bobo, that's the beauty of this place. It's in the middle of nowhere.'

He was so right. Eventually we turned off the road and into a neglected driveway. We passed the gardener's little cottage – judging by the sorry state of the grounds he'd retired years ago. Then all of a sudden there it was before us, a whacking great 'Stockbroker Tudor' manor house, desolate and forlorn. The estate agent who was waiting for us had known Donald from childhood. After the customary handshakes and proper introductions we were let in.

Donald was absolutely horrified at the way the house had been allowed to fall into neglect, not to mention the unkempt garden. As for me, well I was simply petrified of the place. Not only were our nearest neighbours several miles away, but everything about Roundwood was huge and charmless. Although the house had fourteen bedrooms, it had only two bathrooms and the kitchen looked as though it had been built for Henry VIII himself. The more I heard about the sorry state of the manor the more my misery grew, especially after hearing Donald's enthusiasm for all the renovation work that needed to be done. The principal reception room was vast, its cathedral-like ceiling consisting of a tracery of big wooden beams that had been painted black. These, Donald said, would have to be scraped back and bleached to their natural state. I felt nothing could change this loveless barn into a comfortable living room.

We went outside to take a look at the garden, all forty acres of it. This was in an even worse state than the manor. Our shoes sunk into the water-logged muddy grass and made the most disgusting belching noises when we tried to extricate them. The reason for this inundation of the garden, or so we were told, was that the antique drainage system had frozen and burst. Donald, hands on his hips, surveyed the dishevelled grounds.

'I saw this garden about ten years ago. It was like a park then and the house like a palace. It's a sin to have let it go like this, it's been terribly neglected. What do you think of the garden, Bobo?'

Increasingly I sensed that Donald loved this place, but with a last bit of hope that I might change his mind I said, 'Well, we could always grow rice in it!'

Donald threw his head back and laughed. Then he turned to the estate agent. 'With my old girl's sense of humour, you just can't win!' Little did he know I had not been joking.

We left Roundwood and drove through the lanes to a nearby country pub called The Bell, where Donald was received like a long-lost, beloved and admired friend. The discussion with the agent didn't take long. We had a few drinks and before leaving Donald made him an offer of £10,000 for the house. He was in a terrific mood during our drive back to London, making dozens of plans for Roundwood and the future. I had a season booked the following spring in New York's St Regis Hotel and the plan was that Donald would come with me while the Bluebird team worked on Roundwood, painting and cleaning and fitting new bathrooms. I smiled sadly. 'Couldn't they just build a new house while they're at it?' I said.

Donald gave me a quick look and with complete surprise asked, 'You do like the place, don't you, Bobo?'

I was amazed. He obviously didn't believe it possible that anyone could dislike Roundwood. 'I'm not a country girl, Donald, and I can't drive. It's just a little too desolate for me.'

'You'll get used to it, you'll see.'

Secretly, I hoped the vendor wouldn't accept Donald's offer; in fact, the purchase of Roundwood was the fastest property transaction ever. Once contracts had been exchanged Donald was like a boy with a new toy. He became madly busy choosing paint schemes and curtains, deciding which walls to knock through and which rooms to convert into bathrooms. Leo Villa and the team were to organise the work and although they didn't like this too much, apparently they'd done lots of building work in the past for Donald and Malcolm Campbell in between record attempts. Donald occasionally showed me some paint or fabric samples, but only once did he agree with my choice and that concerned our bedroom curtains. I had asked for a bespoke four-poster to be made by the firm doing the decorating. It was to be king-sized, made out of bleached wood and with an antique look to it. This was the sum total of my input to the décor at Roundwood, all the rest was his. I couldn't help wondering what it would look like when finished.

Fortunately, I started getting involved with preparations for my American show. Music and wardrobe were taking over and for a while I forgot the wretched home in which I would very soon have to live.

First impressions of America last a lifetime. To me, it was a childhood dream come true. We arrived three days before my debut at the St Regis and Donald decided to show me New York in all its glory. He found a true delight in my enthusiasm and took me around the many niteries, restaurants and jazz clubs with incredible gusto. For a man who did not like New York or nightlife he seemed very happy. We dined at the Maisonette, the nightclub at which I was booked to appear and which specialised in French entertainers. Later we visited the famous Blue Angel, the Persian Room, the Apartment and many others. The next day Mr Bultinck, the Belgian manager of the St Regis, came to greet us. He was a native of Flanders and was under the impression that I was French, but when I enlightened him he was delighted and we became instant friends.

Springtime in New York was different from anywhere I'd been before and it pleased me tremendously. The weather was much warmer than in England and I was able to walk down Fifth Avenue without coat or jacket. I felt like Alice in Wonderland. The skyscrapers were impressive, the stores beautiful and I loved every moment of the American dream. Donald had gone quite mad and invited all his New York friends for my opening night. The room was packed for the big event. I had a look at the audience before the show and was madly impressed. The table candles flickered as the waiters wafted past, the soft light giving an intimate glow to the room's deep red décor, and the champagne bottles stuck in their buckets near the tables gave the entire place a festive look. Then came the moment of truth.

Waiting backstage behind the orchestra's screens, I had never felt more nervous. I was shaking and wondered why: I had done many big shows before. I heard my name being announced, then the music introduction. I crossed my fingers and thought, *Here I go*. My walk-on was greeted with loud applause, probably led by my husband. I started to sing. At first I could hear the nervousness in my voice and for the first time in my career I was slightly off-key. But little by little I conquered my nerves and relaxed. Nevertheless, I was not enjoying it and when the place burst into applause at the end of my act I was truly amazed. Because of my surprise I completely forgot to thank the orchestra. I grabbed the mike and through the applause, my accent stronger than ever, I said, 'Ladies and gentlemen, please. You are so fantastic, I will sing an encore, but before I do so, I must thank all the men who have played with me.'

There was thunderous laughter, followed by the bandleader shouting behind me something that sounded like '*For* me, *for* me'. I didn't quite understand the commotion and all I could think of saying to him was, 'Later, darling, after the show', which again raised more laughter from the audience and a desperate gesture towards heaven from the bandleader. The show became a success. The next day I read in one of the reviews that part of my charm was the look of complete surprise at my success; I smiled. If the American public and critics liked my show last night, then they would probably go crazy if they saw me on top form. Something was wrong that night, this I knew. It left me wondering whether marriage had broken my enthusiasm for my work.

Although professionally successful, my first two weeks at the Maisonette were a tremendous strain. Donald wanted breakfast early in the morning and he invited a constant stream of guests for cocktails. It seemed as if I was performing all day long instead of for just one hour at night. And another worry: I was gaining weight. I felt very uncomfortable in my show clothes, yet I had no appetite to speak of. Finally, and to my great relief, Donald left for California to visit his friends Ray Ryan, the oil tycoon and owner of the El Mirado Hotel in Palm Springs, William Holden and his golfing companion Clark Gable. I settled down to my own kind of life.

My agent, Barron Polan, took me to some fun places and I was able to unwind. In the morning I slept late and had breakfast at midday, served in bed. In the afternoon I went window-shopping or took in a theatre or film matinee. Barron brought in several important bookers with possibilities for either film or television work. He received many such offers on my behalf, but every time he discussed them with me I became conscious of my lost freedom and my marriage ties. At last, it was Barron who made me face the truth.

'You know, Tonia, when I saw you in Paris I knew at once that you could be a great success in America. How do you feel about that?'

'I don't know, Barron. I'll have to discuss it with Donald.'

He sighed. 'You might as well turn it down right now.'

'Why do you say that?' Barron and I were sitting in a small French-style bistro called Tout Va Bien. He gently patted my hand.

'My dear, Donald is one of the most possessive men I have ever met. I was truly glad when he left. Of course it's charming to be a bride, but the audience don't want to see the bridegroom every night. What's more, it makes you very tense.'

He was right, of course. I had enjoyed the show much more since Donald had been gone. I felt free, not lonely at all. This admission frightened me. I hastened to cover up and asked Barron what he thought I should do next.

'I suggest you take a good look at your life, Tonia, and then choose whichever master you want.'

'What do you mean?'

'Tonia, you can't serve two masters. Some women can. You are the type that can only give herself to one thing. They call it passion. It'll have to be show business, or Donald.' I mumbled sadly and told him that I wanted both.

'It won't work,' answered Barron emphatically.

I left the bistro in a very depressed mood. Barron dropped me at my hotel. While getting ready for the show I remembered a conversation with Donald when he had asked whether I could ever give up showbiz. I had told him that it had been my dream from as far back as I could remember, but that the dream had somewhat lost its appeal since I had met him. Although I didn't think I could give it up, I could pick and choose a little more.

'Well,' Donald had answered, 'I suppose that'll have to do.'

That night, I prayed for a solution. I felt I was growing away from Donald and getting involved again with my work. I remember thinking just before falling asleep, *Please God, don't let me hurt him*. The next morning I awoke with a dreadful sickness. I ran to the bathroom and there was no doubt about the choice I would be forced to make. I was pregnant.

The thought of being pregnant depressed me enormously. I never wanted to get married and I never wanted kids. Suddenly the thought struck me that I should get rid of it. It was still early days so it would be easy. I remembered meeting an American model in Paris called Shereen Trudi who had told me to contact her if I was ever in New York. She was what could be described as an original 'good time girl'. I found her number in my address book and called her up. A tired voice answered. When I told her who I was, the weary voice suddenly perked up.

'Tonia Bern? From Paris?' she exclaimed, now wide awake.

We chatted for a while and arranged to meet for lunch. When she walked into the St Regis restaurant she looked like a million dollars. We hugged and laughed, remembering wild times in Gay Paree. Finally the conversation turned to my problem and the fact that I would have to give up my career. She was horrified at the thought.

'No, no, no, Tonia! You can't do this! No man is worth it!' Then in a hushed tone she continued. 'Ever thought of getting rid of it?'

I smiled and said. 'Yes, this morning, but I don't know anyone.'

She put her hand on my arm. 'I know a very reliable doctor and if you're under three months there's nothing to it. Do you have money?'

'Yes, I have plenty of that,' I answered. She told me to leave it to her; she would call me later. When she did, she said she would pick me up after my last show on Saturday and the abortion would be done early on Sunday morning. This would give me the rest of the day and part of Monday to recuperate, and all was settled. To my shame I have to admit that I felt much relieved and called Barron Polan to tell him to go ahead with the offers. He was surprised and asked me how this sudden change of heart had come about. Needing someone to confide in, I told him the truth. There was a long pause at the end of the phone, then he asked if I was sure I wanted to do this. I told him I was and would call him when it was all over.

That evening when I was getting ready for the show and putting on my make-up I looked in the mirror, but I didn't see my own reflection. Instead I saw the face of my father and it was sad. I closed my eyes and knew that what I was about to do was criminal. This child was made by my husband, a man I was supposed to love, a man who could have married practically anyone, but he chose me. However much I hated becoming a mother I had to go through with it. I called Shereen to tell her. After some protest she said loudly, 'Well, it's your funeral' and hung up. Then I called Barron and told him about my new decision and that I realised it would spell the end of my career. With great magnanimity he said, 'I cry for my star, but I applaud the woman.'

Donald returned from Palm Springs for my closing night. He looked terrific with the suntan he had acquired during daily rounds of golf with the fabulous Clark Gable. He regaled me with hundreds of stories about Palm Springs. In return, I told him about the wonderful offers of work I'd been receiving. His answer was kind but definite.

'Your next show is with me in Coniston. Then, after the record attempt, we can see again about your career.'

'But Donald, it doesn't go that way. People always book ahead, especially with film work, and that's what I've wanted all my life.'

Donald's voice took on the cold tone I had come to know so well. 'My darling, you seem to forget your life has changed. It's our life now.'

'You mean your life, don't you, Donald?'

'If you consider show business as important as a world speed record, then there's not much I can say.'

'You do want me to give it up, don't you?' I asked.

'Frankly, yes. Your career dominates you. You should try to control it. There's more to life than a sing-song. Anyway, those are my feelings – you must do what you want.'

On that note he left me to prepare myself for the show. There was no way out. I knew this would be my last show and I would have to cancel all future contracts. The realisation made me feel cornered and miserable. My early pregnancy didn't help matters either. I would not tell Donald until later – I kept hoping that it was a false alarm. It would take all my strength to give up my life's dream. I certainly didn't feel ready for motherhood as well. That night I closed the show as if my life depended upon it. I was determined to make this last performance a sparkling one.

Chapter 4

FAREWELL TO SHOWBIZ AND MY FIRST PREGNANCY

Donald had given me his attention for my season in New York, but as soon as we were on our homeward flight he made it quite obvious that my career was now over. He spent virtually the whole eight hours in the cockpit with the BOAC crew. On our arrival in London in the small hours of the morning he was met by a posse of sports reporters eager to have the latest news regarding his future water speed attempt. I stood slightly behind him, to no one's interest. I remembered how hectic my own arrivals as Tonia Bern had been in the past. I certainly didn't feel that the title of Mrs Campbell had improved things for me. Leo Villa and his number one, Maurice Parfitt, were waiting for us outside the arrivals building with Donald's Jaguar and Leo's TR. Leo would drive himself and Maurice back in his own car, Donald would take his Jaguar. He very rarely allowed anyone to drive him. We got into the car and headed back to Roundwood. I don't know whether it was tension, disappointment, or simply the winding Surrey roads, but I started to feel sick. I told Donald and got a very unsympathetic retort.

'Do you want to get out now?'

'If you don't mind, yes I do.'

'Can't you wait till we get home? We're nearly there, Tonia.'

I answered impatiently, 'I don't choose to be ill, Donald. I can't wait.' Suddenly I felt very angry and added, 'It's not my fault. I'm pregnant.'

I truly wanted to hurt him by making this announcement in such an abrupt manner. The car came to a screeching halt. Donald's face turned white. 'Are you serious?'

I had already opened the car door and couldn't answer him, the morning sickness having overtaken me. Donald became kindness itself. He helped me along and with his beautiful white handkerchief wiped my face. Feeling better, I looked at him. He smiled softly, put his arm around my shoulder and shepherded me back to the car. For the rest of the drive he was silent. When we reached Roundwood he helped me out of the car, then gave orders to the new house staff that Leo had taken on during our absence, a mature English couple called Sis and Reg.

'Please take Mrs Campbell upstairs and put her to bed. She's not feeling too well.' He turned to me. 'Come on, Bobo, off to beddy-byes.' I didn't argue, feeling happy again with the nice Donald.

While we were away, Roundwood had been thoroughly cleaned and completely redecorated. The newly fitted blue and beige wall-to-wall carpet made the place much more inviting and three new bathrooms had been installed. Stretching out in the big and comfortable four-poster bed I overheard Donald using the phone in my own personal den next to the bedroom.

'No, Matty, I'd rather you came and took a look at her. She's tired and I'm worried. You see, Tonia has a heart defect and before this pregnancy goes any further I want to make sure she's in no danger.'

I had absolutely no idea he knew about my heart condition. As soon as he came into our room I asked him how he'd found out. He sat on the bed and took my hand. 'Two people who love you probably as much as I do. First your father, then Jacques Nellens.'

'Goodness, I thought you two were discussing cars, and cars only.'

'In a way we were. A car is like a woman. If it has a weakness then one must look after it. It's no good winning the race but wrecking the car in the process. And you, my darling, are going to win the race.' Of course, this slick comparison was meant as a compliment.

He ordered a snack for himself in the bedroom. The breakfast served on the plane had been pretty insubstantial and was certainly not up to the standard of his favourite meal of the day, the full English breakfast.

'The smell of eggs and bacon won't worry you, will it Bobo?'

'Not at all,' I lied. 'Tell me, Donald, are you happy about this pregnancy?'

He stood up and walked towards the window, a habit he had when he didn't want to look me in the face. 'I can't answer that one yet.' Then glancing back over his shoulder he continued, 'I've found something I want to keep, and I'm not going to endanger it. Little Georgina is my offspring. Of course I would have liked a son too, but not at any cost. By the way darling, what are we going to do about that little minx of mine, Georgina?'

'You should change her school. She doesn't learn anything at the present one.'

'Frankly, I don't think she'll learn anything at any school. Takes after her old man!' he chuckled.

'Maybe we should have her home for a while, so I can get to know her better?'

'That's all you need, especially now. It's out of the question. I think I'll inquire about a new school.'

'You know, Donald, because of your two divorces everyone's inclined to feel sorry for Gina. The sooner she realises how much you love her, the better it will be for her.'

'It's true, I do love her. Poor kid doesn't know it though. Somehow I can't show it to her.'

'She worships you, Donald, but she's scared stiff at the same time.'

'History repeating itself, isn't it?' He was right. I'd witnessed the same worried look in Gina's face that I had seen in Donald's eyes as a small boy in the Campbell family films. I realised I would have to try to bring them closer together if we were to be a true family.

The first time I met Gina was about a week before we married. We had driven to her boarding school and when Donald introduced me she told him bluntly, 'I know her already. We've seen her on the telly. She sings.' Then looking up at me she smiled and I noticed how charmingly her nose wrinkled. She was 100 per cent tomboy and her looks left no doubt as to who her father was. In actual fact she was a small replica of Donald and he felt it most important that she should meet me before any more decisions were made. He wanted his 'little minx' to be part of all the new excitement in his life. She shook my hand firmly and said a polite 'How do you do?' Later on when Donald went to speak to the headmistress, Gina told me that if I sent her some sweets she'd tell her daddy that I was very nice. I laughed and answered that I would only send her sweets if she herself were very nice. To my surprise she giggled delightfully and said, 'I think I like you and I think you'll send me sweets anyway.' I did.

Matty Banks was a kind but elderly Australian doctor. He specialised in plastic surgery and Donald trusted him implicitly, even for pregnancies and heart defects. He arrived at lunchtime and Donald left us alone for what turned into a very relaxed consultation.

'Have you had a cardiac check-up recently?' Matty asked. I told him I hadn't. 'Well, my darling girl, this should be our first step. I'll arrange for you to see a cardiologist, and after that a gynaecologist. I'll call you tomorrow with the details.'

That week I had a complete medical check-up and the result was not bad at all. The heart was doing its job and an operation was not yet necessary; the pregnancy was normal and should in no way endanger my health. Donald was in heaven and I was in hell. The thought of a baby made me miserable. I was not allowed to move one inch without his help. His attention and care were endearing, sometimes even comical. Several times on the phone I heard him use the dreadful expression, 'Tonia is heavy with child, you know.' It conjured up an image of me a few months hence cradling my huge stomach in both hands. I asked him not to use that phrase, but his answer was that the pregnancy of a woman, his woman, was the most beautiful poetry in the world. To me it was an assassination of my freedom and anything but poetry. More like a lament.

Preparation for Coniston had started. It was to be the first time that I'd witnessed an attempt on the world water speed record. I promised myself I'd remain cool, calm and collected and not add to Donald's worries of the moment. He had constantly repeated to me that this was a man's adventure, but I was determined to show him that this woman could take it.

We left Roundwood in the early morning and headed north on the seven-hour drive to Coniston Water in the Lake District. Donald was silent and moody. I kept very quiet, fighting my pregnancy sickness and a desire to nod off. Donald had just traded his Jaguar for a new high-speed Porsche. Occasionally he mumbled, 'Grabs the corners beautifully, pulls up like a dream.' And in exactly the same tone, 'Feeling okay, Bobo?' His car and his woman.

It was beginning to rain as we approached the Lakes. 'It would bloody well rain, wouldn't it? Typical of the Campbell curse!' Donald said with a grin. 'Well, dear, how do you like it?'

I looked at the high and lonely hills, the narrow winding roads and the hundred different shades of green that covered the landscape. It was certainly a well-watered region. The rooftops glistened with the rain and everything seemed to take on a greyish tinge loaded with depression. It made me wonder what possessed people to come here for their holidays when it was so easy to get to Italy or France. Even Belgium was better than this. I didn't want Donald to see my feelings about the place so I simply commented, 'A little grey, isn't it?'

He smiled. 'The people are warm and sincere and Coniston Water has the right mileage and temperament.'

I didn't answer but looked at the houses spread out along the roads, feeling a growing and puzzling resentment.

'Well, Bobo, there she is, Coniston Water.' Indeed, there it was, right ahead of us, a five-and-a-quarter-mile expanse of grey water rippled by the rain. An immense icy feeling grabbed my heart. I wanted to run back to London, hear a nice tune played on an old piano, see my friends and be happy again. I could not tell Donald how I felt. I could not explain it to him, or to myself. I was afraid of this lake and I knew there and then that one day I would hate it. I looked away.

'I love you, Donald.'

His dry, warm hand reached for mine. 'I know, Bobo, and I'm grateful. I need your love very much.'

I leaned back and closed my eyes. *Please God*, I prayed, *keep us safe*.

Donald had two close friends that he truly adored. Peter Barker, fortyish, was a tall and very distinguished gentleman with a charming but pronounced stammer. His wife, Cherry, was a natural comedienne who could have been a model if it hadn't been for her rather well-fed appearance, about which she constantly joked. Bill Coley was the other close friend, also about forty, short and stocky, intelligent and determined. His wife, Betty, equally short, was one of the shrewdest women I have ever encountered. I was much relieved when Aunty Betty, as Donald called her, decided I could be her friend. I would have been petrified to have been on the wrong side of her. Peter was Donald's public relations and business manager. Along with Leo and the Bluebird team he had been in Coniston for a week before our arrival so that all was ready for a test run when the skipper arrived.

The first run was terrifying. I stood away from the crowds that thronged the lakeside, feeling that no one in Coniston was madly keen on the foreign singer whom Campbell had married. Still fighting my sickness, I was in no mood for diplomacy. Donald waved at me as he settled into the cockpit of *Bluebird*, carrying with him the small teddy bear mascot called Mr Whoppit given to him by Peter Barker the year before. Leo closed the cockpit canopy and suddenly I felt desperately alone. I turned round to look at Peter, but got no sympathy there. He too was scared and looked straight at *Bluebird*. The engine spooled up with a huge whistling noise and *Bluebird* edged slowly forward. She created the impression that some giant force was holding her back, and then she broke loose. High jets of water accompanied her progress, so many that we could barely see the boat herself. Like a fountain of water, *Bluebird* moved slowly forward and then it happened: her nose lifted and from a distance I heard the yells, 'She's going, she's going!' In a flash she was gone like a speeding bullet, leaving in her wake the terrific roar of her engine.

I was shaking like a leaf and tears were streaming down my face. In the nick of time two strong hands came to support me as my legs gave way. This time Peter didn't stammer.

'Come dear, let's both sit over there on that fallen tree.' He guided me over and I calmed down slowly.

'Don't tell him, Peter. Please don't tell him that I was scared.'

Peter gave me his handkerchief. 'Don't worry about it, Tonia.'

'I'll get used to it,' I promised. 'This is only the first time. You'll see. Next time I'll be great.'

'Yes dear, next time you'll be great, but you'll never get used to it. No one ever does.'

Bluebird was back in no time. Donald had reached 195mph which was nowhere near his previous record. By now I had recovered sufficiently to walk over to him. He grinned as soon as he saw me approaching.

'Hello old girl, sorry it was such a slow one!'

The onlookers laughed and one bystander shouted, 'Hey, Donald, if that's how you go when you're slow, nobody will ever catch you!'

'That's the idea, old boy,' Donald called back. 'Let's give the USA a run for it and keep Britain right in front!'

The people cheered, the press made notes and I prayed. Peter was right. I would learn to live with it because I had to. But I would never get used to it.

Five days later he broke the world water speed record at 260.35mph. Never before had it been done so smoothly and so fast. Donald called me his lucky mascot. The new record generated some fantastic press coverage and the news that Donald's new wife was expecting a baby gave the reporters even more to chew on. Everyone was happy and celebrating in Coniston that night and Donald hit the brandy bottle. Here was yet another side to this complicated man. He was the funniest and sweetest drunk I'd ever seen and insisted on me watching every joke he play-acted with 'Look, Bobo, look what I've done!' The next morning he would be his own calm self. He never complained about a hangover. I once asked him about this and the answer, of course, was sheer Donald logic: 'A man can complain about a lot of things, but he has no right to complain about things he has provoked out of weakness or lust.'

I couldn't resist replying. 'Watch it, Skipper, lust can provoke more than just a hangover! You may not feel so tolerant with a small dose of syphilis!'

Donald gave his loud laugh. 'Bobo, please! Anyway, don't worry because my women are strictly bidet types.'

That night something went wrong. I felt heavy and haemorrhaged slightly. Donald took this badly. He settled me into the car and leaving all the luggage behind for the secretary to organise, we drove straight back to London. I'd never seen him so intent and worried, not even before a record attempt.

'Donald, please relax. I assure you I'm fine. And if I miscarry it's not the end of the world. I'm young and we can start again.'

'Don't say that. I don't want to lose this boy.'

He seemed so intense about it that I remained quiet for the rest of the trip. I understood that losing this child would bring a lot of problems to our relationship. For the first time since I'd been pregnant I wanted to remain so, but three days later in the London Clinic I lost my baby. There was no pain, no drama. To my amazement Donald was kindness itself. My room was filled with birds of paradise and he visited me daily, but every time I mentioned how sorry I was he would change the subject, or curtly tell me, 'Please, Tonia, there's no use crying over spilt milk'.

'I'm not crying, Donald. I'm only hoping that one day I'll get pregnant again.'

'Not bloody likely, my girl. Just get better and try to be happy.'

I could not help wondering whether it would have been a boy.

Chapter 5

LOVE ISN'T ALWAYS EASY

My return from the clinic to Roundwood was deadly. Donald's secretary Marian Masters, who had come to work for Donald soon after we married, had now taken over the running of the house. At first she had liked me, but now seemed to resent my relationship with Donald. Sis and Reg had left and been replaced by a dreadful couple. Every time I dared to ask them for something they gave me a sideways glance which was anything but respectful. Then one day I heard them talking in the kitchen. I rarely wore shoes indoors and, padding noiselessly down the stairs, I overheard their conversation.

'She's a very good singer but hardly suited to this lifestyle. Poor Mr Campbell, I think he's starting to regret this marriage already.'

I was thunderstruck but had enough sense to steal back to my room quietly like a thief in the night. I sat down in my den, an unused bedroom that I had turned into my retreat, and mulled over what I'd just heard.

Surely, it could not be true? I had been married seven months. This was the beautiful month of July, with flowers everywhere but no child, no music, no happiness. Why? I would talk to Donald. We were both intelligent and if there was any truth in what I had heard, then I must go. I would not stay with a man who did not want me.

I'd noticed a change in Donald since my return from the hospital, but I'd not dreamed it could be this serious. He arrived home from what had apparently been a very successful meeting. He came upstairs to change into his casual clothes of blue sweater and light grey trousers and I joined him.

'Hello darling, had a good day?'

'Great! A lot was settled. How do you feel?' His tone was friendly, but casual. I answered carefully.

'Not too good. When you have some time I'd like to have a talk.'

He frowned and sighed. 'All right, let's have it. What's wrong now?' He sat down on the small sofa that faced the bed. I leaned against the wall.

'Point blank, Donald, I'm not adding very much to your life, am I?'

He smiled sadly. 'My dear, we made our bed, now we must lie in it.'

I felt angry. 'Oh no we don't, Donald. Marriage is not particularly my cup of tea. I'd rather be a good singer than a bad wife.' Of course it was the wrong thing to have said because his answer was hard and cold.

'Look here, Tonia, this time, good or bad, it's got to stick, whatever the price. Don't you see, woman. I can break all the records in the world, but I'll never get any respect from my people, or my country, if I can't hold down a marriage.'

'Well, you're the one who keeps doing it,' I interrupted, 'so maybe you're the one at fault.'

'Possibly, but you've never been married before and seem to know very little about it. Marriage is not a musical. It's understanding and hard work.'

'Fine, Donald. I agree. But don't you think you should do a little understanding yourself? I gave up all my dreams for you. I used to be very busy and respected. Now I'm not allowed to sing, not even at home. God forbid I should disturb the country quiet. I can't run the house because your secretary wouldn't like it, and every time I ask the staff for something it's like walking on broken eggshells in case I hurt their feelings. I don't know how to drive a car so I can't escape from this lonely place either. Why don't you try to understand that? Maybe you still blame me for my miscarriage?'

Donald took his pipe from the small bedside table and began the precise ritual of filling it. Slowly the words came out, every one of them like a whip.

'I understand only too well. Because you've given up your career, it has left such emptiness that you demand my constant attention in return. I don't think you could run this house. You've not even tried to turn it into a home. I don't blame you for losing the child – that was destiny. But I don't think you particularly wanted it. What you want is a constant romance because that's all you've ever known. You're bored with the countryside without even trying to discover it. All these things are your own problems, and you'd better learn to cope with them without making me pay for it by caging me.'

'Caging you?' I yelled. 'What about me?'

'You, my dear? You caught me and now you try to fry me.'

This seemed so unfair and I was close to tears. 'I don't know who did the catching. The whole thing happened because I truly believed you loved me.'

'Oh I did.' The reply was fast. 'I loved you more than I ever loved anyone in my life. You were the woman, blonde and healthy, whom I desperately wanted to bear me a son.' Dreamily he added, 'I really saw him clearly. Yes, Tonia, I loved you more than you'll ever know, but you managed to destroy that. As soon as you gave up your singing you changed. Maybe I was wrong to demand this from you, but I also believed you loved me more than anything else.' He stood up to light his pipe, then, walking towards the door and speaking more to himself than to me, he mumbled, 'Anyway, one surprise about this sad affair is that you still attract me. The whole thing puzzles me.' And with that he was gone.

I sat there, hardly daring to believe that all this had really been said. My head was empty and my eyes were burning. I remembered strange incidents from my past. I recalled what my first theatrical agent, Janique, had said when I married Donald: 'I cry for you, and for your work.' I truly did not know who was right, Donald or me. All I knew was that I'd never felt so sad in my whole life and was completely unable to come up with a remedy. I went for a walk in the garden where I met Leo Villa in the driveway. Leo was the engineer on the Bluebird team; we all called him Unc. He stopped abruptly and upon seeing my expression asked me what was up. It was no good trying to hide things from Unc.

'Donald and me, Unc. It seems I've messed it up.'

'Messed what up?'

'Our marriage. It's over. Seems the whole thing was a mistake.'

'Oh come on, Tonia, it can't be.'

'Unc, if I can't give Donald the right things, I might as well go. Maybe I'm not right for him, maybe I never was.'

'Well,' said Leo, looking angry, 'when Donald introduced you to me, I said to Joan [his wife], "Now that's a strong, fun and clever girl. She might just be right for the Skipper." But if this is all the fight you are prepared to put up, then I was mistaken.' And with that he walked away, limping slightly from an old injury and putting his trade mark cigarette back into his mouth. Leo had known Donald from the moment he was born, and maybe he was right. Maybe I should fight.

Someone will have to help me with this. There must be a way to win him back. If I still have power over him physically, then surely the other can come back too. Maybe I have handled it wrongly, but this is where I need advice. My long-time friend Vera Freedman came to mind. She might know, being a successful wife and mother, attractive and fun-loving. She might be the right one to advise me.

One week later I met Vera for tea in her home at Hendon, north London. Her house, like all the others in this suburban sprawl, didn't appeal to me, but right then architecture really mattered very little. All I wanted was someone intelligent and understanding to hear my story. She listened attentively and without interrupting. I told her everything and in the most intimate detail possible. When my tale came to an end, she got up.

'You were right to come. I can see exactly what's happened. But first, let me make some tea and get the trolley and then we'll talk. Oh, and I've been and got some Belgian pastries specially for you.'

Vera's tea was always true to the old English tradition. Smoked salmon sandwiches and enough goodies to last a whole week. She poured the tea.

'You think you've lost Donald, but rest assured you haven't. Sex is a good barometer in marriage, and that still seems to be way up, from what you've told me.' Vera passed the plate of beautifully cut sandwiches and then continued with her diagnosis. 'All you're to blame for is that by giving up your career you've given up your personality. You're trying too hard to be Mrs Donald Campbell! Just look at your clothes! Where are the tight slacks, the cute sweaters, and the short skirts? This brown silk suit you're wearing is charming and expensive, but neither the colour nor the cut goes with your personality.'

'Vera,' I interrupted, 'I live in Reigate, Surrey, not Beverly Hills! Can you honestly see me in leopard-skin tights running through an English village? The locals would have a fit and it would embarrass Donald as well.'

'That's just the point, Tonia. Donald fell head-over-heels in love with a free-spirited Tonia Bern. Let's face it, he's had two Mrs Campbells before and we know what happened to them. They lasted two years each.'

'Maybe I should go back to singing, then my own personality would return, wouldn't it?' I asked, seeking reassurance.

'Oh come on, Tonia, you don't need to be on stage to have a personality. Remember how you handled the other men in your life – sweet and loving, but always elusive? Jacques Nellens told me you never asked questions like "When will I see you?" or "When will you call?" He told me how he wondered about your feelings, even in bed. You may not want to hear this, but you can be very irritable when you don't get your own way. Patient you are not and since the realisation that your singing belongs to the past, even I can see the change in you. Donald has been more than tolerant during your pregnancy. Can you imagine how tough it must have been for him during the record attempt with your pregnancy on top of all his worries?'

'Hey, Vera, it wasn't just *my* fault that I got pregnant! I wished the beastly thing never happened.'

Suddenly we both laughed. My words had just given the proof of how right she was. 'All right,' I said, 'so I'm a bitch when I can't do my shows, but, Vera, I miss it terribly.'

Vera didn't give up. 'Start your own life, Tonia. Learn to drive. Buy your own car. You have your own money, you don't have to ask him favours. Come up to London once a week, even stay the night. You can stay here if you like, but don't tell him about it. Let him do some wondering. Don't offer to help with the house or the running of it, just lead your own life.'

'Do you think that will work?'

Vera smiled and poured another cup of tea. 'I jolly well know it will and you'll become nicer to live with.'

I felt relieved. 'Vera, you're wonderful. I was so down in the dumps but just spitting it all out makes me feel much better, and hopeful too.' I left her with the promise I would come and stay the night the following week.

The train journey back to Reigate seemed to go on for ever. It allowed me to think over Vera's advice. To become myself again in dress code and behaviour would be easy, but to be elusive would not. *I've always been too outspoken anyway; controlling this will be a good thing.* By the time the train arrived in Reigate I was actually looking forward to the offensive. A station taxi took me the rest of the way home and I arrived back in great spirits just in time for dinner. I went straight to my room, freshened up and slipped into a pair of my sexiest Italian slacks. There was a knock on the door and the voice of the maid called, 'Dinner is served.' I didn't answer. *To hell with her*, I thought. Ten minutes later I walked downstairs and into the dining room where Donald and Marian Masters had started dinner. I greeted them with a cheerful, 'Good evening, ladies and gentlemen.' Donald looked up from his soup and gave a rather surprised smile at my unconventional outfit.

'Sorry we started, dear, but the soup was getting cold.'

'That's okay, *chéri*, my fault.'

'Had a nice day in London?' Donald asked.

'Very pleasant, thank you. Did me good.'

'You look good.' And the small talk continued. He looked at me askance then asked casually, 'See anyone we know?'

I took a spoonful of soup before answering and without looking up. 'No one that would interest you. By the way, how old is Roundwood?'

Donald was taken by surprise. He thought for a while. 'I think it was built just after the last war, in 1950 or thereabouts. Isn't that so, Marian?'

In the voice I so disliked she replied, 'Yes, Skipper, that's what the documents say.'

The name 'skipper' was only used by the Bluebird team. She was a woman of around forty and had been working for Donald for eight months, but she was not a member of the team. I couldn't understand why Donald gave her so much slack. His voice interrupted my thoughts.

'Did someone ask you about Roundwood?'

'No, I was just curious. It seemed much older to me.'

Although I had believed Vera's advice, I didn't realise how right she had been. I remained casual for the rest of the meal. During coffee Donald asked me what I'd planned for this evening.

'Why do you ask?'

'I'm building a combined gramophone-tape recorder in the office. It will have speakers in every room of the house, including your den. If you like you can help me. Every wire has to have a small label on it. It's a big job you know.'

'I think that's very clever, I'd love to help.' He smiled and got up at once.

'Come on girls, let's go to the attack!'

Of course he had included his secretary in the invitation but she was put out because I had been asked too.

In a meek voice she said, 'If you'll excuse me, Skipper, I'd like to retire. You already have some help.'

'I can use you both,' said Donald.

'I'd rather not,' she replied. 'I have a slight headache.'

'I'm sorry, Marian, sweetie, better look after it then.'

When we were alone together in his office, I mentioned to Donald how nice it now looked with the new salmon pink curtains. He seemed surprised. 'But surely you've seen them before, they've been up for a week now.'

'I haven't been in here. I consider a man's study his personal territory.'

Donald frowned at me. 'Marian told me you were in here yesterday and looked at my diary.'

I was horrified. 'And you believed that?'

'Why would she lie about it?' Donald asked.

I remained calm, trying to bring some kindness into my voice. 'Maybe for the same reason she suddenly had a headache tonight.'

'Yes, that certainly came up quickly,' agreed Donald. 'Don't tell me she was mistaken.'

'I'm not telling you anything, but I do know that I have not been in your office, and I'm not the slightest bit interested in your diary. If I'd wanted to look at it I needn't creep in here to do it. Every night you leave your diary with your other pocket bits on the table in our room.' I laughed, 'I may be many things, but I'm not stupid!'

Donald's reply was very serious and for the first time in many weeks his voice was tender. 'Sorry, Bobo, I'm afraid I was the one who was stupid this time.'

'Come on, let's not talk about it any more,' I answered lightly. 'We've got something more constructive to do.'

Donald reacted with enthusiasm and started explaining every detail of his hi-fi construction. We worked together for three solid hours, holding wires, knotting them and sticking on labels. Every move was explained to me and I understood nothing. When we finished I sighed.

'Wow, that was something!'

'Did you understand it?' Donald asked.

I laughed. 'Don't get me wrong, darling, I listened very carefully, but my brain just doesn't take in such technicalities. After all these explanations, I know just as much as before. You'll have to accept me as the dumb blonde that I am.'

Donald messed up my hair.

'Dumb? You're about as dumb as a fox! You've proved that to me this evening, and I'm not talking about the wiring.'

I was amazed. He obviously had not missed a trick. Gazing at my watch I felt it was time to change the subject. 'Look, it's nearly midnight. Shall I make some Ovaltine?'

'That's a great idea, Poppet, it helps me to sleep.' It had been a great evening.

The next day I booked a course of driving lessons at the motor school in Reigate. I was to take twelve lessons and hoped that I would then be able to try for the test. When I told Donald he said it was a good idea but warned me not to be disappointed if I didn't pass first time. Apparently Marian had already failed twice. I thanked him for the warning but what I didn't say was that I now was more determined to pass than ever.

The days, and sometimes nights, that I spent in London worked like a charm. Donald always inquired about my time; I always gave friendly but evasive answers. One morning while dressing he announced that he had bought a small yacht, a 45-footer with diesel engine called the *Fuchimi*.

'Funny name, can't we change it?' I asked.

'Certainly not! A boatman never changes the name of a boat. It's bad luck. So, do you like boats?'

'I'm sure I'll like this one,' I lied, keeping secret the fact that just to look at a boat made me seasick.

'We'll fly to Monte Carlo next weekend and have a couple of days there. Would you like that? We could even ask Peter and Cherry along. They're always good fun.'

'Wonderful idea, Donald. Shall I ring them?'

'No, don't bother. I'm speaking to Peter this morning anyway.'

The next Friday we flew to Nice on the French Riviera. It used to be an elegant resort in the days when my parents took me there as a child. It had now become far too popular and overcrowded for my liking. We hired a car and drove along the winding coast road to Monte Carlo. The drive was beautiful and the scenery heavenly. When I mentioned this to Cherry she readily agreed and Donald declared there was nowhere like the French Riviera.

'The Italian Riviera is very lovely too,' I pointed out, knowing Italy well.

'I've never been there myself,' said Donald, 'but I'd love to go one day. Just look at these palm trees, the hills, the blue skies. It's a fact that France has everything. The snowy Alps in the Savoie, the elegance of Paris, wines and cheeses like nowhere else. It really is a great country and far too good for the French!' We laughed at this typically Donald remark.

Peter stammered, 'You don't seem to mind the girls over here either, Donald!'

'I don't mind doing a bit of window shopping,' he answered, 'but on the whole, I'm not very keen on French girls. Their heart is a bank account and sex to them is a packet of tricks.'

I kept well out of this conversation, realising that in the last two weeks I'd pulled more tricks than a cartload of monkeys. Arriving in Monte Carlo we headed straight to the harbour. *Fuchimi* was lovely, but from the moment we stepped aboard her Donald changed from a charming host into a fanatical captain. I was constantly corrected. The kitchen was the galley, the beds were the bunks, downstairs was below, and in no time at all I was scared to open my mouth. Donald wanted me to help as we left the harbour and shouted, 'Take the fenders in!' I had no idea what fenders were and must have looked rather stupid for he yelled again. 'They're not going to drop from the sky, you silly girl!'

Peter came to my rescue and took them in. 'Don't worry, Tonia, it's all part of the scene when a skipper gets on his craft.'

Cherry moved up next to me and gave me a wicked grin. 'I don't much go for this scene, do you?'

'Not only that, Cherry, but any minute now I'll dishonour the Campbell name by being violently seasick!'

Cherry was now all heart. 'Are you feeling ill, Poppet?'

'I'm always ill on boats.'

'Oh my God,' moaned Cherry, 'of all the men you must have met, why on earth did you pick on this one? He lives for boats!'

'I know,' I said, 'that's the curse of life. Isn't it strange, Cherry, I have nothing in common with him at all, but I promise you that by the end of the year I'll love boats and all the other things he lives for, too.'

'Including his girlfriends?' asked Cherry.

'No, I don't think I'll love them, but I'll learn to take them as a joke.'

She hugged me, then said seriously, 'Believe me, Tonia, that's all they are. We've known Donald through several romances, but this time it's for real. He's still struggling against it, but I think you'll make it.'

The week was great and I completely overcame my seasickness with the help of some pills. We went all the way to St Tropez where Donald bought me the smallest bikini and a cute black hat with a scarf attached on the inside so I could tie it to my head while learning to water ski. We had a wonderful time with *Fuchimi*. Of course there were Donald's boat tantrums to contend with, but Peter and Cherry coped.

We were taken to several famous restaurants up in the hills above the coast where, needless to say, my favourite turned out to be the most expensive. It was known by two different names, Chez Nestou and Le Vieux Moulin. Nestou, the owner, was an old and handsome rogue, full of fun. At every dinner he performed a ceremony of knighthood on chosen customers and the whole impressive affair was in costume. Donald was already a *Chevalier de l'ordre de Nestou*, having dined there often, but the big secret of the evening was a ceremony for Peter's benefit and it was tremendous fun.

During it all Cherry dug me in the ribs and whispered. 'Look at Peter and Donald. Honestly, two of a kind. One would think they're at bloody Buckingham Palace!'

On our honeymoon in Courchevel. Donald loved messing up my hair. My father did this too. I must have that kind of hair! *Victor Benetar*

Dinner at Courchevel with friends.

Donald adored my father at first sight.

Opposite: Our wedding day at Caxton Hall on Christmas Eve, 1958 – with Gina very much a part of it. *Popperfoto*

Courchevel, 1963. Donald was a good skier, but I was always better at the *après-ski* and the twist!

Nassau, Bahamas. I was not yet able to swim when Donald pulled me into the pool – I just hung on for dear life.

Florida, 1959. Donald clowning around with our host, Dick Pope.

It took me a long time to teach the sugar trick to Whoppit – then Donald took the credit!

Donald's office with the home-built desk he made in four days. *Getty Images*

Opposite: His master's voice. On their walks, Donald and Whoppit would have long conversations – all one sided, I'm afraid. *Getty Images*

To:
Papa & Annie
With love from
Donald
Dec. 1908.

This beautiful portrait of Donald stood on my father's desk until the day he died in 1978. *Yevonde Portrait Archive*

I looked and burst out laughing which didn't go down too well with either of them. The both gave me a dirty look. The evening was a huge success and the men did very well on the brandy, but it quickly degenerated into a demonstration of a bullfight. The fact that neither of them had ever seen a bullfight was no setback. Peter was the bull and on all fours, while Donald, with a red-and-white checked tablecloth, was the matador. The crowd was thoroughly amused by their antics, but not half as much as the boys themselves. When the bullfight was over, Peter dragged me on to the small bandstand and accompanied by the quartet I sang one of Donald's favourite songs, 'I Wish You Love', wondering slightly how he would take the fact that I was stealing the show. I needn't have worried. When I looked across at him it was plain he was the proudest man in the room. He noticed my look and blew me a kiss.

Chapter 6

THE SECRETARY

Within two days of our return to Roundwood, the blissful harmony of the French Riviera disappeared and the atmosphere became heavy. I kept well out of the way. Donald left for London where he stayed for a week. I was not informed of his whereabouts, but then there was no need to because I had a very good idea. I'd been told he was seeing a great deal of a certain girl he'd known before we married. On one of my visits to the Dorchester to meet Vera, I had actually seen them together at the bar. She was tall, with dark hair and buxom to say the least, but not at all pretty like Dory Swan. I'd been able to walk out unnoticed, although somewhat shakily, and met Vera in the lobby.

Most of my time was concentrated on driving lessons. On the morning of my first test Donald called me from London to wish me luck. It was hard not to ask where he was, but I thanked him for having remembered. He told me he'd be home later that day. My test was at 3 o'clock. The principal examiner took me around for forty minutes; when we finally came to a standstill he asked me some road safety questions and then apologised.

'Sorry, I had to take you around twice as long as anyone else, but being Donald Campbell's wife I don't want him to think we pass just anybody. I had to make sure. Now may I congratulate you, Mrs Campbell? You've passed perfectly!'

'You mean it?'

'Most definitely!'

I couldn't believe it. I wanted to fly home. I kissed the perplexed examiner and thanked him profusely, then ran into the driving school where my instructor was waiting. He too was happy, and understanding my haste he took me home. When I arrived, Donald's car was in the driveway. As I walked through the door, Marian greeted me with her usual coolness.

'Skipper is resting and asked not to be disturbed.'

'Thank you, Marian, I wouldn't dream of disturbing him.' I couldn't resist adding, 'By the way, how come a brilliant woman like you failed the test twice? There's really nothing to it.'

I left her standing there without waiting for an answer. I hurried straight to my den and there on the table was a huge bouquet of pink roses with a note that read: 'These are to congratulate or console you. Either way, Bobo, you're quite a girl, and I'm an old grumble box.'

Donald bought me my first car, a blue and white Triumph Herald with a specially personalised number plate, TBC 323. I felt very spoiled by my new toy. The next day I decided to go to London but Donald thought it was too much to drive all that distance so soon. We discussed it over breakfast.

'You don't really know your way around.'

'But things are signposted, aren't they?'

'Yes they are, and going to London is easy. But coming back to Reigate from London, well that's the difficult part.'

'Couldn't you give me a list of directions,' I asked. 'I'm dying to show my new car to my friends.'

Donald frowned for a split second. 'Which friends are you going to visit?'

'Oh, you don't really know them and anyway,' I added maliciously, 'if you don't ask questions, I shan't either.' Donald agreed and I took this opportunity to explain.

'You know, Donald, in an emergency I don't think your secretary would tell me how I could contact you.'

'Yes, that is true,' Donald replied. 'I know you two aren't exactly bosom pals.'

'She does dislike me. That's a fact. And my passing the test hasn't improved things, either.'

'Why do you dislike each other?' asked Donald.

I looked at him and softly lied. 'I don't dislike her at all. Actually, I feel sorry for her and wish I could help. It's pathetic when a woman has only one thing in life, her work. She used to like me, but ever since we got back from America she resents me. I used to live for my work too, but I always had some play on the side.'

He laughed, looking very attractive. 'I'm sure of that! Tell me, Bobo, are you still playing?'

'You're asking questions again.'

'Sorry old girl. You're quite right. What's good for the goose, etc.'

'That's right,' I said smiling, but my heart was heavy. I realised he might have been told that my visits to London were all play. I still wondered how much more had been said and how long I would have to keep up this silly game.

'Well, how about drawing a map for me?' I asked.

'Okay, Tonia, but do me a favour. Ring me from London when you're ready to return, otherwise I'll be worried.'

Had he forgotten the numerous nights I'd waited up and worried, not daring to ask questions when he finally got home? Maybe today I should make him feel the same way.

The drive to London was great. I met Vera for lunch at the Caprice, one of London's most elegant restaurants and also my favourite. Having been a customer for many years I knew all the staff in the place. We had a drink in the small bar while I gave Vera the latest results in the romantic war of wills and explained my plan of attack for the evening.

'I'll call Donald when I leave London, but on the way home I'll stop in Putney. Wendy lives there now. She's bought a flat. I haven't seen her for ages. When I called her she was delighted. I'll have dinner there.'

'Don't you think it's a little bit cruel to get home late from your first car outing?'

'Vera, do you know how often I've cried myself to sleep or wondered whether he'd had an accident? Have you ever seen him drive? He's brilliant all right, but it always looks as if he wants to break a record.'

'Well,' sighed Vera, 'if you go through with your plans then you'd better prepare yourself for an explosion.'

Later on I called Donald from Wendy's. It was around 6.30 and I told him not to wait for dinner. The traffic was heavy, I said, and it might take me a couple of hours to get home. He was very sweet and asked how the car was behaving. Dreamy, I said. We exchanged some more small talk and then hung up. Wendy was clutching a bottle of champagne.

'It's been waiting for you,' she said excitedly. 'You open it, you're better at it than me.'

It was great to be with her again and hundreds of memories flooded back of our days in Chelsea before I went to Paris. I didn't much care for her new apartment. It was more of a showpiece than a home, and much too far out of town. But soon the conversation took over. Wendy told me about her latest adventure and it brought a slight feeling of nostalgia for my days as a single girl. I finally left around midnight. The roads were empty now and I found my way home very easily, arriving at Roundwood one hour later. The driveway was still lit up and to my amazement so was the whole house. As soon as I got out of the car and slammed the door, Donald came running out of the house and grabbed me by the shoulders.

'Bobo, are you all right?' he asked anxiously.

'Yes, of course dear, I'm fine. Sorry I'm a bit late.'

Donald pressed me against his chest so hard that it hurt. There was no anger in him, simply a deep relief. 'Don't do this again, Vixen. I can't stand it. I was already calling the hospitals, and the police, wondering how I'd find you. I was hating the fact that I'd given you a car.'

This time I did feel sorry. I hated the trick I'd played, but I knew I'd achieved my aim. Later, lying quietly in Donald's arms, this was confirmed.

'Bobo, don't ever let anything happen to you. I don't care what mischief you get up to, but keep yourself safe. Remember, darling, you're my one chance, my last one.'

'In future I'll always phone you if I'm going to be late. I promise.'

'Yes,' he answered. 'Do that and so will I. Don't let's ever have those horrible uncertain moments again. While I was waiting for you, I realised how often you must have felt the same way.'

I didn't answer, but in the darkness of the room I smiled to myself. The battle was not over yet. The enemy probably had more secret weapons to use.

The feeling between Donald and me was now warm and pleasant. Each time he stayed in London he would call me, sometimes even tell me the number of his suite at the usual hotel, the Dorchester. I had gained his confidence at least. After one of his escapades to London he did a most unusual thing. As soon as he arrived home, he came to have his afternoon tea with me in my den. He seemed worried and slightly embarrassed.

'I think I shall go away some time in September for a couple of weeks. I want to try to write a book.'

I was amazed. We were only at the beginning of August and this seemed a bit premature. 'You should try to write your own story. It might be much better than all those ghosted books about you and your father,' I said.

'So you agree, Bobo?' He sighed with relief. 'I think I'll go away somewhere quiet.' I nodded, letting him continue. 'I feel I must be alone, with just a secretary and no distractions. I thought somewhere in the South of France maybe. Perhaps even on *Fuchimi*.'

I needed all my self-control because I understood the set-up fully. The secretary would, of course, be some girlfriend; and the book, the excuse. Why couldn't he just admit it and tell me he wanted to roam for a while?

'When are you thinking of going?' I asked casually.

'Oh, around mid-September. You do understand why I should go on my own, don't you Bobo?'

This was where I had to be cautious and not sound in any way suspicious. 'It's good for both of us to be on our own sometimes. After all, Donald, he who's never away will never be missed. Right?'

'Right,' he answered with relief. 'Hey, Bobo, let's go out to some restaurant one of these days.'

'All right,' I said without enthusiasm. I was tired of playing games now and wanted him to leave my den. I had no desire at all for a dutiful outing – and that was all it would be. He didn't seem to want to leave and kept near me all evening. The next morning I drove off to London, having told the staff I would not be home for dinner. I went to Vera's to pour my heart out. Once again she came up with a great solution.

'Look, Tonia, I'm leaving for my holidays next Saturday. That gives you five days to be ready. Why don't you come? We'll be back by the end of August so it won't interfere with Donald's trip.'

'That's not a bad thought. Donald would be home so he could keep an eye on things. I'll tell him as soon as I get back.'

'No,' interrupted Vera, 'don't tell him yet. Next Thursday will be time enough. And don't tell him who you're going with. Just say you're going to Italy with friends. I'll do all the bookings and if the hotel is full up, you can always share my room. I've got a double one anyway. You can drive here on Saturday morning, leave your car in our garage and Donald in the dark!'

I smiled at Vera. 'You know something, I never thought that the most expensive thing in my life would be my marriage. I hope these tricks work, otherwise I'll soon be broke!'

'My girl, by the time that happens you'll have all you want from Donald.'

That night I drove home in great spirits. Italy would be fun. I spoke the language fluently and loved the people. I knew I could easily forget about everything there. I deserved a rest from all this tension and hoop-la-la.

The opportunity to tell Donald presented itself beautifully on Thursday morning. I was sitting on the balcony outside my den reading *Variety*, the international showbiz paper, when Donald came up with a cup of coffee. He'd made a habit of drinking his tea and coffee with me, which I liked. Sitting down on the white garden chair he looked worried again and I told him so.

'I've just paid all the monthly bills. Tell me, is £89 reasonable for a butcher's monthly account?'

'Eighty-nine pounds?' I exclaimed. 'What on earth for? We eat fish twice a week, you're out two or three nights and I eat salad. That's ridiculous.'

Donald readily agreed. 'Do you think you could take over the running of Roundwood?'

I was thrilled, but answered very coolly. 'I'd be delighted, but only if I had my own staff and not that sloppy couple in the kitchen. This house is filthy and every time I say so I get a rude remark from them.'

'Yes, that's true. The house isn't clean. The only thing they keep spotless is our bedroom and your den.'

I laughed out loud, stood up and brought out of my cupboard a huge cardboard box full of cleaning stuff. 'Here darling,' I said, 'this is my do-it-yourself kit. I clean our room and the den with it daily.'

Now it was Donald's turn to laugh. Apparently he'd asked the staff why they couldn't keep everything as clean as those two rooms to which they'd answered awkwardly that there wasn't the time. 'Okay, Bobo, what do you suggest?'

'Keep things as they are for another two weeks. I'll call my dad in Belgium today and ask him to put an ad in the catering trade newspaper over there. He's done this all his life for the hotels and knows the ropes.'

Donald wondered, 'Yes, but will they speak English?'

I laughed. 'Nearly everybody in Belgium does, some of them badly, but they'll pick it up soon enough. I suggest that in September I take over the running of the house.'

'Why so late?' asked Donald.

'I was going to tell you later, but I'm leaving on Saturday for about ten days.'

Donald was perplexed. 'Leaving? Why? Where? With whom?' His voice soared to a crescendo.

'You know, Donald, for a man who doesn't like questions being asked, you're not doing too well. Well now. Why? Because I think it's necessary. Where? To Italy, near Venice. With whom? Friends who've asked me. In two weeks time I'll come home via Belgium to see what kind of staff daddy has lined up. Then while you're away in September I can train them and organise things. By the time you come back you won't recognise the place.'

'Sounds okay,' mumbled Donald. 'I still fail to understand why you have to go to Italy.'

This time I refused to play games any longer and with some anger in my voice I answered him. 'I go, Donald, for the same reason you're going to France in September.'

'That's to write my book,' he exclaimed defensively. He sounded so honest that I realised he truly believed this. Whichever girlfriend had been behind the idea was a clever woman. She had obviously used the excuse of the book to convince him of the trip. It frightened me to know that the woman behind all this was not just a good-time girl, but a clever one as well.

I looked at Donald, and with a note of seriousness in my voice, said, 'I know you believe this, Donald. Just make sure that the secretary who's going with you believes it too.'

'Whatever do you mean?' he asked indignantly.

'I can't explain it now,' I smiled. 'You'll find out sooner or later.'

'Huh, you're speaking in riddles. Anyway, if you must go I won't keep you.' Bad-tempered now, he got up. At the door he turned around and looked straight at me before leaving the den.

'Maybe you're right. Who knows.'

On the morning of my departure Donald was like a lion in a cage. He kept on coming into the room while I was packing then, out of the blue, he asked, 'So that's all this marriage means to you.'

I was baffled. 'What do you mean?'

'Come on, Tonia, no one goes to Italy alone.'

'That's right, I'm not going alone. And whatever this marriage means to me has been your doing. It's my first one, remember? You've made it quite clear to me that you want complete freedom and independence. I've accepted this, but only because it gives me the same rights, which is not such a bad deal after all.'

'I've never heard it called a deal before, but then I hear Belgian girls are that way, businesslike.'

I felt impatient. I stopped packing and sat down on the bed. 'Look Donald, I don't think I've been too demanding. I did give up my work, but I failed to give you a son. This isn't the end of the world, I'm still young and I can repair the part I failed at. I pay for my own entertainment, travelling and clothes, which is more than any of your girlfriends do. I also please you in bed and that's quite apparent. And I'm willing to run your house better and more cheaply than a secretary or housekeeper who's paid for it. What else do you want from me?'

The answer came fast and furious. 'Love. Ever heard of it?'

'You had that too, Donald, but you just threw it back at me. Now you can't blame me for protecting myself.' He turned his back on me and gazed out of the window. Maybe he, too, was remembering the other conversation we had in this very room not so long ago regarding our marriage. How different things were now and how right my behaviour had proved to be. I softened. 'Don't be cross darling, they say the first year is always the worst.'

'So I've heard,' he said, much calmer now. 'All right dear, tell Leo what time you want to be taken to the airport.'

Slightly embarrassed, I said, 'That's okay. It's all taken care of.'

'Is that so? Can't even provide transport for my wife now, can I?'

'You've done that already, Donald. You've given me a car.'

'I see,' he murmured. Then coming over to me, he put both his hands on my shoulders. 'Please wire me, won't you? I want to know you've arrived safely. For what it's worth, I do worry about you.'

Later that day when I was loading my car with the luggage he came to the door looking sad and lonely. I went to kiss him goodbye. He held my head close to his and whispered, 'I'll miss you, Vixen.' I smiled at him and managed to say a very quiet 'Ciao', then got into my car and drove away. I cried all the way to London. The sight of Donald in that doorway had once again reminded me of the family movie I had seen of Malcolm Campbell arriving back on the *Queen Mary* and the sad small boy welcoming him and being ignored. I longed for the day when I would be allowed to show him the kindness he obviously needed.

Italy was wonderful. We were staying in a small seaside resort near Venice called Lido di Jesolo. To my surprise a great many people remembered me from my show days in Italy where I had won the *Passerella d'Ore* for my performance in a musical. In no time at all we had a terrific gang around us. One handsome Italian, Livio, kept me well occupied. Longing terribly for Donald I didn't succumb to his charm, but Livio tried to tell me that a good second best was not so bad and, being typically Italian, he was of course passionately in love with me. I knew he would forget me within a week of my departure, but while I was there he would swear I was the one and only, and be insanely jealous if anyone else dared even to look. We went water-skiing and at night ventured into Venice in a small boat that belonged to him. I smiled to myself, happy at having conquered my seasickness. It was quicker to go to Venice by sea than by road, and much more fun. And in any case, a car is quite useless in the city of canals. Sometimes on our return trip we would stop the boat and let it float away into the ocean. Livio would play his guitar and I would sing. To my shame I must admit that in those moments thoughts of Donald hardly entered my mind, and the intimacy did not make me feel guilty. *Au contraire*, it released the tension of recent months. To me it was not love-making, just a richly deserved therapy – and Livio was a master therapist.

The two weeks were romantic and exciting, but those feelings also passed. I flew to Belgium two days later than originally scheduled, after a heartbreaking goodbye from Livio and a passionate lie that we would meet again soon. My father had received many replies to the notice he'd put in the Flemish paper. He'd interviewed most of them and short-listed three couples for me to meet. I arrived on a Sunday and it was so nice to be in Knokke again. Jacques Nellens picked me up from home that same evening and to my stepmother's confusion I announced I wouldn't be coming home that night. This of course left her a lot of scope for criticism. Jacques took me to all the new discotheques where we drank a lot of champagne and turned back the clock. We were young and only today mattered. I couldn't help thinking how right we were for each other. We shared the same feelings about almost everything.

'Jacques, why couldn't it have been you?'

'Don't ask questions that will make me angry. I've learned to believe that I didn't lose you because I never really had you.'

After this exchange we danced in silence and the rest of the night was spent in perfect harmony. Jacques drove me home again the next morning and pulled up in front of my father's house. He looked straight ahead, impassively.

'Ciao, Jacques. Believe me, a part of me will always be yours.'

He gripped the steering wheel and said, 'Don't worry, I shall love many others.'

I didn't answer, there was no more to say. As I walked away from his car I knew this was one man I could have loved, had I known him better and sooner. But then again, at that time I had probably not been ready for such commitment.

Chapter 7

A BEAUTIFUL VICTORY

That afternoon my father asked what was troubling me. He was one person to whom I knew I couldn't lie and little by little the whole story streamed out. He didn't interrupt but when I'd finished he asked me why I'd brought Jacques back into my life.

'Don't you think that's a little cruel? You know you're in love with Donald. If you must escape occasionally why not do it with a song and a dance?'

'I know, Daddy, it wasn't kind, but what about some kindness to me? Donald has given me hell.'

My father puffed on his cigar, looking at the smoke rings drifting up towards the ceiling. 'My lovely daughter, you didn't marry an ordinary man, so don't expect him to behave like one.' Once again his wisdom struck a chord.

The following day I engaged Louis and Julia Goossens to look after Roundwood. The former butcher and his wife were a young and pleasant couple. On a recent visit to England Louis had decided it was the place for him and Julia, typical of the Flemish wife, shared her husband's desire to the full. He spoke some English and she understood it. They were both anxious to please and didn't seem afraid of work. I told them the hours were completely irregular but this fact didn't seem to worry them. We agreed they would come over in mid-September which would give me enough time to arrange their work permits. When they left I felt happy with my choice, and my father agreed with me. I truly longed to run the house, reorganise the schedules, contact all the Reigate stores – and maybe feel it was my home too.

When I arrived at London Airport at 7 a.m., Vera was waiting for me with my car. I had wired Donald to notify him of my return, but without mentioning the flight number or arrival time. Vera and I had breakfast at the airport and exchanged a few funny anecdotes about our Italian holiday. After taking her home I hit the road for Surrey. It was 10 o'clock when I finally arrived back at Roundwood. Driving past the boathouse near the gardener's lodge, I could see that the team was already hard at work. I drew up in front of the house and as I stepped inside Donald appeared in the doorway of the breakfast room, holding his newspaper.

'Hello darling. It's so good to see you! My goodness, you look gorgeous. A true sight for sore eyes!' He came over and kissed me and I sensed he had missed me. 'Would you like some breakfast while you tell me all about it?'

'I'll have some coffee,' I said, pushing back my wind-blown hair. Donald smiled at the gesture then went into the kitchen to order my coffee. The sun was streaming through the windows of the small breakfast room as I sat opposite Donald's chair with my back to the door. When he returned from the kitchen I didn't turn around. I felt his hands mess up my hair again.

'I've been longing to tousle this blonde hair of yours. If only girls knew how nice it feels to caress hair that isn't set or lacquered, they'd all have hair like yours.'

'I'm glad they don't,' I said quietly.

'Don't worry, Bobo, your hair is not your only endearing feature, there's plenty more besides! Now tell me all about your holiday away from your grumble box.'

I felt embarrassed and didn't know where to begin. My liaison with Jacques came immediately to mind. Luckily, at that moment the maid brought in the coffee and gave me time to think up something. When she left I began. 'Dad has found us a good, honest Flemish couple,' and I told him all about the interviews.

At the end of my report he leaned back in his chair and taking out a cigarette, rolled it between his thumb and index finger and smiled. 'Glad to know we're going to have some order in court. Tell me Bobo, how was Italy?'

'Quite lovely of course,' I answered hurriedly, and continued, 'I've always had a soft spot for Italy. The weather was divine. We swam all day and every day.'

'I can see that. You've got a lovely tan.'

'How have you been, Donald?' I asked, changing the subject.

'All right dear, but for what it's worth, I've missed you.'

'I'm glad to hear it.' I could not say I had missed him too; that would have been a lie. Standing up, I said, 'I suppose I'd better go up and unpack. Do you still want me to take over the accounts of the household?'

'And how! They're growing worse by the day! I'll tell Marian to bring the file up to your den.'

Lovely, I thought. Marian would not enjoy this. The file was duly brought up while I was still in my bedroom. Looking around the room I had a great feeling. Nothing had changed except for one very important fact – for the first time I felt truly at home.

Donald left two weeks later for France. We had shared beautiful days of togetherness and had enjoyed several nights out. With every outing, Marian brought up some detail of the arrangements for his pending trip. This irritated Donald who appeared in no hurry to go. The day before his departure he asked me again if I understood why he was going.

'Of course I do, Donald,' I said. 'After all, I had a nice break myself.'

'Yes, that's true, but this is different. You see, I promised myself I'd do this.'

I realised what was happening. He no longer wanted to go but having arranged this trip several months before with whoever was accompanying him, he couldn't back out now.

'A promise is a promise, Donald, and must be kept, no matter to whom one makes it.'

He looked at me, his eyes softening as they had done so often recently. 'You really understand, don't you? You're a wonderful woman.'

I laughed lightly in answer to this.

'What's the joke?' asked Donald.

'It's not a joke darling, just a giggle of pleasure because of the way you looked at me. You used to reserve that look strictly for Maxie.'

'Well, you know what they say about mad dogs and Englishmen, so when a Scot gives you that kind of look, watch out!'

He left an hour later. Once again my feelings amazed me. I was neither sad nor jealous, just a little sorry for the girl he was meeting at the other end. But then, somebody always gets hurt and this time I knew it wouldn't be me.

The following day the English staff left Roundwood and I was glad to see the back of them. When Louis and Julia Goossens arrived three days later we went straight into the cleaning attack, Flemish style! Marian was going back to her flat in London every evening now, and had asked to have her meals in the office during the day. Louis had got the measure of her and nicknamed her 'Vinegar Miss'.

The house was changing day by day. I went to evening classes to learn flower arrangement, Julia was working hard at her cooking and Louis at being the perfect butler. I also paid a visit to all the old bargain shops in the district and scoured Brighton's antiques lanes where I found some beautiful ornaments. We cleaned them up and together with the flower arrangements, Roundwood was fast acquiring a warmth it had lacked before.

Donald had been gone a week and I hadn't heard from him. The reason for this silence became clear the following Saturday. Marian had not come to work. When the phone rang I answered it and heard Donald's voice.

'Hello darling, so you're home at last!'

'Donald, how great to hear from you! What do you mean, home at last?'

'I called you three times last week but Marian said you were in London.'

'I haven't been to London since you left. I've been much too busy with the house and the new staff.'

Donald was angry now. 'Honestly, what's the matter with that woman? Anyway, Bobo, how are you?'

'Terrific! Louis and Julia are just great fun to work with. You won't recognise the house.'

Donald's voice assumed a gentler tone. 'Hey, Vixen, I miss you terribly.'

I was determined to sound casual. 'I'm glad to hear it, but don't worry about me. We're making your house beautiful.'

'I can't wait to see it. Listen, in the future I'll call in the evenings, okay?'

'Okay, I'll be here.'

'I'll say goodbye now, and God bless.'

'You too darling,' I said, and hung up. I sat on the phone stool, aching all over with longing. This time I felt jealous of the girl who was close to him, the girl who would probably be taken to some cute restaurant and enjoy his charm. Then suddenly I remembered how much Donald had loved Maxie. The dog had learned to wait for his master. *Well, I may not be as patient as him, but I will certainly try to be as loyal from now on.*

One week later the house was shining. Louis and Julia, both now in uniform, behaved as though they had been in domestic service for years. I ordered all our provisions from different stores and found that I could easily reduce our monthly expenses by half. Marian's face seemed to grow a little longer every day. Donald had called in the evenings only and the office messages I relayed to her had been received with icy coldness.

Then came the final blow. On Friday morning she walked into the lounge where I was having my coffee and said sourly, 'Skipper is on the phone for you.'

I jumped up and ran into the office shouting, 'Thank you, Marian.' Picking up the phone I said, 'Hello?'

'Mrs Donald Campbell?' said the voice of the operator.

'This is she,' I answered.

'Go ahead now, sir.'

'Hello, Bobo? How is my girl?' Donald appeared very good humoured.

'Fine darling, especially now I'm hearing your voice. And you?'

'Not too bad, great weather down here. What are you up to today?'

'Nothing special, messing around in the upstairs rooms. They need some attention too.'

Donald interrupted. 'Could you by any chance get on a plane and meet me in Paris tonight?'

A thousand angels were singing sweet music in my ears. 'Could I?' I yelled. 'Just you watch me! Oh Donald, how wonderful!'

'Now don't get too excited. It may be hard to get a flight to Paris on a Friday.'

Now it was my turn to interrupt. 'I'll be in Paris tonight if I have to fly the jolly old plane myself!'

Donald's laughter rang through the phone. 'I bet you would too. Listen dear, I should be there around 9 or 10 o'clock tonight. I'm driving up from La Napoule, near Nice. I'll go straight to that small hotel you've mentioned so often, the Mayflower. If you're there before, wait for me. Book a room right now.'

'Yes, darling, I'll get on with it right away.'

'Okay, Poppet, longing to see you.'

After hanging up I panicked. I didn't know what to do first. I burst out of the office yelling 'Louis, Julia, quick, help!' Both stormed out of the kitchen, Julia still clutching a piece of silver she was cleaning.

'Mr Campbell wants me to join him in Paris tonight!'

Julia exclaimed in our native Flemish, 'That's lovely, I'll go and pack for you. How long will you be there Madam?'

'Just for the weekend I would think.'

'Just for the weekend? All the way to Paris?' Julia shook her head, but her expression remained the same and addressing herself to Louis she asked him what the weather would be like in Paris at this time of year.

'Same as in Belgium!' Louis grinned. I went to phone my old travel agency which said there would be no problem and they'd call me back to confirm the flight. Then I rang the Mayflower Hotel where I had so often stayed in my single days. I knew the owner, Madame Delanoe, well. She was a sweet and well-rounded Frenchwoman, full of life and with a touch of mischief. She was thrilled to hear from me and anxious to meet my famous husband. She said she had followed our lives in *Paris-Match* and was very happy for me. It took me some time to tear myself away from her interminable chatter, but I was grateful for her enthusiasm. This was the tourist season in Paris and I knew she might have to send another guest to a nearby hotel in order to accommodate us, but so far everything was going smoothly. Somebody up there was watching out for me and I wondered whether it was my beloved brother Daniel.

By 5 o'clock Louis was driving me to the airport to catch the 7 o'clock flight. As we drove past the boathouse I waved at Leo. He smiled and waved back, giving me a thumbs-up sign. Louis noticed this and asked what this meant.

'It's a sign of victory,' I told him. 'It's a habit with the Bluebird team, and I feel lucky today.'

'I suppose it is lucky you got your room and ticket during this busy season.'

I smiled. 'Yes, Louis, it's very fortunate.' I remained quiet for the rest of the drive to Heathrow airport, well aware of the true meaning behind Leo's sign. We both knew I had won the battle.

I drove into Paris by taxi. The Mayflower Hotel was in the rue Château Brilliant which was off the Champs Elysées near the Arc de Triomphe. It was small but chic with a very cute bar at the entrance. It had only fifty rooms but each was decorated in its own individual style. Madame Delanoe was at the reception desk when I arrived and exclaimed, 'Ah, ma chère Tonia, welcome back!' Big hugs and kisses followed, then she whispered with a mischievous wink, 'I've put you in the room with the big dark mirror, perfect for honeymooners.'

I laughed. 'Madame Delanoe, I've been married a whole year now.'

'Ah,' she said, 'but this is your first night with him in Paris and we must make it an unforgettable one.'

Serious now, I asked her if she'd heard anything from Donald yet. 'He was leaving Nice by car this morning.'

'It is a long drive from Nice to Paris, even for the fast Monsieur Campbell. He could not be here before midnight. You have lots of time to relax.'

She was proved wrong because just as I stepped into the lift, in walked Donald. Pale blue trousers, open-necked shirt, sunburned face and smiling blue eyes.

'Donald, how wonderful!' I ran to him and was received with enthusiasm.

'Well, I broke another record. I've never driven with such haste in my life. It was tiring but all the time I thought of the trophy at the end of the race, and here it is.' He had completely forgotten his usual British decorum.

Madame Delanoe came over to shake his hand. 'Monsieur Campbell, welcome to the Mayflower, I do hope it will please you.'

'Thank you, Madame. With the charm of La Patronne, how can it miss.'

Madame Delanoe was won over. She personally took us to the room. When Donald noticed the huge smoked mirror facing the lovely Rennaissance bed he gave me a naughty wink, then charmingly said to Madame Delanoe, 'I see you have thought of everything, Madame.'

We freshened up and went to Donald's favourite restaurant, the Dinarzade, a very expensive Russian-style nightclub. To our amazement the whole of London was there, but few husbands were with their wives. I pointed this out to Donald. He smiled and took my hand.

'That's because none of them have a wife like mine. I think we're the only married couple here, Bobo, and it feels like incest! Tell me, aren't you curious about anything?'

'Like what?' I asked.

'Where I've been, what I've done, and with whom?'

'Donald, I am so happy today that yesterday really doesn't matter any more.'

'Water under the bridge, you mean?'

I nodded. He looked at my hand and my wedding ring, then back at me and said, 'I've been a bloody fool. Just like in the story, I looked everywhere for the bluebird of happiness and all the time it was right under my nose. I should have known. But then, I've never in the past known a woman I could fully respect and admire. Hey, darling, you're crying, what's the matter?'

Tears had started to flow slowly down my cheeks, but my voice was steady. 'It's because of the bit about respect. It's the nicest thing you could have said. This is the first time in my life I'm actually crying for joy.' Then changing the subject I asked, 'Tell me darling, did you do any writing at all?'

'I started but couldn't concentrate, though I'd love to write a book one day.'

'You write well, I know you could and I hope you will,' I said convincingly.

Donald picked up his glass of champagne. 'I'll drink to that. Maybe one day we'll both write a book.'

The stay in Paris was delightful. I went shopping on Saturday and bought a very daring dress. That evening I wore it. When Donald saw me in it he smiled and I smiled back at him.

'I know it's a little naughty but don't worry, I shan't wear it at Buckingham Palace!'

Donald laughed out loud. 'I don't know about that. I'm sure old Philip would love it.'

That evening the choice of restaurants was mine. I chose Le Mouton de Panurge in Montmartre, where the waiters dressed as monks and greeted diners with a 'Good evening brother, good evening sister'. The walls were covered with the most erotic pictures. The bread was baked in the shape of a penis and the soup served out of a huge chamber pot. Donald was terribly amused by all this and when he was happy he always wanted to share it with someone.

'I say, Bobo, we must bring the Barkers here. They'd love it.'

'How about Bill and Betty Coley?' I asked.

Donald laughed. 'Somehow, I don't think Aunty Betty would approve!'

While he'd been talking away I had taken two of the penis-shaped breads and broken one in half, sticking it on to the end of the other whole one. It now resembled a twenty-inch organ and I placed it on Donald's plate.

'Follow that!' I challenged.

'You naughty girl!'

He looked down then burst out laughing, placing the bread upside down in his wineglass, much to the amusement of everyone present. Finally, the show was stolen by one of the older waiters who winked at Donald and said, pointing at the bread, 'Ça monsieur, c'est Vive la France.'

Chapter 8

TOO GOOD TO LAST

We returned to England the following Monday. By now autumn was beginning to show itself. The leaves were turning yellow and great drifts of them already lay on the ground; we realised the holidays were over. Roundwood Manor looked gorgeous and Donald's obvious satisfaction at seeing the house transformed gave me the thrill I had hoped for. Louis and Julia looked trim and friendly. Donald liked them instantly.

'I hope you'll be happy with us. What are your names?' Julia's English was poor so Louis answered for them both.

'Louis and Julia, sir.'

'Louis and Julia,' Donald repeated. 'I like Louis, but I will call Julia Julie. She's far too nice to be called Julia!' Julia understood him and from the expression on her face she definitely liked her new boss.

Donald looked around at the changes in the house. He entered the lounge that had been transformed with the careful addition of ornaments, plants and flowers. A dark red marble lampstand topped with an off-white shade stood on a small black and gold table. This motif was repeated on both sides of the big sofa and a low round coffee table with beautifully carved wooden legs stood in the middle of the room. I had spent very little money on all this, having found most of it in small antique shops and then cleaned and polished it all with Louis and Julia.

'I have to say you've performed absolute miracles with this room. It was a big barn before and now it's an elegant salon.' Donald gave me a friendly hug.

Marian had come into the lounge and said quietly, 'Welcome home, Skipper.'

'Hello Marian, Mrs Campbell is here too, you know.'

She looked embarrassed. 'Good afternoon, Mrs Campbell.'

'Good afternoon, Marian. How have you been?'

'Fine, thank you.' Then she turned to Donald. 'Skipper, there are several things that are rather urgent in the office.'

'I'll be there in a few moments, Marian.' Donald's voice was irritable. As soon as she left the room he growled, 'What's the matter with that woman? She looks as if she's swallowed a bottle of vinegar.'

I laughed. 'Maybe that's why Louis named her "Vinegar Miss". Anyway, she's probably just depressed.'

'Depressed? What the hell for? I treat her royally and pay her well.'

'Yes, I know you do, but I think she's disappointed at not being the woman behind the great man.'

'Bloody nonsense,' he said, bad-tempered now. 'No one's great around here and I don't believe in the woman behind the man bit.'

'Yes, but women do believe in it.'

'Do you?' asked Donald.

'No, darling, I don't want to be behind you – just under you.'

'Trust you to find an answer! I hope you never get tired of your old grumble box.'

'Try me,' I dared him. He smiled, messed up my hair, then walked to his office with a sigh.

Marian handed in her notice the following week. I was relieved when Donald told me and he noticed it.

'Don't worry, Bobo, I feel just as relieved. But next time I take a secretary, you'd better interview her first. We don't want a repeat performance of this one, do we?'

Within a week we found the right person in Rose-Marie Fitzgerald, a very attractive divorcee. She was tall and well rounded, with short dark, wavy hair, a great sense of humour and a regiment of boyfriends. She was very serious about her work, extremely competent, and brought a new atmosphere to Donald's office, which both he and I appreciated.

So, little by little, Roundwood became a beautiful and happy home. And 1959 became a very good year, at last.

Spring 1960 arrived with preparations for the world land speed record attempt in the USA. Donald had engaged Peter Carr, a former RAF squadron leader whom he had met previously while Peter was stationed in Nevada during Donald's visit there in 1956. Peter was a great pilot and a calm one and it was for these reasons that Donald decided he would be not only director of the land speed project, but also the reserve driver of the *Bluebird*. Stirling Moss had been his first choice, but Donald later decided he was temperamentally wrong for the job. Peter could be trusted to put the machine before his desire for personal achievement.

The Proteus-engined *Bluebird* car had been designed by the Norris brothers, who had also been responsible for the *Bluebird* boat. Built in Coventry and supported by the powerful industrialist Sir Alfred Owen, the project had so far cost well over £50,000. British Petroleum also had an interest, as had many other firms, but Donald was – and remained – completely in charge. It was an exciting time for both of us.

In our personal lives we now shared mutual understanding. Donald's project was taking us all over England. We enjoyed our free weekends at Roundwood in our new-found home life. Donald was constantly busy. I don't believe I ever saw him doing nothing. If he wasn't pulling up trees in the garden with his new tractor, then he was shooting clay pigeons or doing his own film developing. The amazing thing was that whatever he turned his hand to, it was always done to perfection. My birthday was a classic example of this. It was a memorable occasion and the celebrations – involving birds of paradise and a firework display – were impeccably organised by Donald, I must admit I wasn't that keen on fireworks, but he adored them and so I had little choice but to like them too. In any case, this was one way to make sure he never forgot the date!

Living with Donald during those heady days was a constant voyage of discovery. All the girlfriends had gone from our life and it was rumoured in London circles that Tonia Bern had finally tamed Donald Campbell. He had been transformed from playboy to country squire.

Gina was now settled at a very good boarding school and some weekends we'd collect her and fly to Knokke. First we'd motor to Southend – this normally took three hours, but with Donald at the wheel it took only two and a lot of swearing at the 'fiddle farters', monopolising the fast lane. Then we would drive the car on to the air ferry plane and after a short flight across the Channel we'd drive it off again at Ostend. It was a hugely enjoyable trip and one that we made frequently.

Life seemed perfect now, except for one detail. Donald missed his dog and constantly talked about him. One day I decided I would get him another. Through Donald's sister Jean I found the right dog at a kennel owned by a Lady Spencer. The small golden labrador pup was the only one left in the litter. He was very fluffy, but sad and lonely now that all his brothers and sisters had gone. I immediately fell in love with him and said I'd take him. I signed all the papers and paid the bill before he was put in a big cardboard box pierced with holes and lined with some straw to make him comfortable. I placed the box on the passenger seat of my car and drove off, impatient to see the look on Donald's face when I arrived home.

On the way I bought some blue ribbon and a small card on which I wrote: 'I know I cannot hope to replace Maxie but nobody wanted me, so please take me and give me a name.' I signed it 'L – L – L', for 'Lonely Little Labrador'. I tied the card on to the blue ribbon and then, when nearer home, put it around the puppy's neck. When I arrived home I placed the box on the big table in the lounge, closed the lid and tied the remaining blue ribbon around it. I knocked on the door of Rose-Marie's office. The classic English voice called from inside for me to come in. Rose-Marie had acquired the name of Rosie. She had settled in very nicely and had become a dear friend to me.

When she saw me she exclaimed with excitement, 'Oh dear, have you got him yet?' We'd kept the whole thing a secret from Donald and I nodded my head, gesturing to her to say nothing more as the door to Donald's office opened. Rosie stood up and announced in her official voice, 'One moment, Mrs Campbell. I'll see if Mr Campbell is off the phone yet.' She walked into Donald's office and I heard her say, 'Mr Campbell, is it all right for Mrs Campbell to see you?'

Donald was in a good mood. 'Yes, of course, Rosie. Tell her to order some tea for us all. The break will be welcome.'

After organising the tea and biscuits with Louis I went to pick up the box and carrying it in my arms walked into Donald's office. He was signing some letters and without looking up greeted me. 'Hello darling, I'll be with you in a tick.'

I quietly placed the box on the floor next to Donald's armchair and then sat down in the chair opposite.

'Well, old girl, what have you been up to today?' He hadn't noticed the box so I told him nonchalantly.

'Went to get you a Christmas present.'

'Christmas? You're well in time. We're only in May!' Then noticing the box he continued. 'What in heaven's name is going on here?'

'Nothing very unusual, just a Christmas present which you've got to open now because it won't keep till Christmas. And the sooner you untie the box, the better.'

With a smile he did as he was told and there it was, a little ball of golden fluff, fast asleep and without a care in the world. The ribbon was still tied neatly around his neck. Donald's face melted on seeing him and his voice quaked with emotion.

'Just look at that little thing. Dear oh dear, come here out of this prison!' He picked up the sleepy little bundle then noticed the card and read it. Sitting down, he placed the puppy on his knees and while caressing it he murmured, 'We're going to name you Whoppit, just like our mascot, and we're going to love you very, very much.' He looked up and smiled. When he was emotional, Donald's eyes would become moist.

'My dumb blonde, as dumb as a fox! You're not just a mind reader, you know what goes on in a man's heart. Every time I walked in that garden I thought of Maxie and longed for him. Although Maxie will always remain my wonderful dog, I know this one will give me great pleasure too.' Then he added softly. 'Thank you.'

Whoppit remained in Donald's big chair, puddled all over the place and felt very much at home. When I told Donald that Whoppit should not be allowed on the chairs as he was going to grow much larger, the answer came direct and definite.

'You were a baby once and babies should be made to feel happy and secure. He's only a little one, Bobo. Later on we'll train him.'

'But Donald,' I argued, 'the puddles he leaves will make marks.'

'Yes, I know, but they're only little puddles. Come on, darling, you're his mother, you should understand. And he's intelligent, he'll learn soon enough.'

That night Donald entered our bedroom carrying the new puppy. Not only did he place it tenderly on the bed, but he also rested its head gently on the pillow. Whoppit and Donald became constant companions and I often overheard long one-sided conversations between dog and master, walking together in the garden as if the whole world belonged only to them.

The following July Donald decided we should take a three-week holiday along the French Riviera on *Fuchimi*. On our return we were due to leave almost immediately for the Utah salt flats in the USA. The Bluebird team would leave for America to set things up three weeks before our departure.

Peter Carr had settled in beautifully by now and was to co-ordinate the project. He took over a lot of the work and responsibility and was liked by all involved. Peter was plain to look at but warm and charming, and because of this he seemed to exude an attraction. He also loved a good joke and told many. With him, Leo, Rosie, Louis and Julia, Roundwood became a fun place to be.

We left for France early on a Monday morning in Donald's new Aston Martin, only this time we caught the air ferry from Southend to Le Touquet in France. From there we followed the road to Paris which Donald knew well from his frequent trips abroad. He had also learned that the best French bistros and cafés were those where the wife cooked and the husband was the waiter. We stopped at one such hostelry where we enjoyed a most agreeable lunch, then got back on the road again. We wanted to get halfway before dark so as to be in the South of France by the next day. Donald really stepped on it. He was thoroughly enjoying his new car. All of a sudden I saw him tense up after glancing in his rear-view mirror.

'What's the matter, Donald?'

'We're being chased by the police,' he cursed. 'I must have been speeding.'

What a joke, I thought. 'What do we do now?' I asked innocently.

Donald grinned and, quickly assessing the situation, declared that we had a choice. 'We can stop and face the music, or we can run for it.'

I knew what I'd do given the choice. 'Can we lose them?' I asked.

'With this old girl,' he said (meaning the car), 'in no time.'

'All right, Donald, let's run for it!'

His face lit up. 'Your wish, is my command! Hold on, lady, here we go!' It was an exhilarating moment as Donald put his foot down and the car shot forward. Looking over my shoulder I was amused to see the distance between us and the police car growing wider.

'Watch them, Bobo, and tell me when they're out of sight.' It didn't take long.

'I can't see them any more, Donald. You can relax now.'

'Oh no we can't, they'd still catch us up and then we'd really get it. We've got to find a small lane and get off the main road.'

Donald slowed down slightly, took a swift right turn off the main road and speeded up again till we reached the middle of a small village. He chose a quiet street in which to park the car, then lit up a much-needed cigarette. After taking a deep drag he assessed our predicament.

'Well now, we have another choice to make. We can continue along the road to Paris through the villages, or we can stay overnight in one of them and get back on to the main road tomorrow.'

'Why can't we continue on the main road today?' I asked.

'Simply, my love, because we have just teased a couple of gendarmes. They got left behind and didn't like it. They also possess a little thing called a radio, and although they couldn't have read my number plate, they must have noticed the colour and the make of the car. If we went back to the main road there would be some nice uniformed gentlemen waiting for us around the next corner.'

I admitted I hadn't thought of that.

'Let's get the map out and choose another route, but it means we'll be later arriving on *Fuchimi*.' Donald patted my hand and then continued with a grin. 'But it was worth it, wasn't it?'

I gave him a quick kiss on the cheek. 'Worth it? I loved every minute, but it was over much too soon.'

'Thank your lucky stars it was because we wouldn't half have got some stick if they'd caught us.'

We still managed to get to the Riviera the next day. It had been a lovely drive down and the holiday had got off to a good start. On the road to Monte Carlo, where *Fuchimi* was moored, Donald suggested we stay in a hotel for the night as the bunks were probably not ready.

'Why? If they're not ready I can soon sort them out,' I said. 'No need to spend money unnecessarily.'

'You've just hit a Scot where he feels it,' laughed Donald. But I told him he could not be less Scottish where money was concerned. 'Just give me time, Poppet, we're still on honeymoon, you know!' It was strange how he could still create a melting feeling within me. I leaned back and closed my eyes. 'Hey, is that the effect my tender words have on you? Falling asleep?'

'No, Donald, I closed my eyes to try to stop time for a while.'

We arrived at the harbour and Donald parked the car. Putting his arm around my shoulders he kissed me behind the ear. 'My romantic Belgian blonde, I love you, and what's more I'm in love with loving you.'

We got aboard *Fuchimi* and busied ourselves. Donald was checking the machinery and engines, while I organised the galley and cabins. Later, when all was done, we took a stroll to the harbour bistro for a supper of fish and wine which we ate on the terrace. The beautiful scents of the Mediterranean night air and the balmy warmth filled my heart. I looked at the man across the table, my very own husband. I knew that part of him would always be a stranger, but life next to him was so exciting and I was grateful for every moment. The wine brought a glow to my face and Donald was quick to note it.

'You look beautifully healthy.'

'I feel it,' I answered. 'So healthy, I could explode!'

'That's quite an admission, my love. Well, don't let's waste this mood. It has to be used to the full!'

Donald paid the bill and we left the restaurant. Ambling slowly back to the boat, he squeezed my arm. 'I have a feeling those bunks in our cabin might be a little small for us tonight. How about sleeping on deck?'

The thought excited me and of course we did. That night *Fuchimi* was rocking and it wasn't because of the waves.

A few days later we anchored at St Tropez. This bohemian French harbour town was still the 'in' place in the South of France. We roamed around the coast in *Fuchimi* discovering the loveliest beaches. One particularly beautiful afternoon was the highlight of our holiday. We anchored as close to the shore as we possibly could without fouling our propellers, near a stretch called Tahiti Beach. I'd made lunch and was setting it out on deck while Donald relaxed, sipping some chilled white wine. I saw him bend over the rail and I thought for a moment that he was inspecting the sides of the boat.

'Anything wrong?' I called.

'Shush, be quiet,' was his answer. Curious, I walked over and looked down into the water but saw nothing. 'I must have been dreaming,' whispered Donald, 'but either I saw a mermaid, or a naked girl swimming around.'

Respecting his call for silence, I whispered back, 'Are you sure it wasn't wishful thinking?'

He grabbed my arm. 'There it is again. Look, another one.'

I looked to where he pointed and, sure enough, there was a white form moving beneath the water. 'Hey, Skipper, you're losing your touch, that's a man!'

'Yes, it is! And there's another two, further down. See?'

Suddenly from all around there were naked bodies in snorkels and flippers breaking the surface. The silence was broken when a head popped out of the water.

'Hello there, are you English?' shouted the blond swimmer.

Donald called back, 'Scottish, old boy.'

'Then why do you fly the English flag?'

'That, dear sir, is the British flag. Would you like to come aboard and investigate? Please bring your friends, especially the ladies. In fact, why don't you come and join us for a drink?'

'Wonderful,' answered the swimmer, 'but we haven't got any clothes.'

'You could have fooled me,' laughed Donald. 'If it makes you feel any better, my wife and I will take ours off.'

They swam towards the boat and soon bronzed naked bodies were climbing aboard, still wearing flippers and snorkels. The girls were beautiful, but somehow the sight of all those naked men made me giggle. Up to that moment I had only seen one naked male at a time, but the sight of all those different lengths and shapes together at the same time brought a smile to my face. I couldn't help pointing this out to Donald who laughed when I started to hum the song 'The Long and the Short and the Tall'!

Everyone was shaking hands and introducing themselves. Donald and I had removed our swimsuits and being the only ones with white patches, we were probably not very nice to look at. We prepared salad and sandwiches and poured the wine. Donald was sitting next to a very attractive girl called Danielle who was explaining nudism to him in a natural and uninhibited way. Donald listened intently, sitting on the deck leaning against a bunch of ropes. A few minutes later I noticed he was leaning on his side, and finally finished up lying flat on his stomach.

The group was of all nationalities, but mainly French and German. The lovely Danielle came over to me smiling. 'You have been doing so much work, let me help you wash up a few things.'

'Certainly not! My husband would never forgive me if I took you away from him!'

She laughed. 'Your husband left me ages ago for some German general. Only an Englishman would do that.'

'I wouldn't worry about it, Danielle,' I reassured her. 'I'm sure you had some effect on him.'

She smiled, revealing a set of beautiful white teeth that contrasted with her sunburned face. 'Oh, I'm sure of that, but you'll get the benefit of it later,' and with that she walked away to join her boyfriend, the blond swimmer we had first talked to.

I went in search of Donald and found him in the wheelhouse studying a map with a man I guessed to be the German general in question. They both looked up as I came in and Donald introduced me. Even without clothes, there was no mistaking his nationality. He shook my hand and automatically clicked his heels, though not very effectively without the jackboots. I'd never have believed that a naked man could maintain such arrogance and I nearly expected his organ to stand to attention too. When I later mentioned this to Donald he laughed and told me that the German general was quite a guy. He'd been in Rommel's Afrika Korps and had many interesting stories to tell. He was probably the only German that Donald ever liked. We spent several days among the nudists and it turned out to be a pleasant experience.

After mooring *Fuchimi* we drove up through France en route for home. We stayed one night in Paris, where, still under the nudist influence, I found great pleasure in buying a dazzling, transparent black lace dress, loosely cut and worn with a black silk body stocking underneath. I was not quite sure whether I could ever wear this dress, but I longed for the opportunity to do so.

Back at Roundwood we heard news that the Royal Yacht Club was giving a dinner dance in Donald's honour. For the occasion I dressed in blue velvet. I walked downstairs and asked Louis to tell Mr Campbell that I was waiting for him in the lounge. Donald was still dictating a letter to Rosie. Five minutes later he walked in and exclaimed, 'Bobo, what happened to your dress?'

'Nothing. Why? Don't you like it?'

'Yes, of course, I suppose it's all right. But what about the one we bought in Paris?'

'You mean the transparent black one?' I asked incredulously. 'This is a royal dinner and I'll probably end up sitting next to Lord Mountbatten himself.'

'Good! Let's give the old boy a thrill. Come on, Bobo, quick, go and change.'

'Okay, you're the boss.' I went back upstairs. The change would be fast because no underwear was required. I stripped, put on the body stocking then slipped into the lace. It looked amazing but I still felt it was more appropriate for a cabaret than an aristocratic dinner. I went downstairs and met Donald in the lobby talking to Rosie. They both looked up as I approached. Rosie's eyes nearly popped out of her head.

'Wow!' she exclaimed. 'Take a look at La Bern.'

Donald's tone was one of propriety. 'That, Rosie, is very much Mrs Campbell, at least the one I've always dreamed of.'

'I'm glad you approve, Rosie,' I said. 'We got it in Paris. But I do feel a bit naked in it.'

Rosie laughed. 'It looks a bit that way too!'

'Nonsense,' Donald replied, 'you're covered from head to toe and very dignified.'

'Nevertheless, Mr Campbell, it's a very provocative dress,' Rosie added.

'Good,' he laughed, 'then I'll be the envy of every man there! Come on, let's go!'

The dinner was to be held in the Savoy's private ballroom. We were to meet the Barkers in the public bar beforehand. As soon as we stepped into the lobby people turned and stared. We reached the bar whereupon Cherry immediately exclaimed, 'Tonia, that is superb!'

'Not too provocative?' I asked.

'You're covered, aren't you?' said Peter. 'I think it's the most beautiful thing I've ever seen you in.'

We walked into the ballroom on the announcement of the master of ceremonies. 'Mr Donald Campbell CBE, and Mrs Campbell.' All eyes turned to us; I looked to Donald for support. He was smiling proudly. The Barkers were announced and completely ignored. Most of the guests were looking at me. Donald gave me his arm and led me towards the reception committee. Lady Mountbatten offered her hand and with an understanding smile said how beautiful I looked. Then turning to Donald she said, 'Mr Campbell, we are proud to congratulate you on your achievement and happy to meet your lovely wife.' This was followed by Lord Mountbatten's handshake. He was about the most handsome man I had ever seen – tall, grey-haired and with an unbelievable dignity. His smile had a trace of naughtiness, his voice a warm intimacy.

'What a delightful surprise you are, Mrs Campbell. How do you do?'

I made a slight curtsy – this beautiful man made me feel like a child. Donald introduced me to many famous people whose names, up to that moment, I had only read. The Duke of Argyll was handsomely cool but someone whom I'd prefer as a friend than an enemy; the Duke and Duchess of Richmond were charming and they immediately asked me to call them Freddy and Betty. I did so, but not without difficulty. I also met the blond-haired blue-eyed Lord Montagu and so many others whose names I've forgotten.

When we were finally called to dinner I noticed I was seated to the left of Lord Mountbatten. He looked at me as we approached and once more he smiled, only this time I definitely saw an admiring glance. Even so, I still felt that I would much rather perform the most difficult show than endure a dinner such as this. Lord Mountbatten asked many questions and put me very much at ease by telling me lots of jokes. We laughed and enjoyed each other's company. In fact, he wrote down some of my own stories and used one of them in his speech later on. I met him again two years later at a reception where he walked straight over to me, took my hand and said, 'How lovely to see you again, my dear. Do you have some more jokes for me? I badly need a new supply!'

Chapter 9

THE UTAH CRASH

Our departure for Utah was scheduled for Friday 2 September, much later than originally planned. The day before we left, Donald threw a party for all his friends at the Café Royal in Regent Street to celebrate the launch of his latest land speed record attempt. His attorney and friend, Victor Mishcon, was present and brought with him a document for Donald to sign. At a certain point in the party, Donald gathered the famous Crazy Gang round him in a corner of the room to witness his signature. One member of the comedy team shouted to him.

'Hello, Donald, signing your will? Not very confident, eh?'

'No, old boy,' replied Donald, 'but advisable.' Then walking over to me he said, 'Darling, I've got a surprise for you,' and handed me an envelope.

'What is it?' I asked. I opened it and inside were two plane tickets. I looked at Donald who put his hands around my waist.

'Your ticket to Utah, but with a condition: you're not coming alone.'

I asked him what he meant by that and he told me to take a look at the other ticket, which I did. It was made out in the name of Mrs Vera Freedman.

'Vera? I don't understand. Is she coming?'

'Are you pleased?'

'I'm thrilled, but how? When was all this decided? Does Vera know?'

'Does she know?' echoed Donald. 'Of course she does. We had some trouble convincing her old man, but he finally gave in when I said this would be my condition for taking you.'

'Was it, Donald?'

'Let's put it this way, I feel happier now. I don't want you watching those runs on your own.'

I took his hand in mine. 'Listen, Donald, now don't get me wrong. I'm delighted Vera is coming and it's very thoughtful of you, but one day you'll learn about me and the things I can take.'

'My brave, Flemish blonde . . .'

I stopped him short. 'No, Donald, not brave, just pigheaded.'

We travelled first class and as soon as we could remove our safety belts Donald was invited up on to the flight deck by the captain. Much later, on arrival in Los Angeles we chartered a private plane to fly to Salt Lake City. On the way Donald decided we'd land in Las Vegas for lunch to which Vera and I simultaneously shouted 'Great!' Vegas was a thrill, even just for lunch. We attacked the slot machines with gusto and lost of course. We went to the Sahara Hotel where Donald and the team had stayed for several weeks in 1956 during the attempt on the water speed record on Lake Mead.

'That was before my time, of course,' I primly pointed out.

'Yes darling, well before your time. You were probably still at school!'

'Not quite,' I answered, recollecting those years. 'How did you like staying in Las Vegas?'

Donald smiled, remembering. 'It was crazy. I had a very lovely girlfriend called Susie. She was Marlene Dietrich's secretary.'

'Did you meet the fabulous Marlene?' asked Vera.

'Yes, I met her all right. Didn't like her a bit. Seemed self-centred and hard.'

'Maybe she was lonely,' I said in defence of this legendary beauty.

'Didn't care to find out,' was Donald's curt reply.

Within an hour we met several of his old friends – the sheriff of the town, Stan Irwin, entertainment director of the hotel, and bandleaders Guy Lombardo and Louis Prima. Guy, being a boat racer, bombarded Donald with questions. I liked him the best. We finally arrived in Utah one hour late for the press reception. Peter Carr met us at the airport and when we told him the reason for our late arrival he grinned.

'Oh well, I told the press boys if they wanted a story they'd have to wait till the Campbells were coming!'

'You're right, Peter, good things are worth waiting for,' said Donald, slapping Peter heartily on the back and making him choke.

The press reception was tense: there was a definite feeling of hostility in the air. 'How much money do you make out of this, Don?' asked one reporter.

Donald gave him a cold stare and asked him his name.

'Jim Ruther,' was the reply.

'Right, Jim, mine is Donald, not Don, and the money I'll make out of this is still a mystery to me, but I could tell you in detail what it has cost up to now. Being a Scot, every cent has hurt.' This prompted uproarious laughter and by the end of the meeting the American press had completely melted under Donald's charm.

After the reception Donald wanted to go to the Bonneville flats and look at the run. I asked to be excused and stayed at the Utah Hotel. Towards the evening I became so itchy that I decided to take a bath, and while undressing I noticed lots of little patches and tiny lumps all over my body. I called Vera. She examined me and decided I had food poisoning and that it probably would go away as quickly as it came. Donald called to say that he would stay overnight in Wendover with the team. I was relieved.

The lumps were multiplying by the hour. At around 9 o'clock I could stand it no longer. We called in a doctor. Apparently this was a case of allergy for which he gave me a small dose of cortisone but within two hours of his visit I had swollen like a balloon. My skin was stretched and so painful that I couldn't sit, walk or lie down. I didn't know what to do. I called for Vera who was shocked when she saw me. My lips and tongue had swollen and taken on a grotesque form. Now I could hardly talk. Vera called the doctor again. By the time he arrived the situation had become so dangerous that he was forced to put some tubes down my throat to ease my breathing. This time he gave me a maximum dose of cortisone then, looking at my body, he exclaimed, 'What a beautiful case of allergy! I wish I could photograph it. I've never seen such a good one.' I was grateful he didn't have a camera handy. The injection did the trick and two hours later the swelling began to subside.

Vera and I tried to think what could have provoked this violent reaction. The doctor said it could have been the sulphur medicine the stewardess put on a burn I had acquired by shaking the hand of someone who was holding a lighted cigarette. When Donald returned the next day the panic was over. Vera told him of the events in case of a reoccurrence, but thankfully I was fine.

We stayed at a picturesque motel in Wendover and my first impression of the town enchanted me. It was not unlike a set for an old cowboy movie. Donald's days were busy with the team, the press and countless other problems. Vera and I kept out of the way and spent most of our time by the pool. I kept my nervousness and worry well hidden from Donald, but was grateful I could talk to Vera about them. As usual, she was a great listener and adviser.

All was going smoothly, then Friday the 16th came around. There had been a test run the previous day at which I hadn't been present and I was annoyed at having missed it. That Friday we prepared ourselves for an early departure to the flats for another run. On arrival we were greeted by Tommy Wisdom, who was once described as an old trooper of racetracks and whisky bottles. The *Bluebird* was ready and the team was waiting. Donald put on his special soft shoes and handed me his walking pair. He donned his helmet and I handed him Mr Whoppit. He no longer saw me, this I knew. He was already in the other world, the lonely world of the racer. I was to follow along with Peter Carr, Tommy Wisdom and Vera in another car parked nearby. The *Bluebird* started moving and we all joked as she flew over the salt. I was more confident than ever that Donald would triumph in no time, just like he had on water, again and again. Little did I know that this day would leave a red scar seared into my memory.

After the first run Donald was very bright and cheery. I commented to Vera that he was too light-headed about the whole affair and that it was unlike him.

'Nonsense, Tonia, he's just beginning to like his new baby,' she reassured me.

Then came the return run. First he went slowly, then shot forward like an arrow from a bow. In our car Peter shouted with excitement, as thrilled as a schoolboy. 'Just look at him go!'

Yes, I looked and I saw a scene I would never be able to forget: one big cloud of salt studded with pieces of *Bluebird*, and among that chaos the man I loved. I kept repeating to myself, 'no, no, no'. It was a nightmare. Surely I'd wake up soon? But no such luck.

Tommy Wisdom stopped the car well away from the accident site. He thought it was too late and didn't want me on the scene of the disaster. I leapt from the car and realising that the *Bluebird* was upside down, I stopped dead in my tracks. Suddenly I remembered my brother Daniel. I had loved him too and he also had had to die. I felt a huge hatred towards the *Bluebird* and prayed to Daniel: *Please give me a miracle, don't take him away as well.* At that moment I heard Vera's voice.

'Tonia, look, she's not upside down after all. Come on, it might be all right.'

She grabbed my hand and I flew more than I ran. Leo had been first on the scene and had opened the cockpit. A highway patrolman was lifting Donald out and there was my glorious speed king, helpless like a limp child in the arms of this stranger. Death was still roving across his blood-stained face, but Daniel had listened. This was a miracle. Donald was alive. He opened his eyes for an instant and saw me.

'I'm all right, Bobo,' he murmured. 'Let Peter come with me.' Then he blacked out again. I didn't question why he wanted Peter. I just stood there and would have remained in that spot if Tommy hadn't pushed me to the front of the ambulance. I later found out that Donald didn't want me present in case he died. The driver got in and we started the longest drive of my life. Before the ambulance pulled away I looked out through the window at the *Bluebird* which was a complete wreck and not a very proud sight now. Somehow it reminded me of a dead animal, killed while protecting its master. I hated it no longer. I turned back, staring at the straight road ahead of us and asked how far it was to the hospital. The driver peered at me in a strange way. I must have looked ill for he asked whether I was feeling okay.

'Please, how far is it?' I repeated anxiously.

'About a two-hour drive, ma'am.'

'Two hours?' I sighed in desperation. My eyes were burning, my throat was dry, all my insides were trembling, yet I couldn't cry. The thoughts were running around in my brain. *How bad was Donald? Would he be crippled? Please God, not that.* Then, as if the Lord had taken pity on me there was a knock on the little square loophole that looked into the back of the ambulance. I shifted it open and there he was, poor Donald, trying to joke from the stretcher on which he was lying.

'It's all right darling,' he murmured. 'The main parts are in one piece, the family jewels are safe.'

I nodded and said in an amazingly calm voice, 'You'll be all right. Don't worry.'

When we finally arrived at the hospital in Tooele, Donald insisted on walking out of the ambulance. By now his face was swollen and his eyes were horribly bloodshot. They'd lost their blue colour and taken on a reddish hue. But, typical of him, he walked. The photographers had gathered by the hospital entrance and I dreaded what kind of pictures they would publish in tomorrow's papers.

As soon as we were inside the hospital Donald was put on a stretcher and taken to the x-ray room. I had to wait outside while Peter went to call Leo to find out the extent of the damage to the *Bluebird*. When he returned I knew by the look on his face that the news was bad. He sat down.

'It's a complete write-off,' he said, crestfallen.

'Who's going to tell him?'

'You, Tonia.' It was at that point I realised the moment had come for me to prove my strength. In fact, telling Donald about the wrecked *Bluebird* was easier than I'd thought. When he returned from the x-ray room he looked at me quizzically and asked 'The *Bluebird*?' I smiled sadly and shook my head. Donald looked away. I knew he was crying.

When the results of all the tests came back we were told that he had a fractured skull, two broken ribs and a pierced eardrum. I was horrified by this news but the doctor told us he was extremely lucky not to have broken his neck. Jokingly, Donald thanked the doctor.

'Hey, Doc, thanks for those reassurances but my number just didn't come up and I'm truly happy about that!'

We stayed in the hospital for about two weeks; we should have stayed longer, but Donald was raring to go. We returned to Los Angeles by train although Donald was still far from well. Vera had been wonderful but now she had to go back to her family, having been away much longer than expected, and she left for England together with the Bluebird team. One day after our arrival in Los Angeles we drove to Las Vegas where we stayed for a short while, but on the advice of the neurologist we went to Palm Springs for Donald to convalesce. There, at last, he relaxed. He decided to write his own story. We hired a young American typist and while I tried to amuse myself with the movie crowds (and succeeded nicely) he worked on his book all day and every day.

I fell in love with Palm Springs and had to admit to myself that this was more my kind of world than England. William Holden was partner to our host, the oilman Ray Ryan, and often my escort to the swimming pool and evening dinners when Donald was tired and excused himself. We met the Gabors. Eva was my favourite; she would get into the pool wearing gloves and a sun hat to protect her skin. Harry James and his wife Betty Grable were a very interesting couple. She seemed completely under his spell. Then there was Tony Martin with his beautiful wife, Cyd Charisse, the perfect lady to a not-so-well-mannered husband.

Donald took an afternoon's break to play golf with President Eisenhower who bombarded him with questions about the *Bluebird*. After the golfing was over he saw photographs of the crash. Ike turned to me and said, 'Well, if I had anything to do with this I'd rather race it than watch it.'

Donald winked at me. 'How right you are, sir.'

Palm Springs would remain in a little corner of my heart. As far as I was concerned our stay there was magnificent. It was there I had the greatest birthday party ever – Donald had organised it secretly. In spite of the crash, Donald was offered a great position with General Motors but it meant living in Beverly Hills – and to my disappointment he refused it. But all in all I had a lovely time and, yes, I did kiss William Holden and yes, it was nice, but yes, that was all. One afternoon Bill, as I called him, did invite me to his suite after we had been swimming. He offered me a glass of champagne. I accepted. We talked first about the art of acting but then the conversation changed. I can't remember how it happened but all at once we were analysing what love meant to different individuals. The conversation became intimate. When William Holden looked into your eyes and talked about love you were ready to melt away, but just as I was about to succumb the phone rang. Ray Ryan told Bill that Donald was looking for me. As I stood up to leave, he took both my hands in his, pulled me towards him and kissed me. Then, smiling, he said, 'Saved by the bell, Tonia. Maybe that's just as well.' I knew it was certainly 'just as well' because during that kiss my imagination was running wild and his seductive charm was overpowering. I left in haste.

Six weeks later we drove back to Los Angeles and boarded the plane for England. As soon as we took off Donald handed me a bundle of papers.

'The book?' I asked.

'Yes, the book, for what it's worth. You should be able to finish reading it during the flight and give me your opinion.'

'I didn't think you'd let me in on it,' I teased.

'Not let you in on it? After your wonderful support? Don't ever doubt that, woman. This time I could not have made it without you. I'm in your debt.' With this he looked away and went to join the flight crew for a chat.

I turned the first page and started to read. It began with the Campbells' background, from Donald's father's formative years and his war service as a pilot, through to the record-breaking period between the wars. It then went on to describe Donald's first forays into the world of boats and racing. I eventually closed the manuscript where it ended, up in the air and nowhere near the end of the Campbell story. But the six weeks' typing had been worth it. Donald had covered a lot of ground.

I looked around the plane to see that food was now being served and that Donald had returned from his visit to the flight-deck. Noticing that I'd closed the manuscript, he enquired enthusiastically, 'Well, Bobo, what's the verdict?'

'You write beautifully and I'm glad you started the story, but you've got one hell of a way to go!'

'I know. That's what scares me. So much to tell, so little time to relax and write. But tell me honestly, did you like it?'

'Some yes, some less,' I answered truthfully.

'Tell me about the "less" part,' he said, curious.

'Well, Donald, I feel there isn't enough about you the person in it. People will want to read about your innermost thoughts and feelings.'

'I can't even speak about those so how can I put them on paper?'

'I don't suppose it's easy. Frankly, I couldn't even begin to write all you have done.'

Donald took my hand and squeezed it. 'You, Bobo, you can do anything you set your mind to.' He picked up his script, put it back in his briefcase and added, 'Thanks for reading it, Poppet. Let's hope I give you the next episode soon.'

Chapter 10

DONALD'S FIGHT BACK
TO HEALTH

When we arrived home, Donald had to face up to the worst crisis of his life – what today is called post-traumatic stress disorder. It is virtually impossible to explain why it affected him so badly. He would be perfectly all right for days, then he'd wake me up at night and he'd look like a scared old man. He never knew what he was afraid of. He simply wanted me there to cling to. I could usually ease his fears and in doing so learned a lot about the physical power of a woman. Sometimes he used to accept invitations to social meetings and dinners and would be fine until the time came to get ready, then suddenly he would refuse to go. In the year after the crash I think I must have cancelled hundreds of dinners and other appointments, which was very embarrassing. I encouraged Donald not to accept any more invitations but he wouldn't hear of it, saying he would have to mix with people sooner or later. We saw numerous doctors but none seemed to have an answer. Our bathroom cupboard started to look like a chemist's shop. I didn't know which pills were for what – he was taking them all and I was desperate for a solution. I just had to get this man back to normal and soon, because my own nerves couldn't stand it much longer. In any case, I was terribly bored with life in the middle of nowhere, seeing no one.

Donald had always wanted to be a pilot. On numerous occasions he had told me how heartbroken he was when, after he volunteered for aircrew in the RAF during the war, his father had written to the Air Ministry to tell them about his having had rheumatic fever. Consequently Donald had had to be satisfied with a ground job. Leo suggested to me that I should encourage Donald to use his convalescence as an opportunity to learn to fly. At the time I thought Leo too optimistic, but now I started to wonder whether he was right. The concentration needed might just help him to forget his nervousness. I thought it was worth a try and tackled him about it one morning at breakfast.

'You know, Donald, although you're not well enough for record breaking you should try your hand at something else.'

He looked up and with a bad-tempered expression on his face growled, 'What else is there?'

'We could always go on *Fuchimi* and make films.'

'We're always doing something when those bloody nerves of mine start acting up. I don't seem to enjoy anything these days except sex.'

'I'm not complaining about that! What about learning to fly? We have Redhill aerodrome right here on our doorstep. You could get an instructor and have a go at it.'

He shrugged his shoulders and mumbled, 'I'd probably make a balls of that too. Thanks for the thought, but I think I'll pass.' With that he picked up his paper and left the room.

I sighed. What else could I try? I was now living the life of a recluse. Every outing was cancelled at the last moment and Donald still clung to me as he had done for over a year now. Even the love-making was more of a relaxation remedy than a physical enjoyment. I was at my wits' end. Feeling very depressed I went up to my den, put on some Jacques Brel records and wrote to my father. I'd never been away from home for so long before. Of course my father understood that Donald needed me right now and so he took second place, but I also knew that he'd wonder how long I'd be able to cope with this situation. I was young and full of life and I'd fallen in love with a man who, at the time, was full of drive and energy; but I now shared the life of a man old before his time. I still loved him very much but I hated the life I led and knew I would have to find a way out, for both our sakes.

December was on its way. Gina would soon be home for the school holidays. Maybe I should suggest going to Courchevel? Donald would ski and that might help. Hope flickered within me and I was pleased with myself because I was obviously not going to give up easily. Donald had often said I was a fighter – this time I was fighting for myself as well as for him because I wanted our other life back. That evening we sat together in his study. He was reading *The Carpetbaggers* by Harold Robbins and I was taking up a dress.

'Great book,' Donald said suddenly. Then, more to himself than to me, he continued. 'This is the kind of book that should be written about my dad and me. So far they've only been about the attempts, the hassles – and of course the achievements. Harold Robbins talks about a man's inner feelings, intimate details, even the personal hang-ups. It all goes to make the story bloody colourful and really rather interesting!'

Surprised at this, I asked him if, in all honesty, he would want such things revealed about him and his father. Donald found this amusing. 'Well,' he laughed, 'neither of us was ever very secretive about our sexual appetites!'

'Then Donald, you should write it that way,' I said.

'Don't know if I could, but it's a thought.'

'Donald, may I interrupt your reading?'

He looked up. 'What is it, dear?'

'Gina is coming home next week for the Christmas holidays. Shouldn't we arrange some fun for her?'

Donald sighed. 'Poor little mite, she's not going to enjoy her old miserable Dad. Maybe we should send her to my sister Jean's.'

'No, Donald, no,' I pleaded.

'Why not? She'd be with Peter John, Malcolm and Donald.'

'She's not that keen on her cousins,' I told him. 'They're younger than she is, and anyway she's been away from home too often.'

He agreed with me. 'She hasn't had much home life.'

I took a deep breath and crossed my fingers. 'Why don't we take her to Courchevel? She could learn to ski. She's at the perfect age.'

To my complete surprise Donald exclaimed, 'What a good idea! It'll be great fun seeing her on the slopes.'

'Hey, hold on Donald, she's got to learn first!'

'Well, we learned quickly enough didn't we? Why shouldn't she? After all she is mine.'

And I knew then that we would go to Courchevel. Donald was already looking forward to teaching Gina. I also realised that once again I was using a trick. The first time I tricked him was to win back his love, this time to win back his health. And in the future, well who knows for what reason?

We arrived in Courchevel on Christmas Eve. Donald had turned Courchevel upside down to get us decent rooms at this high season and he struck success with the new and very expensive Hotel Carlina where we were royally received by everyone. Gina's face lit up as soon as Pierre Grunberg, our handsome ski instructor, appeared. Donald noticed this and gave me one of his mischievous winks.

Later, when we were alone in our room, he joked, 'That minx of mine has an eye for the boys – sexy little monkey.'

'Like father like daughter,' I teased, and the holiday got off to a great start.

We dined with Pierre. Gina seemed in heaven. Donald was in a great mood. And I prayed. If this worked I could have another go at the flying lessons. I left father and daughter together as much as I could. Gina was a natural skier and in a few days she was able to follow us. Donald was delighted and very proud of her.

One beautiful afternoon they'd gone out together for some deep snow skiing. I'd turned down the offer of accompanying them, not being particularly keen on the idea, so I decided to go for a walk and have some tea in the village. On the way I heard my name being shouted and saw Pierre slaloming down the mountainside. What a handsome man he was. In no time at all he came to an abrupt halt, his skis throwing the snow up into the air just inches away from me. He beamed at me.

''Allo, beautiful madame! Where is your champion husband?'

'Lost in the deep snow with Gina,' I replied.

Pierre frowned. 'They are not ready for that. It's a different technique altogether.'

'Ah, they know that, Pierre. But it only makes it more tempting to those Campbells.'

'You know them well, don't you? So, as you are alone and I am alone, let's have some hot chocolate and we'll treat it like our kind of adultery. Let's go to the bistro on top of the mountain.'

'Nothing I'd like better, but I haven't got my skis here.'

'That shouldn't stop us,' said Pierre and with that he bent down and yelled, 'Get on my back, madame!' And I did as I was told. It wasn't difficult to sit astride his back. He grabbed my legs as well as his ski sticks, straightened up and walked off effortlessly. Everyone was laughing and shouting and many jokes were cracked as Pierre got on to the ski lift with a blonde clinging to his back. We went to the top of a mountain called La Loze where there was a small chalet-bistro run by a crazy poet called Bouvet. It was a popular venue for hot chocolate and hot rum and we had one of each. I felt on top of the world when all of a sudden it dawned on me that I might not be able to get back down again. In a slight panic I asked Pierre. He laughed. 'No problem. Same way you came up.'

'Really, Pierre, isn't that dangerous?'

His smile became wider and wickeder as he answered. 'It could be dangerous if I did not like and respect Donald so much. Don't worry, you're quite safe.'

'I didn't mean that kind of danger,' I joked. 'I've never considered a handsome Frenchman dangerous!'

'Oh yes,' he replied, 'I heard about you. I once told Donald you were sexy looking and he said "Tonia? Sexy? She can stay without sex . . . for hours!"'

I laughed. 'That sounds like Donald.'

We finished our drinks then said goodbye to Bouvet who shouted something rude after us which made everybody laugh and follow us outside. Pierre put on his skis and bending down again cried, 'En route, Tonia!' Once more I climbed on to his back and to a round of applause from our laughing audience we started our descent.

At first we went slowly but soon gained speed and descended the mountainside faster and faster. Pierre went down practically in a straight line – he was superb, swishing between the bumps. Whenever we flew by some skiers they would first gape in surprise, then laugh and shout. If one of them was an instructor, some rude comment would accompany the shouting. I heard later that all instructors loved to ski downhill with passengers on their backs, but that very few females dared to accept this kind of transport. Personally I loved it and found it exhilarating. Suddenly

Pierre shouted for me to hold on. 'We're going for a jump. Move with me – okay?'

'Okay!' I called. He went straight towards a big bump that looked more like a mountain and – whoops, we flew! We must have been airborne for at least six yards. I was fully prepared for a crash landing but to my surprise we touched the ground so smoothly that I hardly felt the thump. Pierre shouted over his shoulder, 'You move well, my lady!'

'So I've been told!'

With peals of laughter we reached the bottom of the mountain. Pierre made a beautiful slow-motion stop and again we were applauded. As I dismounted I felt younger and happier than I'd felt for a long time.

'Pierre, you are by far the most handsome horse I've ever ridden.'

He laughed at my comparison. 'It is the first time I have been called a horse. Most of the time they call me a stud. But with you, madame, I can only offer a ride, so whistle for Pierre the horse any time you like.' We both laughed but were interrupted by the chiming of the village clock.

'Wow, it's 5 o'clock! Donald will be wondering what's happened to me.' And with that I ran off, calling back over my shoulder that it had been great fun and that I'd see him again soon. He waved and went on his way. Fortunately I was first back at the hotel and went to my room. I took a quick bath and had started dressing when Donald came in.

'Well, Bobo, what's this I hear about your performance this afternoon?'

My heart sank. *Here it comes*, I thought, *I've been too happy . . .* I looked up but to my relief Donald's eyes were smiling.

'Oh Donald, it was such fun. Wish you could have seen us swishing down the mountain.'

'Who said I didn't?' he laughed.

'You did? Where?'

'Gina and I decided to tackle the Loze and were dithering slowly down the mountain when we heard somebody shout "Hey, look at that lady on the back of the instructor". I recognised you at once and shouted back "That's no lady, that's my wife!"'

'Trust you to think of that!' Then I changed the subject. 'You know, Donald, Bouvet's little chalet on top of La Loze is really great fun and he's a terrific character too. We should go there more often. How did your afternoon go, anyway?'

'Lovely,' he replied.

Donald came over to me and put his hands on my shoulders. His blue eyes were serious when he spoke. 'I only hope my daughter grows into the kind of woman you are, a woman who can make a miserable man like me happy. Bobo, am I ever going to rid myself of this nervous trouble?'

Without hesitation I said with complete confidence, 'Yes, you will Donald – we will.'

The evening was pleasant. Gina had gone dancing with Pierre at the St Nicolas discotheque and we went to the one at the Carlina run by a lovely man nicknamed Bebe. The club was called Chez Bebe and that evening the place was packed with VIPs. There was Commandant Weiller, a big shot in the French airline world; Princess Mia Pia, daughter of the former King Umberto of Italy, with her mother; the composer Claude Bolling and his lovely wife; Rubirosa, the famous diplomat and jet-set personality, with his glamorous wife Odile; Brigitte Bardot; and a beautiful society girl named Helen Grinda, sister of the tennis celebrity, and we befriended her. Donald was in great form. He seemed his old self again and invited everyone to dinner the following evening. Deep inside I hoped I wouldn't have to cancel it.

The next morning he left very early. I didn't see him until the afternoon and I'd already started to wonder what to do about the promised dinner party. I was having coffee on the Carlina terrace when I saw him ski down the slopes towards me. He stopped and pulled up his goggles before shouting, 'Well, Bobo, it's all organised. Now we've got to alert the guests and get them informed of the programme.'

'What do you mean by programme?' I asked, puzzled. Donald took off his skis and joined me.

'Here it is,' he said. 'I've hired the ski lift for 8 o'clock tonight as it usually stops at 6. All our guests are to gather with their skis at the ski lift by 7.30 and champagne will be served there. At 8 o'clock we all go up the mountain, where at the top Bouvet is preparing a great meal. Then at midnight we all ski down the mountain with flaming torches!'

'Donald, that's crazy! How can we carry burning torches when some of us can't even manage our ski sticks properly?'

'Ah, now then. Skipper has thought of all that. Twelve ski instructors have also been invited to join the party and some of them, as well as the good skiers, will carry the torches. The more amateur ones can follow behind in the light. I've also got six blood wagons for those who don't ski at all, like the ex-Queen of Italy.'

I couldn't believe my ears. 'You have invited the ex-Queen?'

'Yes, and she accepted with great enthusiasm.'

I sat back in my chair with resignation. 'Now I've heard everything!'

Donald smiled and slapped me on the back. 'Come on, Bobo, we've got work to do.'

To my amazement everyone accepted, except for Brigitte Bardot who had returned to Paris that morning, and Commandant Weiller who said he had some work to do. My feeling was that he didn't like someone else throwing such an original party. Frankly I had always found his dinners extravagant but dull.

All the guests arrived on time and were excited about the whole idea. Gina and Pierre had organised the champagne which stood chilling in the snow beside the ski lift next to a wooden bench of glass tumblers. The corks popped and Gina and I started pouring drinks while Donald made all the introductions. I asked Gina who the two blonde girls over by the lift were.

'Ah them, they're two waitresses from Courchevel 1500.' This was the village beneath Courchevel 1850 where we were staying. 'Daddy invited them because they are expert skiers. They do look a bit rough though, don't they?'

'It's probably the yellow hair, dark lipstick and gold earrings that make them, shall we say, a little unusual to be introduced to a queen, even an ex-one.'

Gina laughed while pouring her umpteenth glass of bubbly. 'Don't worry, Ton,' she said. 'Leave it to the old boy.' So I did and it turned out to be one of the greatest party nights Courchevel had ever known.

We all went up the lift in different ways – with sticks, without sticks or tucked into a blood wagon. Bouvet waited at the top with bowls of steaming onion soup, spit-roast chicken, salad, cheeses and delicious crêpes Suzettes –

all served with limitless glasses of wine. During the evening I asked Bouvet where I could find la toilette. He said simply that it was behind the chalet in the open air, but preferably on the right-hand side. He explained that the snow on the left was used for melting water for the kitchen.

'Charming,' I said, 'but what if someone has no sense of direction?'

'Aha,' laughed Bouvet. 'That does happen quite often, but it only gives more taste to the onion soup!'

Somehow anything seemed possible up there in the darkness. Clouds had descended on the mountaintop and with the full moon shining it all looked like a scene from a Christmas card. I wish I could have photographed the scene around the table inside the chalet. There was the erect and severe-looking former Queen listening with great interest to the stories of one of the rougher ski instructors, while opposite her, also listening, was one of the blond waitresses madly picking away at her teeth with a long hairpin. Her Majesty looked at her, smiled stiffly and declared, 'They look very useful, those hairpins. Very useful indeed.' And for a horrifying moment I was afraid the waitress would offer one to our royal guest, but instead she smiled shyly and after wiping it, replaced it in her hair. Gina had noticed my expression. She laughed out loud and shouted across the table.

'See, Ton, only Daddy can bring complete democracy to the top of the mountain!'

It was a beautiful sight of togetherness among people from very different worlds. We all skied down the mountainside in the wee small hours of the morning, slightly tipsy. It was remarkable how the less expert skiers suddenly became very accomplished under the effects of the wine. We sang old French songs, English and Italian, all mixed in together, and everyone was laughing when we finally reached the bottom. The plan was to meet at the St Nicolas disco for a nightcap and to make sure that no one was missing. After a head count we raised our glasses and all became rather quiet. We contemplated that for the past few hours we'd been living in another world, a fairy tale world. Pierre Grunberg put it into words: 'Tonight was a night we will never forget thanks to the amazing Mr Campbell.'

Donald looked embarrassed. 'Oh, you overestimate me! Nature in this village is beautiful, the food satisfying and the wine took care of the rest.

The real reason for its success was the people and the beauty they had within them – that's all.' He put down his drink, took Gina and me by the hand and added, 'It's time to put the Campbell girls to bed.'

Much later, just before going to sleep, he murmured more to himself than to me, 'I think the old girl loved every minute of it.' I knew he meant the ex-Queen of Italy. She may not have been Queen of England, but for that evening at least she was Donald's queen. I hope she realised this, because I knew that the entire fabulous event had been intended to give her a good time and Donald's only enjoyment was the pleasure he took in looking at the fun around the table.

The next morning we met many of our dinner guests who all thanked us for such a great time. It was then that Donald noticed an old friend of his, a doctor called Victor Benetar. He came over and we invited him to join us for breakfast. Victor introduced us to his very beautiful companion, a model by the name of Laura Elisson-Davis, whom I recognised from her pictures in fashion magazines. We hit it off at once and the breakfast table became very jolly. Victor had a movie camera and got up and started to film us. Suddenly he shouted, 'Come on, don't just sit there – do something!' With that Donald got up, put several of the white serviettes into his trouser belt and began to dance an extremely comical ballet, to the delight of all.

We left Courchevel after three wonderful weeks. Donald seemed to have forgotten his health problems and was his old self once again. Gina discovered there were other things in life besides horses and developed amazingly during our holiday. And I was allowed some fun again, although deep in my heart I had misgivings about returning to Roundwood.

The day before we left Donald and Gina had gone skiing while I went shopping. On the way I met Pierre who invited me for tea in his flat. We talked and laughed, but then he suddenly took my hand and kissed it. I tried to joke and said, 'Careful, Pierre, I may want you to continue the kissing elsewhere.'

He looked at me seriously and said, 'You might?'

I adopted his seriousness and said softly, 'Yes, I would.' The room seemed to be filled with the scent of forbidden fruit.

Pierre released my hand. He never looked more handsome than at that moment; he said, 'Making love to you, ma chère Tonia, would be a dream, but doing this to Donald would be a nightmare.'

I didn't respond. I knew I had been politely turned down. Even a Frenchman knows where to draw the line – and in my heart I was grateful.

The following day Donald, Gina and I drove from Geneva, back through France and then flew home across the Channel in the air ferry, this time to Lydd. I noticed a change in Donald as soon as he drove away from the airport. Gina noticed it too and gave me a sad smile. I think she felt sorry for me. She was, after all, going back to school the next day and was obviously glad of it.

As soon as we entered our bedroom that night Donald sat down on the bed, groaned and took his head in his hands.

'What is this? I'm petrified again and I don't know why. I thought I'd recovered, but all the way from Lydd I've felt this coming on.'

'I know,' I said comfortingly. 'I saw your face grow tense.' Donald looked at me. He'd that lost-boy look and my heart ached when he asked me what we were going to do. I didn't answer for a while, but then suddenly a thought came to me. A doctor I knew years ago, Dr Carl Goldmann, could well be the answer.

'Donald, we're going to see one more doctor – mine.'

'Oh, Bobo, what's the use? He'll only give me another pill.'

'Not this one,' I said. 'Dr Goldmann will find the answer and tell the truth. He's cured me many times from all sorts of complaints. I believe in him blindly. I don't know why I didn't think of him sooner.'

We went to see Dr Goldmann. Tests were carried out on Donald and finally we were in his consulting room for the results.

'Mr Campbell, the news is good and bad at the same time.'

'What do you mean, Doctor?' asked Donald, surprised.

'If you had a definite medical problem we could remedy it, but unfortunately I can't do that. You're the only one that can fight the problem you have. Don't get me wrong – you do have a problem. A lot of fighter pilots used to get this during the war. Some got over it, others didn't. You, Mr Campbell, crashed in *Bluebird*, and although you always knew this could happen you never really thought it would. The surprise and shock of it has brought you this anxiety because subconsciously you have realised for the first time that you could lose your life. So each time you think of your record breaking or get any reminder of it, you get those shakes. In Courchevel you were away from it all and busy skiing, but on the way home the whole thing came back. So either you give it up, or you start one hell of a personal fight completely on your own, because I don't even think psychiatry would help at this stage. It's in your hands completely.'

Dr Goldmann stopped and looked questioningly at Donald. I didn't dare to look at Donald because I felt sure he would never accept this kind of talk. But I believed Dr Goldmann. Then Donald spoke, very softly.

'Well, doctor, thank you for telling me the truth. In other words I have become a cowardly wreck.'

Goldmann smiled. 'No, Mr Campbell, not a coward but also no longer a small boy playing with boats and cars. You are now a grown man who has suddenly realised his dream involves playing with death. Loving life as you do, your whole body and mind are in revolution. Physically you're perfect, there's nothing wrong with you at all. But you wouldn't pass a pilot's physical because of your mental state.'

Donald stood up. 'Thank you, Dr Goldmann. We mustn't take up any more of your time.' They shook hands and Donald walked out of the consulting room. I lingered awhile. Dr Goldmann put his arm around my shoulder.

'Tonia my dear, it's not going to be easy, I don't think he believes me, and as long he doesn't face it there's no cure.'

'What do I do now, Doctor?' I asked.

He thought for a while and then said, 'Find something for him to do away from record breaking, something that would demand his attention. But above all don't become a "yes" girl with him. Fight him – he's had enough sympathy.'

We said goodbye and I joined Donald in the lobby. We drove home in complete silence. When we arrived at Roundwood, Louis told me there had been a call from a Craig Douglas. I was amazed at this because I knew Craig Douglas was a young pop singer from the Isle of Wight with about twenty hit records behind him, and although I was very worried about Donald I couldn't help wondering why he'd called. Donald had gone straight to his office and before locking himself in told Rosie that he didn't want to be disturbed.

After the door closed Rosie looked at me and asked what had happened at the doctor's. I told her that Dr Goldmann had said there was nothing physically wrong with Donald.

'But that's wonderful isn't it?'

I sighed. 'Is it, Rosie? I wonder.'

As usual she sympathised with me, and then told me to ring Craig Douglas. 'He's rather dishy, and I'm dying to know what he wants!' she added.

I was grateful for the diversion. Rosie dialled his number and a voice answered. She said very professionally, 'Mr Douglas? Mrs Campbell's returning your call.' She handed me the phone to speak.

'Hello, Mr Douglas. I understand you called me. What can I do for you?' His speaking voice was very attractive, with only a slight Hampshire accent and more grown-up than I remembered it.

'Thank you for calling back,' he said. 'In a nutshell, I'm calling you on behalf of Janique Joelle. I know you two don't see one another any more but you have always been her favourite friend. You see, she's too proud to call you herself but I know she'd love to see you again.'

I hesitated a moment then said 'Mr Douglas . . .'

He interrupted. 'Please call me Craig.'

'All right,' I said, 'Craig. Janique and I have such different lives. She chose this break, I didn't. She lost interest in my life when I left show business and I don't really see why we should meet again now.'

The voice at the end of the phone was even softer now. 'Because she needs you. She always talks about you and she is going through some rough times. She needs another woman to talk to – someone she respects and loves.'

'Well, I don't mind meeting her again,' I said grudgingly, 'although I don't really know what I can do if she's going through problems of which I know nothing.'

I would have preferred to say no. But I thought of my own problems with Donald and just as I was going to say so I remembered Dr Goldmann's words: 'Fight him – he's had enough sympathy.' Maybe it would be good for Donald to see me go out and about with my own friends, so I agreed to meet for lunch the next Monday at the Caprice, and that was the end of the conversation.

Donald and I spent the evening seeing very little of each other. After Rosie left to go home, Donald stayed in his office and I went up to my den to read, but I couldn't concentrate. I finally rang the Coleys and talked to both Betty and Bill for a while. Bill suggested that I contact Peter Carr, enquire about flying lessons and try to coax Donald into it. He said it had always been his life's desire and it seemed to be the answer to the problem. After my call to them I realised they very much agreed with Dr Goldmann's opinion.

Donald never came up that night. I spent hours wondering whether to go to him. Finally, exhausted from worry, I fell asleep on my studio couch. Early in the morning, still half asleep, I had the feeling I was being watched. I opened my eyes to see Donald sitting in my chair looking at me. Sleepily I murmured, 'Hi there.' He leant forward and answered, folding his hands over one knee.

'Poor old girl. What a life I'm giving you.' I decided not to answer and as if in a dream I heard Donald's calm voice continuing. 'I'm going to Redhill aerodrome to find a flying instructor.' He smiled and winked at me before continuing cockily, 'I don't believe your quack. Typical of the doctors when they can't find what's wrong they put it down to nerves. It's an easy way out. Anyway, like I am, I can't go into any *Bluebird* cockpit. I daren't risk smashing another one, so I may as well take time off and learn to fly. I've always wanted to.'

I sat up happily. 'Marvellous idea. Let's have some tea.'

'Tea, or are you changing the subject?'

I sat back against my pillows. 'Darling, I tossed and turned all night and finally fell asleep on this couch. Now you cheerfully announce to me that I needn't have worried at all! You're going to do exactly what I wished you would do.' Then becoming very much Tonia Bern, I added, 'And I want my tea – voilà!'

Donald smiled, stood up and called Louis. 'Tea for her ladyship, Louis, and fast or we may have a French turn!'

Donald went to Redhill alone. I felt this had to be a boy's adventure so I found the excuse of having to organise the weekend's shopping. He was loyal and he would have included me, but I knew he was relieved at my absence. He found a great young instructor by the name of Tom Williams – handsome and ex-RAF of course. Donald spent practically the whole weekend at Redhill. He came home on Sunday evening with Tom who was to become a frequent visitor to Roundwood. It was great to see the change in Donald. Rosie was worried because he completely neglected all *Bluebird* matters and the letters from firms involved with the building of the new *Bluebird* were becoming pressing. Sir Alfred Owen of Bristol Siddeley had announced he would build another car stating: 'If Campbell has the guts to drive it, I will build it.' Rosie had worried unnecessarily because after coming home from a flying lesson he called her and me into his office. Sitting behind his desk, he pompously said, 'Take a letter, Mrs Piellow, and you Miss Bern-Campbell listen carefully.'

He dictated a magnificent letter to Sir Alfred, first apologising for the delay, then explaining that he'd been learning to fly, feeling this to be most important because his next venture was to be in Australia. He continued that he wanted to find a salt lake with more mileage than Utah and had heard of several possibilities in Australia's outback. Apart from the fact that he would be making the attempt within the Commonwealth, it might also be less expensive than the United States. To achieve this he wanted to fly over the outback in search of the right place and flying the aircraft himself would be so much more to the point. He continued the letter saying there was a place called Lake Eyre that might be right, and that if his hopes were answered the next land speed record would be set up within the year. He ended his letter by saying he had just made his first solo flight and was confident that within the next week he would receive his pilot's licence.

'That's it, Rosie! Duplicate it to all firms concerned and let's get those letters off by tomorrow.' Then looking at me he winked. 'What do you think of it, Toniacha?' I sat dumbfounded. Rosie had left the office with the excuse that she had better start at once, but I knew she was being her usual discreet self. Donald left his desk, came to sit in the chair opposite me and took out his pipe.

'I'm back you know, but it wasn't easy. While I was up in the plane solo I had the worst attack of nerves yet. I shook from head to toe. I was right in the middle of clouds and it seemed I couldn't get out of it. It was all I could do to keep control, but I did and then suddenly the clouds were gone, the sky was blue and the attack gone. I felt happy and free. I knew I could still do it. All it needs is my own self-control and I have that.' Then he added, mockingly, 'You'll be proud of the old man yet. Coward my foot – I'll show that quack!'

I smiled at him. 'Well done, Skipper. I never doubted that you'd eventually beat the problem,' I lied. What I didn't say was that the doctor whom Donald had called a quack had performed the miracle. He had obviously known that Donald, being the proud man he was, would react this way.

Donald had made all these new plans without my knowledge and had shown me once again that in the long run he walked alone. How deeply worried and confused he must have been through all of it. But it also proved that he could never be content with the simple life. The thought of preparing for a new record attempt and knowing that he could still do it, while associating his new-found flying skills with the attempt, brought back all his drive within a few days. The nervous problem was over and now we were to ride the speed rail once more.

As Donald was his normal self again I decided it was time to visit my father who was thrilled to see me. I arrived on a Thursday and intended to stay a week. It was great to shed the worries and responsibilities of the last few months. My cousin Maurice was now running the hotel and my father had moved into his beautiful villa, called The Flamingo, with my stepmother Annie. They lived a well-deserved restful life. Annie suggested that I stay at the hotel, knowing that their early bedtime wouldn't suit me.

Maurice had always been like a brother to me. He was married to a very nice woman called Lucie who was more attached to the Carlton than he was. This suited Maurice perfectly – he was a bit of a Don Juan and loved his freedom. On the Friday after my arrival we decided to hit a few of the discos along the Belgian coast, leaving Lucie to take care of the business. Maurice knew everyone and everyone loved the tall, lean and fun-loving man. The last place we visited was a club in Zeebrugge. The owner was the fashion-conscious and handsome Marcel Arnault. He was a master of the Madison, the in dance at the time, and soon showed me the steps. When Maurice wanted to call it a night I was still enjoying the evening so we decided Marcel would drive me back himself and Maurice left.

At 3 a.m. Marcel closed the club and suggested we sleep off the effects of the evening. He would take me back to the Carlton later that morning, he said. His extreme elegance and dancing perfection had led me to suspect that he was of a different persuasion, as we say in showbiz (meaning homosexual), and I agreed to stay. When we reached the bedroom I laughed out loud – the bed stretched practically from wall to wall! I don't know whether it was the soft lights of the harbour shining in through the window or Marcel's *savoir faire*, but it soon became clear that he was no homosexual. The night was full of surprises and great sex, yet with the dawn I felt nothing but guilt.

Marcel called me repeatedly during the days that followed but each time I told him that I wanted to spend time with my father, which was the truth. This was just as well because on the Sunday Donald arrived with the Barkers. Thrilled about his new flying skills he had chartered a plane to come over and surprise me. As soon as I saw him looking happy and healthy my heart leapt with joy and I hated myself for my weakness. Later we were all enjoying an aperitif at the Carlton when, to my horror, Marcel drove up in his Alfa Romeo. He stepped out of the car looking like a model from the cover of *Vogue* and waved at me.

'A friend of yours?' Donald asked. I replied that he was just an acquaintance. To my dismay Donald then beckoned him to join us. As Marcel approached Cherry exclaimed, 'Wow, Tonia, what a handsome specimen!' and Peter joked, 'Control yourself, Cherry, for goodness' sake.' I didn't know where to look or what to do. Marcel accepted the drink he was offered by Donald and chatted nonchalantly to all of us.

Donald had been watching me very quietly and suddenly I felt his hand on my knee. Squeezing it, he said softly, 'It's all right, Bobo. I love you and I understand.' But the tone of his voice was incredibly sad. He never spoke of or hinted at this again.

The flight back was pleasant. Donald obviously enjoyed handling the plane and the Barkers were on great form. I often wondered how much damage my stupid frivolity had done.

Our life became madly busy. Donald was promoting several products – from gloves to Ovaltine, from oil to safety belts – but before giving his name to any product he investigated it thoroughly and at length. The Campbell name was not to be associated with anything doubtful. He received enormous fees for the endorsements and they provided our main income. Although Donald had secured sponsorship from many companies for the record attempts, he was proud of the fact that he financed most of it himself. The other firms involved used his name for advertising and they, too, were investigated by Donald before they could join the record attempts.

Donald left two months later for Australia. From Sydney he would charter a plane and fly to Adelaide in South Australia with another pilot and an expert from British Petroleum. From Adelaide they would start the search of the Australian outback. He told me it would probably take a month. His cheerfulness left him at London airport and his eyes were very serious when he said goodbye. After he'd gone I felt lost. This man was sometimes husband, sometimes stranger. Whether he made me miserable or happy, as long as he was there beside me I was alive. From the balcony at the airport I stared at the plane that took him away until it was a small black dot in the sky. I felt my spirits had flown with him and an empty shell was returning to Roundwood. Later that evening I would write to him. I always looked for funny cards, 'lovey-dovey' ones, hoping they would make him smile. I spent a miserable time until his first letter arrived. I memorised it.

22 October 1961

My Darling

At last a moment to sit down, think and write. I miss you so much more than I ever thought it possible to miss anyone. Your very welcome card was waiting when we returned from Canberra and Melbourne. I do hope you are fit and well. At the moment I have another call in to you but always the lines are busy, out of order or closed down.

To try and tell you something about it all. We have been well received on all sides so far. I have had two meetings with the Premier and one with the Prime Minister, they seem interested but whether we will get all the support needed or not remains to be seen when we have come to a conclusion on the salt.

Lake Eyre is the most desolate area you can imagine. From ground level or from 5,000 feet up you can see nothing but flat, nothing in the middle of nothing, it's very frightening and you can so quickly get lost if not very careful. The whole of the middle of this vast continent – the size of America – is just flat barren desert, not a hill, not a tree, just nothing. It's nevertheless full of life – kangaroos, emus, dingo dogs, snakes and millions of insects. What they eat goodness knows. Lake Eyre is a dried out salt lake (of which there are a number) in the middle, or rather on the southern side, of this sand desert. The salt was left all over the desert by the sea millions of years ago. On the very rare occasions when it has rained the water dissolves the salt and then it all collects in these dried out lakes. The sun evaporates the water leaving the salt which is very hard and thick, in places 12 inches thick.

Eyre is some twenty-five miles long and fifteen wide. Unfortunately right across the middle occur three salt islands, some at 150 feet, maybe more, across and perhaps ten to twelve inches high. If they are scraped down they wound the undersurface which will not heal. The longest unobstructed run is only seven miles and we have therefore had to find a method of moving them without damage to the undersurface. Of course they have to occur right across the middle and not at either end, but such is life. We have evolved a cutting machine which is in fact a face milling cutter with carbide tip teeth (tell Les, he will explain in more detail). The cutter is driven by an electric motor and is all rather like a milling machine mounted on the side of a Land Rover. Power is supplied by a big diesel generator mounted on the back of another Land Rover. Both vehicles left this Sunday afternoon for the lake, one driven by a BP assistant manager, the other by a topping press chap – Tony Lucas. They should arrive tomorrow night. John Pryce and I leave by air tomorrow morning in a chartered Cessna 172 (how I wish we had the Apache). Incidentally had to sit the Australian Pilots' licence exam on Saturday and do a flight check!! Will not know if failed or passed until Monday morning!?

Up at the lake we stay at a sheep station owned by Elliot Price. It's a little settlement 35 miles from the lake – otherwise known as the 'outback'. The back of beyond!

Our telephone call has just come through – how wonderful to hear your sweet voice. I wish the line had been better. How I long to be home with you.

Elliot Price's sheep station is fantastic. In the middle of nowhere he has 12,000 sheep and is reputed to be worth half a million pounds. He cannot read or write but knows how many beans make five! A grand chap. How the sheep eat beats me, all there is is a bit of salt bush! Yet they all seem fit, not that you see many of them for they are spread over miles and miles and miles. Its lamb chops for breakfast, lunch, tea and dinner!! It puts me off. The water comes from an artesian bore where under terrific pressure it pours from a pipe in the ground which goes down 3,000 feet! Nearly a million gallons a day come forth and it forms a little river, in fact very muddy. Around it grow a few scruffy looking trees and all along its banks. The water has a very high content of sodium carbonate (washing soda) so you cannot drink it and no green life (vegetables, grass etc.) as we know it can live in it. You drink rainwater stored in huge tanks (there's been no rain for 24 years!). One keeps a fair watch out for snakes, which scare me stiff, although no one else seems to take much notice.

Out here by and large they are a grand crowd of men. The BP chaps from managers downward are absolute crackers. The assistant manager of the South Australian branch here in Adelaide started his long service leave yesterday (his long holiday) and started it by driving one of the Land Rovers up to Lake Eyre (450 miles of hard road) to be with us. (I can't see many of the English managers doing it.) John Pryce, Dennis Druitt's opposite number, has been with me throughout the trip. What a difference! One doesn't have to spend the whole day and most of the night drinking and talking about crumpet! If Dennis comes to Eyre I don't know what he will do – either go mad or the sheep will have to run fast.

We are just off to have dinner with Norman Gilbert, the branch manager, another cracker-jack of a man. Both John Pryce and Norman Gilbert are English but have been here for years and years. Pryce looks like a film star! Andrew Mustard, the Dunlop chap you may remember from Salt Lake last year (ginger beard!), had done a fine job.

Another problem – Eyre is owned by the state and a number of smart arses have now applied for leasing! I hope to scotch this one with the Premier tomorrow before leaving.

Haven't seen much of the women – one or two of the air hostesses have been quite attractive but a little clueless. Anyway it's just as well.

I just long to be back in your arms and if you cannot put some life in me its certain no one else can.

Fondest Love my Darling
Ever yours
Donald

Needing to do something to assuage my misery in missing Donald I met with Janique and Craig Douglas and the three of us got on very well. Janique was going through an emotional storm and like most of us needed some distraction. In her work as an agent, Craig and I were her very own professional discoveries. She was proud of us and felt that she had created us artistically. On top of this we had the same sense of humour; we could make her laugh and forget her worries.

Donald had also met Janique before leaving and although she was very friendly with him, she was not one of his favourite people. But then whatever power Donald had over women, Janique was one person on whom it had no effect. Maybe he wasn't trying. Funnily enough I had very little time for Janique's husband, Bunny Lewis, having always considered Janique far too good for him. Of course, when Craig Douglas met Donald much later, Craig instantly became Donald's hero. Donald looked upon Craig as the kind of son he would have liked. He felt Craig was a boy to be admired because, although from a modest background, in a very few years he'd become a man of the world. The two were to become great golfing partners and friends.

To me Craig was everything I had given up – showbiz, music, success and fame. I loved him for his great smile and his unaffected enthusiasm. He was young and handsome and we became inseparable during Donald's Australian trip. Craig was closer to my age than Donald and we had a lot in common. I followed him on his concert tours in my car and whenever Janique could free herself from office and family ties she would come along too. We had tremendous fun whenever we were together. Show business had taken me in again. Of course Donald was always at the back of my mind, but the lure of showbiz was like a drug and I craved it. I didn't even mind when the gossip columns said it was nice to see Tonia Bern back in circulation (shrewdly they added 'in the company of Craig Douglas').

One night after a concert in Chester I invited Craig to my hotel room and told him the gas fire was not working properly, which happened to be true. I was wearing a lovely black chiffon negligee when Craig arrived. He tried earnestly to repair the fire. Not succeeding in this endeavour he naively offered me his own room where the fire was working. He escorted me back to his room. After he left I sat down on the bed, laughing quietly to myself. Then, looking in the mirror, I said aloud, 'Surely you're not going in for cradle snatching?' I fell asleep with a smile on my lips. In later years Craig and I became the closest of friends but there was never any romantic feeling between us. His attitude to me was one of brotherly protection. In a certain way he brought Daniel back to me and I loved him for it.

Donald returned to England after an absence of seven weeks. His letters home were beautiful, warm and superbly written, and I treasured them for they kept the loneliness at bay. On his return I stood at London airport and faced him alongside a barrage of cameras and reporters. He came off the plane wearing an Aussie hat and carrying a big toy kangaroo – he was never afraid of the ridiculous. As soon as he got near me he grabbed and kissed me while the press photographers clicked away and had their fill. I was glad to see him looking so well. For seven long weeks I had lived the life of a free spirit and the sight of Donald brought back with a sudden shock the responsibility of being Mrs Campbell again. In no time Donald noticed my mood, but held back from commenting until we were in the car that took us to Roundwood. He spoke of Lake Eyre which was near an outback station called Muloorina in South Australia. To Leo Villa and Maurice Parfitt he gave technical details. He had started the ball rolling and we were to go over there in about six months' time.

All Lake Eyre needed was the odd bumps scraping here and there, and with some fifteen miles of driveable track this task would take about six months to complete. Through all this talking to Leo and Maurice, Donald never spoke or turned towards me but his hand clutched mine very tightly.

After we arrived home at Roundwood and were finally alone in his office, he put both hands on my shoulders and looked seriously into my eyes.

'Am I welcome, Bobo? Or has a certain girl been naughty?'

I didn't answer. I couldn't. I knew I had strayed more than once in thought. I smiled and shrugged my shoulders. He went to sit on the chair and proceeded to take off his shoes.

'Well, I never thought the day would come that during seven long weeks I would want one woman only, and away from her would want no other.' Then looking up he added, 'And what's more fantastic, I'm actually happy that this kind of thing can happen to a man like me.'

I wish my dad had known this. I could stand it no longer and went and sat down by his feet. I said softly, 'I'm sorry, darling. The only fling I did have was with show business. I enjoyed being back in that atmosphere so much that I now feel guilty. You deserve more loyalty than that, Donald, but I want you to know how weak I really am.'

His hand was caressing my hair. 'Don't worry, Bobo. I read all about that fling.' Horrified I asked him how. 'There are gossip writers in Australia too, you know! Come on, old girl, whatever you did was done for a reason. You're a damned attractive woman and I must admit Craig Douglas is one hell of a handsome lad, so there's nothing wrong with your taste.'

'But Donald,' I protested. He stopped me at once, putting his finger on my lips.

'Hush, my love. No more about this. You're my girl whatever you do. A naughty girl perhaps, but I never did want a saint! And you didn't look like one the very first time I saw you. So cheer up and give me that Bern smile I've longed for all these weeks.'

Week ending May 19 1956   EVERY THURSDAY   4°

Picturegoer

THE NATIONAL **FILM** AND
ENTERTAINMENT WEEKLY

THE
WOMAN
BEHIND
THOSE MARRYING
GABORS

LOREN
wins her
BATTLE

DON'T CALL ME
BIG
'EAD
says Max Bygraves

TONIA BERN

This was Donald's favourite photograph of me, but he had to put it face down on his desk during meetings for fear it would distract him.

A laugh a minute during an evening with the Crazy Gang, who were Donald's favourite entertainers.

Donald in the sound box during one of my recording sessions in 1966. I think he loved it more than I did! *Agence Dalmas/SIPA Press*

A jam session in Courchevel with Rubirosa on tom-toms and Claude Bolling on piano.

Left: Donald with that lost boy look – it really melted me.

Below: At Roundwood with house guests, American socialite Eleanor Franks and her Italian boyfriend Pierre.

Below: Happy days in our beloved Courchevel.

Above: At our wedding reception Terry Thomas had said to Donald, 'After two rehearsals' (meaning Donald's previous marriages), 'you should be ready now for a good show, what?'

Left: Time out from showbiz and record breaking, beside the wishing well at Roundwood.

Right: Arriving at Heathrow Airport from an overseas trip.

Above: Coniston, 1959. My first experience of a record attempt. I was scared stiff – only Donald's love kept me going. *Getty Images. Below*: The Bluebird team with their skipper. Donald is flanked by the Villa brothers, Tim and Leo. *Mobil Photo Library*

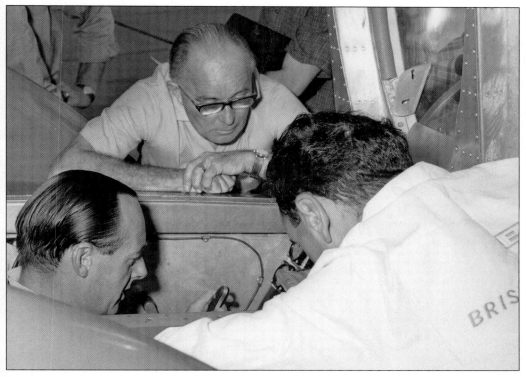

Donald, Leo Villa and Maurice Parfitt going through final checks before the record attempt at Bonneville salt flats, Utah. *British Petroleum*

The *Bluebird* car on Lake Eyre, Australia. It was my job to rinse the brake parachute after every run to ensure no salt residue was left which would damage the chute. To make sure, I had to taste it after rinsing it repeatedly. Bon appetit? I didn't think so!

Preparing for the return run on Bonneville salt flats with a cigarette and a Coke. Not long after this picture was taken on 16 September 1960, the *Bluebird* crashed and Donald was seriously injured. *British Petroleum*

Donald never knew that nothing really happened between Craig and me, and he never asked. With all my heart I gave him the smile and the love he wanted. Craig continued to visit our home, spending more time with Donald than with me. They went flying together, spent weekends golfing in Le Touquet, and the affection between the two men was complete. Seeing them heading off to golf one day and probably thinking there had been some goings-on during Donald's absence, Rosie couldn't resist commenting.

'Mr C. must have read the gossip about you and Mr Douglas.' Then shaking her head she added, 'Can one ever begin to understand the old boy?'

'No, Rosie, and one shouldn't even try. All I hope is that if ever the roles are reversed I can be as loving and understanding as him.' In later years I was to have this opportunity and although I outwardly succeeded on the understanding bit, on the inside I was eaten up with pain. Then I would remember that maybe Donald had known this pain too when looking at the young and handsome Craig Douglas, and the thought of this gave me the tolerance I needed.

Chapter 11

A Girl Called Fred

Six months later and it was the month of March, the height of the cabaret season in Europe. But there I was on the opposite side of the world standing dreaming on that horrible desolate salt flat called Lake Eyre. *What would it bring me?*

I remembered as a small child seeing Maurice Chevalier and deciding that being a stage star would be my life. I used to lock myself in my room for hours and try to copy him, dreaming all the time of having my name up in lights.

'Hi Tonia, how about some tea?' With a sudden shock one of the team brought me back down to earth and the desolate reality that was Lake Eyre. The cheery voice belonged to a north countryman called Carl Noble who was a popular member of the Bristol Siddeley group.

'Okay, Carl, I'll get the kettle going,' I said, and went back to the tent which had been erected by the team. It was a rather crummy-looking affair, but useful. I lit the Calor gas ring, filled the kettle, put it on the stove and waited.

Lake Eyre was an endless horizon of unbelievably lonely grey salt stretching for miles, with occasional patches of bubbly crust which made it look like a giant diseased skin. Digging into the crusts one often discovered the sad remains of birds or rabbits. Alone on Lake Eyre no one could survive, nor even find their way without the aid of a compass. It felt like the end of the road that leads to nowhere. Conditions had been anything but good since we arrived on 16 February 1963. Rain kept falling on the track and softened it, making it impossible to continue the preparation work. There had not been any rain in that part of South Australia for twenty-four years and it made us feel particularly unlucky.

Donald wanted to break John Cobb's land speed record of 394mph, but the weather looked as if it might put paid to his chances. In addition, there were floods all over Australia and the Cooper river which ran into Lake Eyre was flooding. If it continued to rain like this, we would have only two weeks before the Cooper flooded Lake Eyre. Hoping against hope we continued with the work. Thinking of all this and worrying as usual, I had prepared the tea and called in the men. They never came until they had wrapped up *Bluebird* to protect her from the rain. I filled their cups and took one over to Donald who was talking to Ken Norris, *Bluebird*'s designer. We called Ken the Mighty Mouse and beneath his calm exterior I always felt there was an undemonstrative but big sentimentalist struggling to get out. I couldn't help but overhear his last phrase.

'Well, she really wasn't designed for a soft track you know, Donald.'

'Tea, Ken?' I asked, to cover the fact that I'd overheard him.

'Lovely,' he answered, and went off to the tent with his little book of figures under his arm. I gave Donald his tea and said I had to go back. As I turned away from him he called to me. I looked back. He gave me one of his little-boy smiles and said in Australian slang, 'Stop worrying, darling, it'll be all right directly.'

I grinned back. 'I'm not really worried, darling,' and I felt my heart jumping as if it was ashamed at hearing such a great big lie.

As I approached the tent Leo Villa emerged from beneath the dripping canvas to tell me what a good cuppa it had been. Leo's nickname was Unc – because of little Gina, I suppose, but it could equally have been because of little Donald! As Chief Engineer to Malcolm Campbell many years before, he had lived and worked through all the Campbell records. He was always friendly, helpful and ready for a good joke, first on the job and last to leave. A true diamond in the Campbell clan's crown.

I cleared up the mess in the tent then climbed into one of the Land Rovers to drive thirty miles along the red dusty road to Muloorina sheep station where we were based. I usually flew back in Donald's plane, a

Piper Aztec, but tonight he was staying on with the boys. I would go ahead to help with supper preparations for the team of thirty. Driving along this bumpy road in a grimy old Land Rover I kept hearing Ken's words again and again: 'She wasn't built for a soft track.' Once again my memories turned back to Wendover and the Bonneville Flats in 1960, and the fateful day of Donald's crash in the first *Bluebird*. In show business terms I hoped this new understudy would be safer than the original star.

I could see it happening all over again but before I knew it I had arrived back at the sheep station. Louis and Julia, our Belgian staff, had come with us to Australia because we couldn't possibly have found another such hard-working and honest couple in so short a time. Julia did the cooking while Louis helped the team. Roundwood and the dogs had been left in the capable hands of Rosie and a couple we had engaged to look after things during our absence. Gina was at boarding school and on free weekends would go to Donald's sister, Jean Wales. Louis and Julia had created quite a few laughs because of their poor English.

The track that led to the station was soft and muddy in parts. Driving along it could be compared to driving in soft snow, but without the picturesque landscape. In fact, the only landscape worth speaking of was three or four miles of so-called salt bush that resembled rusty barbed wire. The other features of this unlovely road were the occasional fly-blown corpses of a bird or a sheep that dotted its margins and the bleached white skeletons of animals that had died of thirst and hunger.

As you approached the station the surroundings became less barren and hostile. A cluster of trees surrounded the bore hole and on the rare occasions when it rained, strange-looking flowers sprung up and carpeted the ground with dots of colour – though it was still not a painter's delight. The sheep station itself consisted of seven houses, all self-built and therefore very similar in appearance. The only evidence that we were living in 1963 was the modern cars parked outside the houses, one car per house. Yet the great people who lived on the station would never need a psychiatrist's help at any stage.

Old Elliot Price was the head of the family from whom we had requisitioned the sheep station and his eyes gleamed brightly when he told me on our arrival that this was his kingdom, and 'the most beautiful sight in the world'.

Yes, Elliot, I thought, knowing the place a little better now. *It is to you . . . and after all, beauty is in the eye of the beholder.* But all the same I wondered how much longer I would have to stay in his kingdom.

It had only been three weeks since we arrived and already it seemed like a year. I longed for the relative civilisation of Adelaide some 500 hundred miles distant. It was a pleasant enough town full of friendly people, many of whom were Italians – the so-called new Australians. They brought a lovely continental flavour to the place and made me feel at home.

Just as I arrived a flustered Julia appeared and told me that once again the meat hadn't turned up. I rushed over to the caravan we used as an office, which also doubled as the home of our public relations officer David Wynne-Morgan. Sadly, Peter Carr was no longer with us because he didn't want any more lengthy absences from his wife and children; this time Donald had chosen a bachelor. I entered the caravan to find June and Pat, the two Australian secretaries, giggling with some army chaps who were there to help us with roads and communications. Authoritatively I asked June what had happened to the meat we were expecting. She turned to Pat for information, but Pat told her that David had organised it, and so I was none the wiser. David was still out on Lake Eyre and by the time he came back the boys would have to eat.

All food had to be flown in to our camp and Marree, some thirty-five miles away, was the closest settlement. Surrounded by Aboriginal missions it really only had one general store which provided basic foodstuffs for the local sheep stations. This was pretty plain fare and consisted of smelly sausages, hard flour and tasteless lollipops – very little use to the Bluebird team. We put our heads together and decided to concoct a spaghetti bolognese. Julia, knowing the very special recipe that I'd been given by the chef of a top restaurant in Bologna, exploded with protest.

'But Madame, we have none of the stuff we need.'

'Don't worry, Julia,' I reassured her. 'Miracles do happen!' We had an arrangement with the Price family that they would take their meals with us. I went in to the kitchen where I gathered up several tins of corned beef, cut up onions and tomatoes, poured in some brandy and with a lot

of goodwill prepared what could pass for a bolognese sauce. The fact that
the garlic was missing didn't really matter because none of the English
boys would have appreciated it anyway.

When the crisis in the kitchen was over I returned to our own caravan
where the aura of peace and cleanliness was very welcome. Taking a
shower I thought of my numerous theatrical friends – Hughie Green,
Craig Douglas, Maurice Chevalier, Jack Benny and so many others – who
could have made great jokes about this place, which to me was the ugliest
spot on the face of the earth.

After taking a shower I decided to dress up a little to boost my morale.
One always had to wipe off the sand after having a shower, because the
bore water was full of it. To prevent my skin from drying out I rubbed it
thoroughly with lotion. Then I took a look in my cupboard. I hadn't
brought many glamorous clothes with me, but I did have a tight-fitting
pure silk Italian one-piece jump suit. I decided on that. While completing
the final touches of my toilette I heard Donald's plane coming in to land,
so I hurried to the homestead kitchen to help Louis and Julia. On the way
there I bumped into Elliot. He was a strange mixture of obvious toughness
and hidden sweetness. His enthusiasm when he welcomed us had at first
surprised us, but we soon learned where his real interests lay. If he could
have charged us for the air we were breathing he would have done so. Yet
there was a soft spot in the old ox. He smiled as he saw me.

'You look like a real nice sheila, Mrs Campbell. Any reason for the get-
up?'

'Of course, Elliot. Don't you know I'm in love with you? I want to find
out if you really have a heart.'

'Don't you worry about my old ticker, girl. It's there all right.'

'I wonder,' I said mockingly. He roared with laughter, not the least bit
offended by my teasing, and trailed off surrounded by his grandchildren
who adored him.

I never did find out which kids belonged where, but what I did know
was that there were too many of them running around. However, they
were nice kids and very grown up, afraid of nothing and disgustingly
happy with nothing – much nicer than kids in the sophisticated world,
and it did make me wonder whether civilisation was really the answer.

They always seemed to be around when they really weren't wanted. Their school was an old shed where there was one teacher for everyone. His name was Ian and he was positively the most unattractive young man I had ever met. Still, 'à la guerre, comme à la guerre' as they say at home.

The tables were ready and the boys started coming in. There was only one bathroom in the house and that contained one sink and an old bathtub. The men used it communally. The bathroom was situated on the verandah and right next to it was the extra gas-stove we had flown in for our cooking. It was placed there because of lack of space in the kitchen where a big old wood-burning range was in use all day. With a daytime temperature of more than 100 degrees, the added heat from the stove made things pretty uncomfortable. As the boys were having their baths and washing I was mixing some powdered milk, fresh milk being unobtainable in those parts. Donald entered.

'Boy, it's been hot . . .' he started, then stopped abruptly. A look of complete surprise crossed his face as he noticed my outfit. Then in a severe voice he continued, 'Tonia, I would like a word with you at once.'

From his tone I knew something was wrong. I looked at my half-whipped milk as if the explanation might be in it.

'Well, are you coming?' He let me pass through the door first and walking to the caravan with him I felt like Marie Antoinette going to the guillotine. When we were safely in the caravan he could barely suppress his anger.

'What do you think you're doing in that outfit?' he exploded. The expression on my face was blank so he continued, tearing my heart apart. 'You look quite ridiculous. Don't you realise there are ten women to 150 men on this station. Some of these chaps haven't seen their wives for over six weeks, so what's the big idea? Do you want to make things more difficult for them by wearing those bloody tight trousers?'

I felt revolted at the time and all I could say was, 'Sorry, I didn't think it was as sexy as all that.'

His mood became worse as he mumbled, 'Sex. That's all you females think about. For God's sake change before you go back to the kitchen.' And with that he left.

Later on I would see the funny side of this, especially where sex was concerned, as he thought a great deal more about it than I ever did. But at the time I felt deeply hurt and didn't return to the kitchen. Instead I sat in the caravan and wrote to Vera Freedman. I missed her sensible advice and poured my heart out, saying I was, after all, still Tonia Bern and this was anything but the right place for me. I wrote three long pages of self-pity and complaints, then re-read them and tore them into very small pieces. I then took another piece of paper and began all over again.

'Dear Vera, things are not too easy out here and I get very depressed at times – but then I knew it would not be a sleigh ride, so don't worry. All is well and I'm still smiling.' And that is just what I did – I was smiling when Donald returned.

That night I woke up with a start. I heard the sound of rain falling like pieces of lead on the caravan roof. I didn't dare move in case I woke Donald who was still fast asleep. As if he'd read my thoughts, he opened his eyes and said sleepily, 'There we go again. It'll be on the track again tomorrow, you'll see, Tonia. I have a feeling we won't make it, you know. Too much is against us.' There was an infinite sadness in his voice and there was little I could say because I agreed with him.

The rain kept falling all through the night. Donald and the boys left at the crack of dawn to inspect the damage to the lake surface. After I'd cleaned up inside the caravan and settled the food situation for the day I walked over to Lorna's house. She was the eldest of Elliot's three daughters and one son, all of whom lived on the same station with the exception of his youngest daughter. Lorna was buxom and good-hearted. She was married to Bluey, a big and colourful red-headed fellow, the sort of man one could only associate with the outback. They had four children. She offered me a cup of coffee and apologised for the rain.

'I mean we should be glad, of course, because we need the rain urgently. We've had twenty-four years of drought you know, but let's face it, after waiting all those years another four weeks wouldn't have mattered. Here, have some cakes. I made them myself.'

I ate the cakes gratefully. Eating was the only pleasure I had left and I'd already gained two pounds since arriving at Muloorina. Anyway, tight clothes were forbidden so to hell with my figure! We were having a cosy chat when Andrew Mustard came in. He belonged to the Dunlop team and had been closely involved with the design and development of the tyres for *Bluebird*. He spoke English with an accent I could only describe as BBC Third Programme and I was often at great pains not to laugh. He informed us that the track was not too wet after all and then rolled off some figures and descriptions of the salt conditions. Before he left we both nodded sagely, having understood absolutely nothing.

'He's all right really,' said Lorna. 'If only I could understand him! Gee, he speaks funny.' She looked so worried about it that I found the situation rather comical.

We were interrupted by one of her sons who ran in and called to his mother. 'Can I go for a swim? Grandad is taking all the boys and some of the army officers to the creek.'

'Of course you can go,' said Lorna. 'Why don't you take Mrs Campbell with you? She'll enjoy a swim in this heat.'

At this the boy looked troubled, but I thought it was a wonderful idea and I longed for a swim, so Lorna ordered her son to wait for me while I fetched my swimsuit. When I returned dressed in my costume with a towel wrapped around my waist, the boy said we'd have to take the kids' car. This contraption was home-built, with four wheels and a dozen pipes connected to them, but it worked and off we went.

The creek was situated about 300 yards along a dusty lane but my driver stopped about 50 yards away from it, looking very pale. Then I saw the reason for the boy's embarrassment – a very white and completely naked body belonging to a policeman was climbing up the 50-foot windmill that drove the water pump. The windmill looked like a giant ladder with a big round fan at the top. Not knowing that a woman was going to join them, none of the men had bothered with swimsuits. The boy turned scarlet, jumped from the car and ran to them shouting, 'Mrs Campbell is coming for a swim! Mrs Campbell is coming for a swim!' I stayed behind, of course, laughing softly but giving them time to don their swimsuits, and those who had not brought one, their underpants.

The swim was a big disappointment. The creek was muddy and covered with flies. Stepping into the water I could feel my feet sinking into a slimy ooze and the odd things that floated about in the murk, brushing against my legs, not to mention the thought of the snakes, didn't help with my enjoyment of the experience. Needless to say, my swim was short and sweet. The drive back was even worse. Hundreds of flies covered my body and because I was wet, the dust from the road stuck to my skin. Somehow I knew this would be my first and last swim at this 'resort'!

Donald came back that evening in a much better mood. When he entered the caravan he kissed me affectionately. I think he was trying to make up for the harshness of the previous day, but he needn't have worried. I'd already forgotten it.

'Well, Bobo, the track's not too bad. It'll be dry in two days and then we can continue the work and maybe have a go soon.'

I was wearing a loose-fitting plain shift dress, no make-up and flat-heeled sandals. My hair was brushed back. He looked at me and smiled, then suddenly he became very serious.

'Tonia, I want you to know something. You've never looked more beautiful than you do today.'

It was his way of saying thank you, his way of telling me that inner beauty was more important than all the Parisian and Italian outfits in the world. It made me feel good. We spent a harmonious evening together. When we were getting ready for bed, Donald told me that he would fly to Adelaide the next day to collect all sorts of machinery as well as some of our personal friends who wanted to come up. Because of that there was no place for me in the aeroplane, but as it was only for one night I wouldn't really mind, would I?

But oh, how I did mind! How I longed for a bath in clean water, a visit to the shops, the chance to listen to my few French records on the gramophone in the house we had rented in Adelaide. Maybe a trip to the hairdresser as well. I would have felt like Alice in Wonderland, but with my back to Donald, I lied.

'No, of course I don't mind. I've got too much to do here anyway. David has made a complete mess of the food orders, so I'll have to reorganise them myself.'

Just before going to sleep I heard Donald say, 'It's pretty awful isn't it, Bobo? But it won't be long before you'll be like Tonia again, you'll see.'

I answered softly, 'It's okay, Skipper, I only miss my music.' We turned to sleep and the night took away our worries.

When Donald took off for Adelaide next day I felt terribly left behind. I worked hard on my tapestry (one of my hobbies), wrote some letters home and organised the food. Later in the evening David Wynne-Morgan came to the caravan. He slumped down on one of the bunks and told me that the press were getting impatient.

'They all feel we're wasting time and Donald is not very cooperative.'

'Don't they know about the rain?' I exclaimed. 'Don't they understand Donald's worries?'

'I suppose they do, but what they want is action.'

'Well, David,' I said, 'with a record attempt they will just have to wait.'

'I suppose so,' answered David. 'Well, it's not easy for anybody I guess.'

I sighed. 'Do you mind, David, I must have some fresh air, although frankly there isn't much fresh air about here. Still, as it's dark now, at least the flies will have gone to sleep.'

I left my caravan, which had suddenly become stifling, and went for a walkabout, being sure to take a torch in case I encountered any snakes or scorpions. At night there were no flies and the fresh air was soothing. I walked past the first house, which belonged to Hazel and Bill Mitchell. Hazel was Elliot's second daughter, the only slim one in the family and a natural-born comedienne. She had two sons, but I think her laughter had kept her from producing any more children. I could hear the sound of music drifting on the night air and stopped a while to listen. Hazel's husband, Bill, owned the only gramophone on the homestead but his records were old and scratchy. Even the radio didn't prove much of an alternative. The signal reception on the station was very poor during the daytime, due largely to the eccentricities of the home-made electricity generator. Still, it was good to hear some music again and I felt like going inside, but I was not in a talking mood so I decided to make an early night of it.

Re-entering my own caravan, I felt the absence of music even more keenly. Softly I began to sing an old French song 'Que reste-t-il de nos amours' ('I wish you love'). As I was preparing to go to bed I glanced over at Donald's mascot, Mr Whoppit, who seemed to smile in thankfulness for the song. I grinned and said out loud to him, 'I can do even better than that given a piano, Whoppit. Just you wait and see!'

When I went to sleep that night I had the strangest of dreams. All my songs came alive and seemed like ballerinas dancing around me. I was just about to join them in 'The Roundabout' when the music changed. The ballerinas stopped dead and the music became the loud shrieking noise of the *Bluebird* engine. It became louder and louder until suddenly there was a huge explosion and all the ballerinas disappeared. I woke up with a start, looked about me at my silent caravan and felt very scared. I got up, took a sleeping pill before returning to bed and eventually faded away into a heavy slumber.

Early the next morning I decided to have a walk and shake off the feeling of the dream that was still haunting me. As I walked around the homestead, welcomed at once by the thousands of flies, I came upon Pat Crowe, a press photographer with the *Adelaide Advertiser*. A happy character with a Clark Gable flair about him, he was loading up his Land Rover with cameras and other equipment.

'Hi, Pat!' I shouted. 'What are you up to?'

'Going to take some shots of the outback,' he called back. 'My editors keep screaming for news and photos. It's not easy for us you know, Tonia.'

I looked at him. 'It's not easy for anybody, Pat. Record attempts never are.' He stopped his loading and came over to me, chuckling.

'Ah! Excuse me. I spoke out of turn. Look, why don't we take some shots of you? I've got a great idea. You, sitting in the water, washing the boys' laundry. We'll do it in the bore halfway to Marree.'

'But that water's boiling hot, Pat!' I said.

'No it's not,' he answered, 'only a little bit. Oh come on, it'll be fun! We can take some soap . . . some washing powder, and put it in the bore to make some bubbles.'

The idea began to appeal to me and Pat must have noticed this because before I could say anything more he pulled me into his Land Rover and off we went. We stopped at Hazel's for the soap. She hooted at the idea and gave it to us at once. Pat was great for a sing-song and the whole army repertoire came out as we drove along. I joined in, of course.

In a pretend shocked voice he said, 'Mrs Campbell, I had no idea you could sing that kind of song!'

'Ah well, Pat, one lives and learns, and Donald knows them all.'

He looked ahead and for a brief moment he became serious. 'I love your voice with that funny accent. I'm mad about it. Ever since I met you, Tonia, I've been looking through the whole outback to find a sheep with a French accent!'

I laughed and asked, 'Won't a cow do?'

'Yep, even a cow, so long as she speaks like you.'

Our small talk continued. Pat wanted to know why Donald needed to have reserve drivers. I explained that so much was involved in setting up a record attempt that he felt if ever he couldn't do the attempt for one reason or another when the conditions and car were perfect, then it had to be done with or without him.

'He's quite a guy, isn't he? I don't think the general public realises that.'

I smiled sadly. 'The general public does, Pat, but the big shots don't.'

We arrived at the hot water bore. While I tried to get my feet accustomed to the temperature of the water, Pat was sprinkling the washing powder in the waterfall, tripping all over the place. Neither of us expected the scene that followed. In a few seconds the whole creek was filled with a riot of bubbles. Pat ran to his car to collect a giant bathtub filled with all sorts of laundry which Hazel had loaned him and shouted very excitedly, 'Tonia, this is fantastic! Now, you get wet . . . completely . . . and come and sit in this bathtub. It will make a great shot with all this foam. Hurry before it dies down!'

There was no need to worry about the foam dying down because it got higher by the minute. My loose and unattractive attire became a beach outfit once it was soaked. I climbed into the tub which Pat had placed halfway into the water and we had a great time, Pat taking the shots, me blowing bubbles. While changing positions from which to shoot, Pat had to scream at me to make himself heard over the noise of the waterfall. It sounded quite mad.

'Legs up!' he screamed, then 'Now Tonia! Okay, now one down . . . try them up . . . arms above your head throwing the foam . . .'

And so it went on and on with soap bubbles everywhere – and I mean everywhere! When finally the session was over we were both exhausted and I changed into dry clothes again – borrowed from Hazel – behind the Land Rover. I joined Pat who was still beside the creek but now looking slightly worried. When he saw me he told me the reason for his concern.

'You know, Ton, we never thought of those poor cows and sheep who'll drink this muck, did we?'

'Oh my God! Pat! That's a terrible thought. Why didn't Hazel think of that and warn us?'

Then I remembered the numerous skeletons that littered the outback and hated the thought of maybe having contributed to this. Our drive back had no sing-song and was very quiet. We went straight to Hazel's house where her husband Bill was having coffee. She smiled at us.

'Well, you two, have some coffee. How did it go?'

Pat looked sheepish. 'We made a lot of foam, you know.'

'Good on you,' said Hazel, 'but why are you so down about it? Didn't it work out?'

Hazel,' I said, 'we made some great photos but we ruined the bore.'

Bill stood up at once, looking serious, and asked what we meant by that. 'Come on, let's have it,' he taunted us, a note of aggression in his voice. Then we explained. They both laughed out loud.

'You can both relax directly,' said Bill. 'A bit of soap never hurt anyone, least of all here in the outback. I would drink the blasted water myself, although I prefer a pint of beer. We don't hurt easy out here, human or animal, and speaking of the animals, they won't be constipated for a while!' With that he walked out laughing, calling us 'town cissies'.

We spent a good time telling Hazel all the details, but they were really only funny to us. The photos were later published in *Paris-Match* and were very much the pride of Pat Crowe, who continued to look for a sheep with a French accent, but never found one.

Donald landed about noon the next day. I couldn't understand why he taxied his plane right up to our caravan. It was not like him to be inconsiderate and the plane was stirring up big clouds of dust. As soon as he stopped the engine I jumped out of the caravan to tell him off. Then the door of the plane opened and I had the surprise of my life. There stood my great friend Lorrea Desmond. I couldn't believe my eyes and didn't dare. Lorrea and I had become friends in London many years before when we were both struggling our way into the limelight. A Belgian and an Aussie. It had been lucky then and I think those years were by far the most carefree I had known.

Lorrea was now famous in her own country. As she stood there smiling at me in her beautiful turquoise outfit, splendid hairstyle and divine long red nails, she brought to mind all the fun and the excitement of those years. We kissed and hugged and talked, all at the same time. When the first excitement had passed I turned towards Donald to thank him, and there was yet another surprise waiting. I could not hold back the tears for in his arms he held my gramophone and next to him was a case full of records. It had all been organised very rapidly.

Florence Ulve, a great friend of ours who owned the only continental-style nightclub in Adelaide, had booked Lorrea for a season. When Donald heard of this he went to see them and together they decided to take pianist, drummer, the lot and go to Lake Eyre. They'd give the boys a show and me the thrill of seeing Lorrea who by now had become Australia's top TV star. Lorrea was a sight for sore eyes and the whole evening was spent laughing and joking and madly making plans for the show that was to be held the next day because Lorrea had only two days free. That night I went to bed a happy girl. Donald was going to sleep in the tent with the boys and Lorrea was taking over his bunk. We chatted till the wee small hours of the morning, drank the Australian champagne she brought, and of course we went down Memory Lane.

The next day, while the boys were out working on Lake Eyre, Lorrea and I prepared the show. It was to be held in the army tent at around 6 o'clock which just gave the boys time for a wash and shave. Then after the show the meal would be served and the celebration would go on. News travels fast in the outback and the whole of Marree was present as well as the team and all the army chaps. To us it was the greatest show on earth. Lorrea put all she had into it, and she had plenty. This was real talent from a big-hearted, lovely showbiz girl and it made everyone very happy. Even Elliot Price kept mumbling, 'That's a really lovely sheila if ever I saw one!' But old habits die hard because he made her pay for a salt block souvenir of Lake Eyre, telling her that she had to buy it as it would bring her luck!

Donald was due to fly Lorrea back to Adelaide the next morning and was going to use the trip to bring back more food. Before she went Lorrea wanted to see Lake Eyre and *Bluebird*, so it was decided that David Wynne-Morgan and I would accompany her and Donald to Lake Eyre. To my surprise she wore no make-up and just a simple pant suit. I guessed Donald must have explained to her the problems of lack of female contact in the outback. We gave her a conducted tour but soon the time came to say goodbye. I didn't say much – I just kissed her and then she walked up the steps of the plane. Just before the door closed she waved to me, then Donald started the engine and the plane began to taxi. To make light of the moment I ran along beside the plane for as long as I could until I was out of breath, then I stopped to watch it take off, hoping that my running had made her laugh a little. Instead, I heard later that she had cried softly and said, 'Poor Ton. How I hate to leave her there, so terribly alone, so terribly out of her own world. She must love you a lot, Donald.' Apparently, he didn't answer.

Down on the ground I went to the tent to prepare sandwiches for the team. The boys had only one subject of conversation – Lorrea. Carl Noble, a north countryman with a dry sense of humour, had only one worry on Lake Eyre: where to find girls. But his quest was quite hopeless and with genuine feeling he sighed, 'Coo, it was nice to see a real woman again.'

Pretending to be terribly hurt and shocked, I exclaimed, 'Carl – what am I then?'

First he looked surprised, then shrugged his shoulders and said 'You? Didn't you know? You're Fred.' Everybody laughed, and that's how I became a girl called Fred.

The days that followed were full of anxiety. With eyes full of fear we watched the threatening clouds hanging over Lake Eyre. Donald had done his trial runs for the press and that had kept them quiet for a while. Finally he decided to go ahead on the half-dry track, but first he would fly to Adelaide to collect timekeepers and officials and then return the following day for a run the same afternoon. As soon as this decision had been taken, a strange fever infected Muloorina. Old Elliot was going around frantically giving all sorts of details about the approaching record attempt, as if he had done it dozens of times himself. There was no need to say that these details were anything but accurate, for Elliot, being hard of hearing, had misunderstood most of what was being discussed.

When Donald took off for the lake I stood on the dusty red strip, waving until my arm ached. I looked around me at the dried-out trees and the primitive shearers' quarters that were now full of press and other people who were paying £5 per day for Elliot's hospitality. Once I told him jokingly that this was the price for a single room with private bathroom at London's plush Dorchester Hotel. 'Oh,' he said. 'But I give them food as well for that.'

The fellows didn't complain about the food but then there was no alternative and I must admit that my own cooking arrangements were anything but organised. Looking around, I felt a stronger dislike for the place than ever before. How could people like Hazel and Lorna still live here after having seen other places during their holidays? I suppose it must be in the blood.

I admired Elliot in many ways. One of them was the remedy he had come up with for his hernia. Whenever it troubled him he climbed up on to his fridge and jumped off. After doing this a couple of times all was well, he used to say, and so it seemed. I often wondered what the Harley Street men would say about that miracle cure.

I went to the homestead to find Mrs Price, who rarely showed herself, and found her busy on the radio transmitter which was her only amusement and hobby. It was built into the corner of her dining room and from here she could call other sheep and cattle stations for miles around. But the main purpose of this invention was to contact the Flying Doctor Service. If an ailment was described over the transmitter, the doctor would attempt to diagnose it then tell the caller to use medicament number seventy or eighty-five or some other number stuck on the medicine bottles or powders. These were contained in a small black case. The first time I heard this conversation I felt like saying 'Faites vos jeux', but this was no roulette. It was a gamble with life and only when the patient was seriously ill did the flying doctor appear in person.

Mrs Price was a dear old lady who let us take over her house completely and accepted with gratitude our insistence that we would not allow her to do a stroke of work. She was very heavy, like most women out there, and had the most frightening swollen legs covered in varicose veins. From the moment Donald had met her his heart wept with pity and he insisted that we were especially kind to her. He told me that here was a woman who had worked and slaved under the most primitive conditions and was now completely worn out, yet never complained about her lot because she had her beloved transmitter and could chat with her neighbours several hundred miles away.

Elliot could neither read nor write so she was kept very busy with all the books and correspondence, but whenever she was asked to send a telegram through her transmitter, her face beamed with joy. Then her voice, happy but unmusical, screeched away. 'Ajas Muloorina, are you receiving me?'

That afternoon she was speaking to a woman called Mabel on some far-away station. Yes, she had her usual headache, she said, but the doctor's pills were very good and it was Glen's birthday very soon. She would give him a bow and arrow. Did Mabel hear about Dan Moss? He was in bed with 'flu. She'd heard it on the wireless two days ago.

And so there were no secrets in the outback. For whether you were having a cold or a baby, everything was broadcast on that famous wireless and everything was numbered for a bottle or powder from that little black box. And so I named the radio receiver of Mrs Elliot Price the 'gossip calypso'.

Mum Price finished her daily interlude at last and I made her a cup of tea. I was always able to make her laugh and she told me the most fascinating stories of how they had started out. But somehow she never made it sound hard and miserable. To her it was life – love, children and success at the end of it all, with lots of lovely grandchildren whom she adored. I was glad to know that the children loved her too and that she was a queen in their hearts.

That same night we were all having dinner and chatting away when suddenly I heard a strange noise. It was as if bombs were falling everywhere. 'That's rain, if ever I heard it,' shouted Mum Price. Rain, I thought, it sounded like torrents, and we all realised that this time the heavens had really opened. I looked up at Leo Villa. He had suddenly aged ten years and shaking his head, mumbled, 'That does it, that does it!'

Donald returned the next day about noon. The observers on the lake had reported that the rain had not spread and the track was almost dry.

The timekeepers had brought a fever of excitement with them. Together we boarded the plane and Donald flew us to the track. When we landed I caught sight of David Wynne-Morgan waving his arms to usher us away. As we left the plane Leo came towards us with his slight limp. I couldn't help but notice how much older he was looking.

'I don't like it, Skipper, it's not dry enough and there are still plenty of clouds about.'

Donald looked up at the skies and I knew he agreed with Leo. I broke the tense atmosphere and asked whether anyone would like some coffee.

'Best idea I heard today,' said Leo.

Walking towards my canteen tent I felt so helpless I could have cried. *Oh please weather,* I thought, *settle down, just for one day.* But somehow I felt nobody was going to listen to me. Coffee was soon prepared and the boys came in, grateful for the break. They chatted for twenty minutes, mostly about *Bluebird,* then one after another they drifted back to work. I began clearing up but I was never to finish for with a sudden roar the tent was filled with a most violent gust of wind that threatened to whirl it up into the air. Cups, saucers, sugar and biscuits flew everywhere. Without knowing what was happening I tried to save some of it, but all along I could hear screams and shouts from the team who were trying to save their own equipment. That's when I realised these were the desert storms I'd heard so much about. Donald ran into the tent shouting. 'Darling, drop everything, we've got to get the Aztec off the ground before it gets damaged. *Bluebird*'s safely covered and chained down, the boys have taken care of that.'

He was calm, as usual, and had taken a firm grip of my arm. As I left the tent I realised why – it was all we could do to keep our feet on the ground. We held on to each other and struggled to the plane. It took two of the boys to wrestle the cabin door closed behind us. While Donald was starting her up I fastened my safety-belt. The propellers began to turn and off we went. I don't know how we ever managed to take off. The plane was blown right and left and up and down, but somehow Donald managed to control her and up we climbed above the storm where all seemed much calmer, but not for long. My eyes wandered around the cabin and I noticed with horror that I'd forgotten to secure the door's safety latch. I told Donald.

'My fault,' he said. 'The pilot should always check the door before take-off. Try to pull it down.' I reached for the latch but was too late. There was an almighty bang, the door flew open and the plane pitched down like mad. Donald immediately tried to open the small cockpit window on his side, hoping that the flow of air might steady the plane, but it seemed jammed. He tried to straighten up but the situation appeared hopeless.

'We have to crash land, hold tight!' he shouted.

All I could yell was, 'No, no!' My voice was firm.

Swiftly I tightened my safety-belt and leant out towards the open door and the emptiness. My two hands grabbed the door and pulled. I'll never know how I got the strength but the door hinged back slowly towards me. Donald was able to get the plane back under control and in a voice full of admiration he congratulated me. For ten minutes, which seemed more like ten years, my hands clung on to the struggling door. I couldn't close it but I didn't dare let go. Only after we finally landed was I able to let go and it was only then that I noticed blood on my hands. The door had cut right through the palms of my hands. I hid my injuries from Donald and went to the caravan to disinfect the cuts. I knew these minor scratches were nothing compared with what might have been.

Outside the caravan I heard Donald's voice describing the flight and the courageous actions of his wife. The fact that he could have blamed me for failing to fasten the door latch when he himself had so much to do obviously never entered his mind.

That night I had organised a Lancashire hotpot and the boys were thoroughly enjoying it when Inspector Bredner came in. Bred, as we called him, was a lean, strong Australian and a perfect police officer. He had a very soft spot for singers and was always charming to me, but I don't think he understood my presence there with the team. I'd never seen him as worried as he was that night.

'Can I see Donald, Tonia? I'm afraid I've got bad news.'

Standing by the stove as he spoke, I completely forgot whose meal I was dishing out and I left it there. 'Come on, Bred, the food will wait.'

We went into the dining room where Donald took one look at us and instinctively knew something was wrong. Bred nodded.

'Yes, I'm afraid that's it. It's pouring down on the lake and the floods are approaching at a rate of knots. I reckon the lake will be alive in a few hours.'

I could sense the feelings coming from the boys, a mixture of panic and doubt as to the accuracy of Bred's statement. Donald had a steely determination on his face and it made him look tall and strong. His voice was beautifully calm as he spoke and once again my admiration for him was unlimited.

'Boys, I'm asking for volunteers. We've got to get the *Bluebird* off the lake at once. That's the main thing now.'

'I don't think there is any urgency, Skipper,' said Andrew Mustard. 'There will only be a few inches of rain by morning and that won't move the heavy weight of *Bluebird*. It'll be much easier in the morning. Anyway, you won't find her in the dark if she's floated off.'

'We'll find her,' said Donald in resolute mood. 'I will not take the risk of letting *Bluebird* break through the salt and float away. Too much has gone into the '*bird* and you know what salt can do to her. It literally eats up all the mechanisms. You can never wash it out completely even after a run, let alone if she sinks through.'

With that, Donald stood up and so did the whole room. There was a hint of tears in his eyes as he continued. 'Thanks boys. I expected nothing else.' Then, quite cheerfully, he turned to me. 'Fred, keep some hot soup ready and sandwiches. It'll be a long, wet night.' And off they went.

Typically British, Donald was at his best when everything went wrong. The team knew they had lost the record for this year and that this was the end. But somehow they could only think of rescuing *Bluebird* from the dangers of the lake as if she were a damsel in distress. When they left I prepared the sandwiches and a huge pot of soup which kept me quite busy. Those of us who were left on the station had no idea how long we'd have to wait, but we all knew we couldn't rest until Donald and the team returned.

The story of the rescue was later told to me by Ken Reaks. He was a true RAF type and bursting with admiration for Donald. In the event, Andrew Mustard had been proved completely wrong because they found floodwater everywhere and everything was already afloat. It was pitch dark and Donald had to sit on the bonnet of a Land Rover holding two torches to help them find the way, the vehicle's wheels half-submerged in the salt water. When they reached the tent where *Bluebird* was 'hangared' there was no sign of her. Some of the boys panicked. Ken told me Leo looked like a man whose child had just died, but Donald told him not to worry. They'd find her. With his customary tremendous sense of purpose Donald organised a methodical search pattern to ensure that none of the boys got lost. It is not easy to appreciate the difficulties of conducting such an operation unless you've experienced the big and desolate Lake Eyre at first hand. The mental picture I was given of Donald – soaked to the skin with salt crusting his face, sitting on the bonnet of the Land Rover clutching a torch in each hand – made my heart melt with compassion. Then suddenly a scream of joy rent the night air, a scream that echoed again and again over the vastness of the lake.

'There she is!' The Skipper had found his ship.

Shouts from the boys came from all directions. 'Hooray, well done Skipper!' At that point even Andrew must have realised Donald was a true leader, but thoughts of Andrew were completely forgotten in the euphoria of the moment.

It was 4 o'clock in the morning before they all returned to the station. Until 6, the time was spent telling and retelling the tale of the rescue, drinking soup and eating sandwiches. Then, and only then, came the sad realisation that it was time to depart. We had to pack up and wait one month, two months, maybe even a year, for the lake to dry up again. No one knew how long it would be before a fresh attempt could be made.

On our way to the caravan Donald pondered aloud whether there was another lake somewhere in Australia that could be used. I knew he would have to look. 'You know darling, I'm going to get stick from the press because no one would believe these rains unless they saw them for themselves. No one would believe we lost *Bluebird* because she's so big, and because very few really know the outback or Lake Eyre. All the people involved in this record attempt who are sitting comfortably behind polished desks in London will never believe I did all I could.'

The next day was spent packing and preparing for our departure and then finally we boarded the plane. After a flight that lasted several hours we arrived back in Adelaide. The house we had rented overlooked the sea, but it was now cold and damp because it was June and the Australian winter had set in. In England there are lovely log fires to keep you warm in winter, but down under it's darned cold inside as well as out and dark at 6 o'clock, winter or summer.

While hectic preparations continued for Donald's planned trip around the outback to find another lake, I went on a shopping spree for my forthcoming visit to Sydney. I was to stay there with Lorrea until Donald's return. Lorrea had married Dr Alec Gorshenin and had just returned from her honeymoon. When we called her she was thrilled and said she would prepare my room at once.

As soon as I'd unpacked I decided to have a look through all the press cuttings that Florence Ulve had saved with her usual thoughtfulness, realising that we had no papers at Muloorina and that I would want to know what had been said about my man. Apart from a few criticisms, the press coverage wasn't too bad. Somehow, word of the bad luck at Lake Eyre had spread across the continent. Old Elliot had given several reports of the unbelievable case of rain, which of course was good for him, but for poor Mr Campbell, as he put it, the thing was awful. Looking at the press photos of Donald and myself was no treat at all, for on most of them we really looked like Donald and Fred. I wondered if I'd ever live this down with my showbiz crowd.

Donald left Adelaide with three team members. He said he would keep me informed whenever he was near a post office or telephone which, in those parts, were rather rare. Then he took my head in both hands and said, 'Go have a fling in showbiz, Bobo. It'll do you the world of good.' The day after his departure the remaining team members flew back to England but I'd accepted two TV shows in Adelaide so I had to stay behind.

The day of my first TV show came and as I walked towards the camera singing 'C'est si Bon', which was Australia's choice of French song, the lake, the rain and the hardship all went and once more I was myself. Within two weeks of my TV appearances I had created quite a stir in Sydney. I was offered every possible programme and the critics used phrases such as 'She monopolises the screen', 'Her singing and her sharp, contemporary wit are a delight', and 'It will be a sad day for Sydney and

Australia when Donald Campbell jets in to take her away'. Reading all this, I realised every article mentioned Donald: with or without him I would always live in his world. All this was, of course, the greatest medicine to make me forget the disappointment of the lake and when, after three weeks, I received news from Donald saying the trip would take another twelve to fourteen days, I wasn't too unhappy. I missed him, of course, but Mr Showbiz was a great stand-in, if only a stand-in.

I decided to look for a flat so that Lorrea and Alec could have some time alone, especially as Lorrea was leaving in about two weeks for a cabaret season at Surfer's Paradise, Australia's answer to the Riviera. When Alec came home that evening I told him of my plans. I'd heard of a nice studio flat in the same district. He looked quite horrified and asked me to stay.

'Don't go, Ton. It's been fantastic having you here. The old girl can talk shop to her heart's content and when I come home she's relaxed and quite willing to listen to my conversation. Before you came all I heard was showbiz which is a strange world to me. I couldn't go through all that again. Please stay, just for a while?'

I wasn't sure what I should do but when Lorrea came home and the matter came up again there was no more argument. She refused to let me go. So I stayed.

Donald had already been away for an extra ten days when I took a call one morning from the operator. She said she had Donald on the line for me from Alice Springs, but when she put him through I just couldn't seem to hear him, only clicks and more clicks.

'Can't you hear him?' asked the operator. When I told her I couldn't she said she'd try once more. She came back in seconds.

'There's nothing wrong with the line but your husband can't talk to you. He's afraid you won't be able to take it. It sounds as if he's crying.'

I wasn't sure what was happening. Suddenly all sorts of terrifying possibilities came into my head and this time I really screamed. 'Please ask him to talk to me. Tell me what's wrong. Is he ill or has he had an accident?'

Again, clicks and clicks and then a silence which seemed like forever. The operator spoke again.

'He's sobbing now. He said there won't be any more trips. He left the hospital an hour ago and is in a phone booth. He can't talk to you but says he will talk to a Miss Desmond.'

I became hysterical with worry but fortunately Alec and Lorrea immediately took control of the situation and contacted the police on their other line. It soon became clear that the whole thing had all been a cruel hoax. I was too ill to feel relieved by this news and I remember going to bed that night praying I would hear from my man soon. I'd believed the call because it was just like Donald not to want to give me bad news if I was on my own. This experience made me realise more than ever that he was my whole world.

The next day, a Tuesday, I received a telegram. It read: 'Haven't been near a phone for days, but hope to ring tomorrow. Miss you terribly. All's well. Love, D.C.' It was only then I realised what very sick minds some people have. Although the police did their utmost we never found out who made the call. Frankly, I didn't really want to know.

Unfortunately, this was not the only bad thing to happen in the weeks that followed our departure from Muloorina. Sir Alfred Owen arrived in Sydney and was quoted in the papers as having criticised Donald's handling of the world record attempt. This was just what the press wanted to hear. They had been writing about Donald for months but now they really had some ammunition! Sir Alfred's arrival might have been a very small item in the papers under different circumstances, but the criticisms he made generated a controversy that grabbed the headlines and it was reported worldwide. When Donald next called me I had to report this to him. He didn't comment, but simply said he would return as soon as possible to cope with the problem.

He arrived the following weekend; although it was a joyful reunion there were storm clouds above our heads and I could feel them. He was very hurt when he read the reports. Over the next few days he appeared on several TV shows to answer the criticisms. His performance was superb and I was more proud of him than ever. There was not one bitter word against Alfred Owen. Indeed, as he said on television, he was surprised at the behaviour of such a great English gentleman who'd been so supportive of him and he failed to understand his reasons. Donald continued to say he would have expected such criticisms to have been made to him personally. He understood that it was necessary to explain to people sitting behind a desk what the outback was really like, but there was no need to explain anything to the people of the outback who knew what a great catastrophe the team and Donald had suffered. He also pointed out that they had saved the *Bluebird*, a very close-run thing. In later years Donald was to write a complete account of his response to these particular criticisms and events.

To the people of Adelaide, Donald came out of the incident a great gentleman. But unfortunately the bad publicity had not done his reputation any good in England, and that was the real pain Sir Alfred Owen had caused him. As for me, well, I was not as charitable towards Owen as Donald had been. I called him a publicity seeker and a hard businessman. In my view it was now quite obvious why he'd backed Donald: it was purely and simply for his own reputation and nothing to do with winning the record for Britain. I hoped that Donald would start a libel case and sue Owen for damages. Although I knew that in time Donald would forgive and forget, I never would.

Donald had failed in his quest to find an alternative track in the outback, so we would have to wait until Lake Eyre was dry again. As this would take several months, Donald decided to return to England where he would face the music and try to repair the results of the media damage. We left on a Sunday and the airport was crowded with friends, business associates and press. One reporter came up to Donald and asked, 'What now, Mr Campbell, any plans?'

With a sad look in his eyes, Donald smiled and said, 'Yes boys, one plan, we're coming back.' Although he said it softly I had the feeling that no one there doubted his words.

Back home in England the press reported to Donald that Stirling Moss had also criticised him on a recent trip to Australia. Moss had arrived at Sydney airport and was asked by reporters for his opinion on the comments levelled at Donald Campbell. The press reported him as saying, 'Donald Campbell should leave the cockpit to a younger man.' This was later denied by Moss who said the quote had been taken out of context. On the same day as Moss passed through Sydney airport the English carpet tycoon, Cyril Lord, arrived there too. He was asked for his view of Moss's remark and answered that such words 'were pure sour grapes'. When Donald was told the story he chuckled good-humouredly: 'Good old Cyril Lord, true English loyalty, just what I expected.' As far as Stirling Moss was concerned Donald didn't seem to mind, and although he himself never criticised Moss he also never complimented him the way he did Graham Hill, Jack Brabham, Jackie Stewart, Craig Breedlove and many other speed personalities.

Back in England we soon felt the damage caused by what had been said and lost the support of several firms. I told Donald that I thought he should sue Sir Alfred Owen for at least £50,000. At first Donald said he couldn't do that. I asked him if he didn't feel outraged at the injustice of it all. He told me that he felt more sadness than outrage.

'I've had let-downs before. The firms I'm losing I can replace. I intend to break that record and I will. Then all this criticism will go away. But I admired Sir Alfred. He was a father figure to me. That's why it hurts.'

Some time later he reconsidered my advice and went to see our solicitor, Victor Mishcon (later to become Lord Mishcon), to ask his opinion about claiming damages. Victor didn't feel this was right and said that instead he should seek a public apology. By then the Owen group had realised the truth of the events on Lake Eyre; Owen himself agreed to an apology and a gift of £5,000 towards the next attempt. I tried hard to get Donald to refuse this offer and go for the £50,000, but he said that Sir Alfred had been too good in the past in his support of the record attempts and therefore he could not, in all conscience, seek more money.

The press needs controversy to sell newspapers. The apology statement came low down on their list of newsworthy stories and as a result it made a very small paragraph on the back page of some newspapers. Very few people read it. I told Donald he should spend the £5,000 on magnifying the apology into a huge advertisement and put it in several papers. He laughed at me.

'Bobo, you are quite a defender of the Campbell Clan but frankly I want to forget the whole nasty affair and get on with the future.'

Chapter 12

A DOUBLE TRIUMPH

One year later, 1964, we were back in Australia with the same friends but different backers. The criticisms had done their damage and I knew the atmosphere was different as soon as we arrived at Sydney airport. One reporter sarcastically asked Donald when the record attempt would take place. Donald remained calm and smiled.

'That's in the hands of your weather, old boy. As soon as the weather behaves, I'll take my chance and not before.' As always, he handled the situation brilliantly.

We stayed in Sydney for two days while Donald organised an Aero Commander charter plane to take us on the five-hour flight to Muloorina. He simply couldn't wait to get to the lake. Louis and Julia had not come over so I wondered how I would manage things this time. I had learned a good deal about cooking the previous year and hoped my friends in Adelaide would help us with the delivery of food.

Before we left Adelaide in 1963, I'd become very friendly with Florence Ulve who was the proprietress of the Lido nightclub. She had introduced me to a man called Graham Ferrett. Graham had curly red hair and was certainly no Robert Redford, but he was full of drive and had a great love of fun. His humour was rather on the basic side but this suited his personality perfectly. He had left his job with York Motors to join the Bluebird team and replaced David Wynne-Morgan. I was thrilled about this because it would mean we'd get some laughs.

After a long and uneventful flight we arrived at Muloorina. As I looked down on the station somehow it didn't seem quite as ugly as I remembered. With its red sand and green roofs, sheep and kangaroos it seemed like home in the middle of nowhere and from the air I could see people rushing out of the few houses to greet our arrival. We made a perfect landing. I jumped up and opened the cabin door. Hazel, Lorna, Elliot, the kids, even the dogs, were there to welcome us and in front of them all stood Graham, beaming away.

When Donald climbed down from the aircraft everyone clapped and cheered, especially old Elliot. With last year's *Bluebird* benefit he had bought his life-long dream – his own private plane – and had also renewed his sheep stock, so we were welcome, very welcome. But to Mum, Hazel and Lorna our return meant company, friendship and fresh news. Those things were rare delicacies in the outback where the women are especially warm-hearted. Donald had made me buy loads of glossy magazines with details of the latest fashions that he knew they would love. We all had tea in the main house and while the men were making plans I told the girls all the female gossip. They lapped up my words as if they were champagne.

This time we had no beautiful caravan. Instead, Donald and I would take the room next to the kitchen which Louis and Julia had used last year. Two young students were due to arrive the next day to take care of the housework, and a secretarial girl, too. As I walked into my room carrying Donald's mascot, Mr Whoppit, I looked through the window to see the crummy verandah covered with dozens of camp beds and festooned with socks, shirts and shaving brushes. I could hear my mother's voice as she used to show very chic hotel rooms to her guests. 'And just look at that view, monsieur. As you English say, the best money can buy.'

I smiled and squeezed little Whoppit in my arms. How long would it be this time? How many socks would I wash, how many potatoes would I peel, how many tears would I shed? *Enough self-pity, let's get on with the job.*

I never had much practice in cooking before Muloorina but I did remember how to make a good old Flemish soup. The author John Pearson, who arrived to write the story of the attempt on Lake Eyre, later described this as one of my greater talents. The boys often teased me, especially one of my favourite members of the team, Tom Lawson. He used to say, 'Well, Fred, how about some of your Belgian Lancashire hotpot?' It was always said with tongue-in-cheek but stories of my unappetising gravy did the rounds of the team and half of the outback before the press eventually caught on. One newspaper reported my culinary prowess like this: 'She lives on Lake Eyre, among thirty men. She sings a great song, but when she makes gravy, it comes out very wrong. Guess who? A girl called "Fred".'

Thankfully, the two students arrived. They were terrific girls who were on a working holiday around Australia. Greshenda was the daughter of an English professor. She was small, plump and bonny and we decided to call her Ricky. Christel was a German art student and the hardest-working girl I'd ever known. They both settled in beautifully and I realised at once they'd be a wonderful help. Then came the secretary, Valerie James, an attractive young woman.

Work on the track was progressing but Leo was not happy with the condition of the surface. It was still too soft and damp. Andrew Mustard, who was in charge of track preparation, kept saying all was well, but as time went by a definite rift began to appear between him and the men. It was clear that even here in the outback the criticisms by Alfred Owen had left their mark.

A few days later the car was ready for action. Andrew declared the track was fine, but Leo didn't agree with him. Feeling the pressure to get things moving, Donald decided on a run for the next day. Unc walked away after the meeting shaking his head. As he passed me I guessed he was thinking that Malcolm Campbell would not have done it this way and not on that track, far too dangerous. And Malcolm Campbell would have said 'balls' to the criticisms. I made myself the firm promise there and then that if anything happened to Donald I would pursue all those who had criticised him to the bitter end.

Dawn was still a long way off when the homestead started to wake up at 2 o'clock on 14 May 1964. Outside my window I could hear the boys getting ready. Elliot was already in the kitchen – because he was hard of hearing, his voice was always very loud. Thank goodness Donald was still sleeping. It never ceased to amaze me how he could sleep through most things. I had arranged with Ricky and Christel that they would prepare breakfast so I wouldn't disturb Donald by getting up to do it myself. He did not have to be ready till 4 o'clock and I wanted him to get the benefit of a little more sleep.

The boys were to drive to the lake, a journey that took just over an hour, but we would fly there in only fifteen minutes. Several team members came with us in the aircraft. They took it in turns except for Unc who always wanted to be there first, just in case.

I was relieved when Christel knocked on the door. The fever of getting ready had left its mark on me and I was just keen to get going, hoping that Andrew would be right after all and that maybe tonight we would celebrate the new record. While Donald was in the one and only bathroom with Ken Norris and Elliot, I cleaned up our room. I was making Donald's bed when I had the strangest feeling. I can't describe whether I was scared, excited or both. I sat down on his bed and with my hand caressing his pillow, I whispered, 'Please God, whoever and wherever you are, don't take him from me. I'd be lost. Let me make his bed again tomorrow morning.'

We arrived at the lake where *Bluebird* was waiting for her master. The atmosphere was electric and everyone was tense. I walked behind Donald carrying his helmet and Mr Whoppit. My head felt as if a banjo string had been tied tight around it. Andrew came over.

'Everything's checked, Skipper. Wind is okay too.'

I wanted to stop Donald and tell him to listen to Leo's words of caution about how dangerous it was to use a damp and soft track. I wanted to scream and beg him not to walk so deliberately to his death, but then I remembered his words when he took me on his first record attempt after our marriage: 'Bobo, an attempt is no place for a woman. It's a man's adventure so you'll have to forget you're a female and become just another member of the team. It's a lot to ask but I have a feeling you can do it.'

I swallowed my fears and as he climbed into the cockpit I handed over the helmet and Whoppit. My heart seemed to be banging my brains out. Donald looked at me and somebody somewhere gave me the strength to smile and wink at him. His face was serious when he said, 'That's my

Fred. Well done that girl.' The cockpit closed. Once again I was the loneliest girl in the world. He gave his signal and the roar started – *Bluebird* came alive.

I had my fingers tightly crossed as I walked back to the car that would drive me to the other end of the measured track. I climbed inside with my eyes still on *Bluebird*. 'There she goes!' shouted one of the boys and within seconds Donald had disappeared from view, leaving behind him a trail of wet salt. We were doing ninety in our car and it seemed terribly slow. At last we got to the other end. Everyone was moving fast to get prepared for the return run. Donald had lifted himself out of the cockpit and was calmly smoking a cigarette. He looked tired as he explained to the boys how it had felt. He said it seemed like a huge brake was holding *Bluebird* back and he'd only reached 300mph. We were nowhere near success yet. He smiled sadly as I approached. At that moment a member of Andrew's crew arrived. He seemed excited as he spoke to Andrew who turned calmly and said, 'Apparently, the track is slightly damaged'.

This time Leo didn't keep silent. In a voice remarkably strong for his small size and mature age he said, 'We can't have the return run before we've checked that.'

Donald knew he was right and the three of us went for a trip down the track. It was heartbreaking to see the damage. Two huge rails had been gouged on and off along the track, about ten inches deep, and water was already surfacing. This proved Leo's point that the salt crust had been too thin for a record run.

'It's had it, completely and utterly, Unc,' said Donald with quiet sadness.

'Yes, Skipper, it's had it, but you haven't. Believe me, Skipper, you're the luckiest man alive.'

During the evening that followed there was a terrible atmosphere. In our hearts we'd hoped for success but now came the anticlimax. This is where Donald was usually at his best. From the kitchen I could hear his voice full of reassurance, telling the boys not to worry, that today had been a test and that's all it was supposed to have been. So now they'd learned that the salt crust had been too thin. He told them they would prepare another track where the salt was thicker. Little by little the feeling of renewed hope was born. Skipper had done it again.

Graham Ferrett had become my close friend on the lake and very often helped with the washing-up after dinner. He was doing so again that night.

'Fat Ferrett, do you know what really irritates me?' I asked him.

'No, Fred. Let's have it.'

'Well, I can never wash when there's a test run. The bathroom is always occupied and although I can brush my teeth and wash my face in the kitchen, hallelujah for the rest. I really don't like this! It makes me feel uncomfortable all day. It's horrid!'

'Yes,' said Ferrett sagely, 'I agree. Bloody horrid. We really must have a conference about this problem!' And with his basic sense of humour, the whole thing was to become a big joke. The most ridiculous suggestions were made, like a swim in the muddy creek a mile away at 4 o'clock in the morning. But many a true word is spoken in jest and when the idea was brought up of a small basin that I could fill with water and keep in my room, I decided to follow this through quietly. The very next day a special order was sent to Adelaide's main store, David Jones, through my good friend Florence. The order read, 'fifteen pounds of frozen beef, ten sacks of potatoes, thirty corn on the cob and one small basin'.

My basin arrived that week and served its purpose admirably. I worked out a perfect system for washing myself from head to toe. It involved some awkward positions, of course, but after some practice all went well. When not in use my treasured basin was always tucked away safely beneath my bed.

Donald had found his thick salt area and the whole team was now hard at work getting the new track ready. Ferrett had taken over the works and all was hectic. This track would be twenty miles instead of thirty. Donald was determined it would be a success and worked on it all day and every day. After ten day's hard slog it was ready for a trial run. That night a meeting was held in the shearing shed and it seemed to go on and on. I heard the boys getting restless and irritable because the conversations were leading nowhere and no one seemed able to make a decision. Donald was in the very delicate position of having to satisfy sponsors, press and difficult members of the team all at the same time but finally it was Graham who spoke up.

'Well, how about having a Billy Graham,' he said.

'I know who he is but what is it?' asked Donald.

Ferrett smiled at him and said, 'Donald, "Let's have a Billy Graham" means, let's have a decision for Christ's sake!' There was a great peal of laughter.

Men like Graham Ferrett are worth their weight in gold on any record attempt. When the laughter died down the decision was announced. There would be a parachute test with the *Bluebird* the very next day. Everyone went happily to bed.

'Tonia, Donald, three-thirty!' Ricky's voice always sounded cheerful, even at this hour. 'Time to get up!' After kissing hello to Donald (our sex life was definitely on hold because we did not have the privacy of a caravan) I climbed out of bed, took out my basin from underneath it and kneeling, I put my hands in the water. I was just about to wash my face when Donald spoke with a certain urgency.

'What in heaven's name are you doing?'

'Washing, of course. This basin is my own private bathroom!'

For one moment Donald's expression was like a big question mark. It was immediately followed by a huge grin and a laughing voice that said, 'Fred, please don't wash yourself in that! I saw it during the night and I thought it was there for another purpose, so I used it!'

At first I didn't quite understand, but when Donald began to laugh the truth dawned on me.

During the days that followed there were several test runs, work progressed and Donald learned a great deal about the car. By 1 June he had reached 352mph and on one occasion a top speed of 406mph was achieved. Then 2 June brought with it strong winds, so the waiting game started again. Every day I went to the lake where I sat in the tent writing my diary, continuing with my embroidery or making tea for the boys, hoping all the time that the wind would drop but at the same time dreading it. At about 3 o'clock we usually gave up and returned to Muloorina to prepare the evening meal.

The station was alive and well. John Pearson, who was writing the story of *Bluebird and the Dead Lake*, was never at peace because every-one, especially Elliot, wanted to be mentioned in the book. The poor man had dozens of conversations, many with people who had no importance to his book at all, but his patience seemed angelic. Some had expected a dirty, bearded, tall bohemian, but instead John was of medium height and slim build, tidy in appearance with slightly waved black hair. He looked delicate and walked with the poise of a ballet dancer. I think some of the boys entertained private thoughts about how long John would last in this rough and tough outback world, but he was to surprise us all.

John had now been with us for several weeks but he was still as polished as the day he arrived. He asked questions in the most self-effacing manner and was always the perfect gentleman. How he kept his elegance in this dismal place I never knew. The only time I saw a glimmer of passion in his eyes was when he spoke about my Flemish soups which he seemed to like very much. One night he was drinking a tumbler of beer while standing next to one of the more difficult members of the team, who seemed to have a lot to say about what Campbell should or should not do. Every so often this little fanatic of a man spilled some of his beer on John's feet, pretending not to notice. John quietly looked down at him.

'You're making my shoes dirty and I don't like it!'

The little man, obviously poisoned by the opinions of the hostile group in the team, continued to pour little drops on to John's feet. Well spoken and with his voice perfectly under control, John said again, 'If I were you I'd stop talking nonsense and please stop pouring beer on my shoes!'

Again, the little man ignored this and then it happened: John's arm went up very slowly, so did the tumbler in his hand and with great elegance he emptied its contents over the little man's head. The latter began to burn with fury and his language became stronger than ever. John remained full of dignity and with a faint but very attractive smile said, 'Shall we go outside and settle this matter?'

But the little man was frightened by this turn of events. 'I don't fight with anyone,' he stammered.

John placed his tumbler delicately on the wooden table, treating it as if it were made of crystal, looked at the embarrassed man and just before walking out uttered one word, with great emphasis but still very calm.

'Pity.'

When I heard the story from Ricky I went straight up to John and congratulated him on his exemplary behaviour. His only response to my enthusiasm was a very friendly, 'I don't like my shoes getting dirty. That's all!' Nevertheless, from that day on he was known as 'Knuckles'. What a shame John had to leave before Donald made his triumphant run. I'm sure he would have been thrilled if he could have seen how everyone with absolutely no exceptions, including the little fanatic, loved and admired the Skipper.

One night while preparing my soup over a hot stove I was overcome by a feeling of dizziness. I sat down, hoping it would pass, but it slowly grew worse. When Valerie came in she commented straight away on how white I looked and advised me to lie down. I went to my room where I stretched out and felt much better. Valerie came in with some brandy which I swallowed readily. The burning feeling seemed to ease the mysterious pains around my heart.

'What's wrong, Tonia?' she asked, concerned. I felt I owed her some kind of explanation and tried to make it as short and unaffected as possible.

'I was born with a so-called "heart condition". Most of the time I feel perfectly all right, but last year in London a specialist said I needed to think about having an operation to correct it. Frankly, I don't like to think about it too much.'

Valerie was standing by the window and came over to sit down on my bed. She unbuttoned her blouse, removed her bra and there I saw a big, red scar across her chest.

'Why?' she asked. 'There's not much to it, you know. It sounds more dramatic than it really is.'

I sat up in bed. 'Valerie, that's fantastic! You've had this done?'

'Yes, last year. I was home within three weeks, and believe you me I felt better than ever. And when your husband breaks that record you'll see me dance, laugh and drink more than anybody here!'

I suddenly felt much better and sitting back I thanked her. She rearranged her clothes and, smiling a little, said, 'The day you decide to do it, don't spend months thinking of how dangerous it is, just make the decision and go for it.'

I couldn't face staying in bed and as the boys had not yet returned from the lake I got up and took the opportunity to wash some of my underwear. I collected it all together and went into the bathroom. How funny the place looked! It was bedecked with bath towels bearing little notes that said, 'her name is Sheila, and she's mine,' or 'I love her – she loves me well,' or 'hands off – she's mine'. Why anyone would want to touch these towels was beyond me, and their shaving brushes were not much better either! But for once the bathroom was mine and so I proceeded to do my private laundry. Then I heard the first cars arriving back from the lake, so I hurried over to Hazel's to hang my smalls on her hidden line. I thought it would be bad for morale if the boys saw this kind of laundry blowing in the wind. As I finished the job I realised that one pair of panties was missing. I ran back to the house, but it was too late: once again I'd lost the bathroom and by the sound of it there must have been twelve of them in there already. I knocked hard on the door and shouted. 'Hey boys, I've left some of my laundry in there. Have you seen it?'

There was a kerfuffle and some masculine laughter, then a firm answer, 'No, Fred, nothing.'

Days later I was to find out from Valerie that my bikini panties had been borrowed in turns by some of the boys. Apparently they'd put it under their pillows at night hoping it would produce sweet dreams and it was now doing the tour of the army camp!

Monday morning came around and once again the frozen meat had not arrived. I asked Elliot if he could help me out.

'Well,' he said scratching his head, 'it's rather difficult. The sheep are miles away at the moment. I don't know if I can get one this quick. Anyway leave it to old Elliot. I'll find something somehow.' With this I went to the lake, knowing very well that Elliot would get me something.

Another day dawned on the lake and again no luck. The wind blew stronger than ever and the team was getting restless. There was a 'make or break' mood in the air and we knew it was dangerous. On the way back, sitting next to Donald in the Aero Commander, I hoped very much that Elliot had found something for me and that the evening would bring a good meal. The boys would need a good supper to keep up their morale.

But I needn't have worried for back at the homestead Elliot had kept his word.

As I approached the house I saw two of Elliot's grandchildren looking at me with tear-stained eyes. When I asked them what was the matter they ran away: I soon found out why. As I entered the kitchen I noticed a glistening heap of red meat lying on the table waiting for my attention. With shock and horror I realised why the children had been crying: the meat on the table had once been my little pet lamb, Coco. I had found him as a newborn, lost in the salt marshes. I had loved and nursed him into a healthy, affectionate pet who followed me around wagging his tail just like a little dog. And here he was, diced into hundreds of pieces. I prepared the evening meal and even smiled when the boys told me how good it was, but I didn't eat one single piece of meat that night. Poor little Coco had served his purpose, and what a futile purpose it was – one single meal.

7 June dawned. Once again a 4 o'clock start and off to the lake. We were all very despondent. These days of hanging around on Lake Eyre while the wind blew a mixture of salt and sand into hair and eyes were very depressing. Something had to happen soon, especially for the team's sake. Leo's wife, Joan, had arrived. Donald had sent for her. Unc was happily married and although he never complained, he missed his wife terribly. Donald arranged for her to travel to Australia from England and when she arrived, Unc was the happiest man alive. Of course, this gave the boys something to tease him over, but Unc took the nicknames of 'Italian lover-boy' and 'the Casanova of Lake Eyre' with great humour, and even some pride. Joan also turned out to be a wonderful help to the two students and me.

After we arrived at the lake Christel and Ricky made tea and coffee while I doled out the lunchtime sandwiches to the boys. We were very tired and the conversation was poor, in fact practically non-existent. Maurice Parfitt was one of my favourites in our personal team – always the same smiling face and with a terrific sense of humour.

'Well, Maurice,' I said, 'how are you enjoying this holiday resort?'

'You know Mrs Campbell,' he answered, 'I was seriously thinking of buying a plot to build a bungalow here, but with all the publicity it has had recently I suppose the price will have gone up, so I think I'll leave it.'

I laughed and walked back to the tent where the girls were standing outside gazing up at something. Ricky's voice was excited as she said 'Look, Tonia, look! The flags are quite still now!'

I looked up. There was no movement in the flags. She was right. As I turned to look towards Donald who was standing near *Bluebird*, I realised at once that it was time to collect his helmet and mascot.

Everything was ready in no time and here it was again, the excitement, the hope, the run, the agony . . . and once more the disappointment. He improved his speed from 365 to 390mph, but once again it was a test run and not the real thing. The ugly spirits of Lake Eyre refused to give us our success.

Thankfully, the track was not too damaged this time but it needed to be repaired. The sad, heavy mood that had been in the air now overpowered me. I walked towards the deserted tent where I sat down on one of the wooden boxes. How I hated it all. How long would it go on? I started wondering about the legend of Lake Eyre.

Elliot had mentioned a superstition about a curse that had been placed on Lake Eyre by a witch doctor after a white man had raped and murdered an Aboriginal girl there many years ago. The rain spirits had cursed the lake and decreed that any white man who walked on it would be swallowed up by the waters. No happiness would ever come to the place unless the Aboriginal tribe could walk on the lake again and forgive the murder. Was the story of the murder fact or fiction? We were never to find out, but apparently no Aboriginal would ever come near the lake. I am somewhat superstitious, but I had laughed a little when Elliot told us the story. Now, sitting in the tent with one failure after another to think about, I didn't laugh any more and wondered about the legend. Maybe I could get some Aboriginal people from Marree to come over? They did know me, because after Lorrea's show they had asked me to do one myself in Marree.

When Donald joined me later I told him of my plans. He smiled sadly.

'It will take more than a visit from an Aborigine to give us what you want Bobo, but go ahead. It can do us no harm.' Then, more matter-of-fact, he continued. 'We're interrupting trials for a three-week period. Everybody needs a rest and so does the track. A little civilisation and comfort will do us good so we'll fly to Adelaide tomorrow afternoon. Okay darling?' I knew he was doing this for me.

The very next day there were crowds of photographers and reporters waiting for us on our arrival at Adelaide airport. They stormed at Donald, 'Are you giving up, Donald? Has the lake won? What are your plans? Please give us a smile, Mrs Campbell.' I felt like a monkey in a zoo. There was scepticism all around and it was very upsetting for Donald. *If only they knew how genuine and determined he was they would respect him and believe in him.* If I'd been in his shoes I would certainly have lost patience with them, but not Donald. He was perfectly calm and cooperative and ignored their mocking attitude.

When we got to the home of our new-found friends, John and Helen Swain, we were made to feel very welcome. John told us about certain critical articles in the press, but Donald said it was bound to happen because of the duration of the trials. We discussed the pros and cons of all this and came to the conclusion that when we finally broke the record it would be the greater and better for it. We talked late into the night and everything seemed much more cheerful by the time we finally turned in.

For two weeks I was kept very busy with several broadcasts and personal appearances on TV, but I couldn't escape from the disagreeable questions and mocking remarks of comedians and compères. Everyone wanted to have a dig at Donald through me and this was one time in my life when I didn't enjoy show business.

Donald could barely wait to return to Lake Eyre and his maddening track. In return for her help in getting us all the frozen foods we needed at Lake Eyre, I had accepted a short season at Florence's Lido restaurant. We decided to leave for the lake immediately after I had fulfilled that commitment. Florence was in her element and business was flourishing. I didn't feel on form and I couldn't give a true performance until the third day, but then it came – that certain something the audience waits and cheers for. Florence couldn't get over it and in the weeks that followed every artiste who performed at the Lido had to suffer her unending descriptions of my show. I enjoyed that week of glamour and fun and it was with fresh courage that I returned to Lake Eyre with Donald on 9 July.

The track seemed to have improved little in our absence, but all the same we set up camp. I decided to execute my plan with the Aboriginals of Marree. Christel and I drove up there together and parked the car in the main square. As soon as they saw me the people gathered around and shouted, 'Sing Miss, Sing'. In no time at all I was sitting on the bonnet of the car singing to them and making them clap their hands and join in to 'Waltzing Matilda'. More and more people crowded in until I decided this was enough music and that I now needed to convince them about coming to Lake Eyre to see the *Bluebird*. The older ones would not hear of it, but the younger ones were more adventurous and less impressed by old superstitions. Finally three of them decided they wanted to come along – two boys and a girl. They were all I needed; I pushed them into the car and drove back along the soft dusty road. I avoided stopping at the homestead in case they changed their minds and wanted to turn back. I was determined not to stop until I finally drove on to the lake and then there would be no turning back. I had to open all the car windows because my three passengers were anything but clean and their body odour was rather fruity. The red dust from the road made no difference to their complexion but it sure did to mine and Christel's. By the time the car came to a halt and the doors were opened the team saw not three Aboriginals, but five! It was Carl Noble who noticed the difference first and laughed, 'Well, if it isn't our Fred gone native!'

We all had a really good laugh and as I watched the Aboriginals touch the *Bluebird* I felt strangely happy and at peace. At that moment I was convinced there was magic and power behind those people and I hoped my premonitions would prove right.

On 11 June I woke up with a start. It was 7 o'clock and Donald's bed was empty. I dressed at once. There was no one in the kitchen but cups and plates were strewn everywhere as if the Indians had arrived and everyone had fled. As it was now bitterly cold, I took my new kangaroo coat with me and went outside. Everyone seemed to be standing around and the whole place had the atmosphere of a funeral parlour. As I walked towards them Lorna saw me. She met me halfway and sighed.

'Isn't it awful? We need rain so much and it keeps falling where we don't want it.'

Poor Donald. How much more could he take? I walked back to the homestead feeling that I couldn't face him right now. I had to think. Was someone telling us to give up? I would have given a fortune at that moment to know what to do or advise, but I felt helpless and very despondent as I heard the plane take off. I was still in the kitchen when Donald and the boys came back from the lake. I couldn't believe my eyes: everyone was cheerful.

'Bonjour, Freddie,' said Donald as he walked in. 'Come on, coffee all round. We need it!'

'What about the track?' I asked.

'Well, maybe your Abboes did kill the curse because there's not a drop on the track, only around it.'

Donald's eyes were tired but they had a soft smile and I got the feeling that he knew more than he wanted to tell. When we were alone, he spoke to me.

'Bobo, I know I should give the whole thing up. Everything points to failure, but there's a little demon inside that keeps nagging me to press on. Do you understand? I have to go on. I can't give up now.'

He was desperate. I knew this was the perfect moment to ask him to stop, to think of John Cobb who killed himself trying to break the water speed record, and so many others – dead because of their love of speed. I felt I should remind him of those who loved him, Gina and myself, how utterly lost I would be without him. I wanted to tell him that England no longer cared for record attempts, that his achievements for British prestige would not be cheered, the flavour of the moment was long-haired pop groups. There was so much I could have said, but the only words that passed my lips were, 'You'll make it, Skipper – I know you will.' And with all my heart I prayed he would.

The next day we flew to Lake Eyre and landed near the track. There was expectancy in the air again. How could they still hope after so many disappointments? I looked at Leo but he didn't look back and went on with his work in a world of his own. It was my world too now, and a very insecure one. The wind was blowing so I knew there would be no run today.

The next morning, Friday 17 July, I was woken sharply. 'Fred!' It was Donald's voice, tense. 'Come on, hurry up, darling. This is it!' I rushed out of bed and was ready in no time. We walked to the plane and I understood what 'record run weather' meant. There was the strangest feeling in the air, a complete stillness just like the lull before a big storm. The weather on the lake was just the same as at the homestead. All was ready. Donald climbed straight into the cockpit and didn't even look at me when I handed him Mr Whoppit. When they shut him in I knew he had gone into another world. I closed my eyes and thought of my brother Daniel who had died and Paul, my other brother and a sportsman too. Maybe they would protect Donald, help him. A million thoughts raced through my head. It was Graham Ferrett who grabbed my arm and led me to the car just as *Bluebird* had fired up. We drove off first. I was on the back seat where I had been placed just like a doll. I had been scared too often, I had prayed too much, I had nothing left, not even hope.

Bluebird flashed by and I didn't even see it. There was a lot of excitement in the car. Everyone was talking, but it all sounded far away, as if I had water in my ears. When we reached the other end the boys had nearly finished the preparations for the return run. Donald was sitting on top of the car, smoking his customary cigarette. Walking over slowly I heard whispers of 403mph. I reached *Bluebird* and looked at Donald, hoping for a smile. But there was no signal, no smile. Only a determined look straight down into the cockpit as though he was watching something inside. I turned back to the empty car and got in. I felt lost. I had never felt this lonely before. Suddenly they all came running over: *Bluebird* was leaving again. Graham took my hand and squeezed it.

'That's it, Fred,' he said, 'just a little while longer and it will all be over.'

But this was not the dentist's chair. Didn't he understand? Could anyone understand? We soon arrived at the other end where *Bluebird* was at a standstill and Leo was opening the cockpit. Donald pulled himself out. Then the water seemed to run out of my ears. Very clearly I heard the radio operator shouting, 'That's it, that's it! 403.01mph. He's done it! He's done it! The record has been broken!'

Everyone now ran towards *Bluebird* – everyone except me. I sat glued to the seat of the car. It was over. The waiting, the misery. It was over and he was alive. This was the first run he had done since I'd brought the Aboriginals to the lake.

'My God!' It was Valerie's voice that brought me back to reality from the strange make-believe world I was in. 'Come on, Tonia,' she shouted. 'Donald wants you.'

'No, Valerie, no! This is his moment, don't spoil it.' But she was followed by Graham and old Elliot who were all shouting, 'Donald wants you, Fred.' I looked towards *Bluebird*. Donald was still sitting on top of his cockpit, shaking hands with excited team members, but I could tell his eyes were searching for me and when at last he saw me he smiled. The crowds went silent as I approached. Donald kissed me, took my head in his hands and his words were the greatest gift I ever received.

'Fred, we've done it. It's our record.'

'Hip, hip, hooray!' shouted Ken Norris, and the Bluebird team carried off their skipper on their shoulders. History had been made. This time there was none of that famous English reserve. Everyone cheered, including the men who had not believed that Donald would be successful in his latest record attempt – even Andrew Mustard – and I even suspected that they were glad they'd been wrong. There was no cooking to be done that night, thank goodness. The army and police had organised a barbecue for all in their main tent.

Valerie was running around beaming happily. She had made a bet a while ago with John Pearson that she would make the grade with the handsome but very serious and elusive Gregory Waters, an Australian army officer. The bet consisted of a bottle of champagne. She'd not missed the opportunity presented by the festive mood. As I was uncorking one of the bottles Florence had sent over for the big day, Valerie walked up to me. She took it out of my hands laughing. 'I'll have this one, Fred, and when you see Pearson back in England, tell him to return it to you. He owes me one.' Looking at her watch she added, 'Since about two hours ago!' I looked at Graham, who was chuckling away because we all knew about the famous bet.

'What I want to know is where and how?' laughed Graham with a twinkle in his eye. There are no secrets in the outback and we soon found out it had happened by the dirty creek in an army Jeep.

The celebrations went on until the early hours of the morning but Donald and I walked back to the homestead with Graham before midnight. It was a beautiful night. Donald was holding the torch and shining it along the ground in front of us in case of snakes. We watched the dancing beam of light out of habit. I smiled, thinking that soon all this would be but a memory.

'It'll be strange not to worry about wind and rain or snakes any more,' I mused.

'Well,' said Graham, 'we had to worry about something or else we'd have gone mad.'

Donald answered, as if thinking aloud. 'You know, Graham, I feel empty. Maybe I've waited and hoped too long. This doesn't seem a victory. Oh, I know it was more than we thought we could ever do on such a rotten track, but I so wanted 450 and she could do it so easily on a hard surface. Now she'll never prove herself because we're entering the jet age, travelling to the moon, and soon *Bluebird* will be a has-been.'

There was no answer to give him because he was right, and suddenly I knew once again that this would not be the end. His reference to the jet age probably meant that not long from now Donald would be planning to build a jet car.

We left Muloorina the very next day. As the plane took off I looked through the cabin window at the small crowd of inhabitants on the ground below. Somehow they looked lost and sad. Would they ever be able to pick up their normal lives again in the desolate outback? We had brought excitement, and we might have spoiled things for them all. I hoped not.

'I'll bet you're not sorry to see the last of that place, are you, Fred?' asked Graham.

Donald answered for me. 'Fred might be a little sorry, but Tonia will soon take up her real life again.' He was right, of course.

Flying over Lake Eyre at low altitude I could see a little black mark right near the track. 'That's where we had the tent. That's where Fred was born.' I waved and Graham, noticing this, asked me what I was doing. 'There's no one there, Fred!' he laughed.

I smiled. 'Oh yes there is, Graham. I'm waving goodbye to the evil spirits of Lake Eyre who were good enough to break the curse for one day and let us be successful on their lake.'

Helen Swain knew how I felt about cold Australian houses and she had put all the fires on full. We sat around discussing a possible parade with *Bluebird* and the team. The town of Adelaide had asked for it and Graham and Leo were in favour, but Donald, as usual underestimating his achievement, said no one would be there and the whole thing would be silly. After we put it to the vote the parade was organised and everyone became very busy.

So often had I heard people say, 'This man should have a son to continue the Campbells, born to speed.' And while everyone else was occupied I started to think about this. Although I wholeheartedly agreed, I couldn't help wondering what would happen if the son took after his mother and became a wandering troubadour or a pop singer. I smiled as my imagination conjured up the picture of a young man singing along to a guitar – 'Malcolm Campbell and the Rolling Stones'. No, this could not and should not ever happen. Anyway, whoever heard of a mother called Fred? After my last pregnancy Donald had decided categorically that I should not go through it all again and I began to agree with him. Bluebirds would remain our only babies.

When the day of the great parade finally arrived the streets of Adelaide were filled with thousands of cheering people as the *Bluebird* drove through at a stately 10mph. I was standing in front of the town hall where Donald was supposed to stop, take his bow and make a speech, but as the car approached people went wild, screaming and cheering. The children broke through the police barrier calling 'Good on yer, Donald!' And suddenly I was pushed to the back of the crowd and became one of them, so I grabbed a flag – I never noticed from whom – and joined in with the cheering like a child. I stopped abruptly as I felt a hand on my shoulder. It was Graham Ferrett supporting his small son on his arm. His face was beaming with pride.

'Well, Tonia, there it is. Success at its highest. You know he's out-numbered The Beatles! Over 200,000 people, the police said, all here to salute that man. It's great – it's marvellous, isn't it?'

I didn't answer. Tears were streaming uncontrollably down my face. Gratitude, love, excitement, pride, all mixed up together, were bursting out of me. Graham put his son down and gave me a hug. The little boy looked up at his father and asked him who the lady was.

'That, my boy, is a wonderful lady, but you can call her Fred.'

At that moment I understood why Donald always impressed upon everyone that a record attempt was teamwork. Graham was a member of the team; so were Leo and Maurice and Carl Noble. They were all beautiful sportsmen. Whether I was in the streets of Adelaide among a cheering crowd or performing on a Las Vegas stage, I knew that a part of me would always remain Fred, a member of the Bluebird team, and I was terribly proud to have been part of this great adventure.

Donald's speech started on a light note, making jokes about the press whom he called 'yesterday's enemies but today's friends', then slowly but surely it turned serious. He spoke of the team, the police, the outback people whom he called pioneers, and he thanked them all. Then last but not least came the words I would never forget, and neither would the media who even reported it several years later. He said – and this time it wasn't 'We' but 'I' – 'I think not of the speed and personal pride that comes with it, but of my wife looking on. For Tonia's sake, and I love her so very much, I must end this life of danger and speed. When everyone cheered as I got out of the cockpit I looked for her immediately. Her face was white and she looked so damned pleased to see me in one piece. When we kissed I realised that with Tonia I have found real happiness for the first time in my life.'

The crowd exploded, Graham took my hand and squeezed it and I cried.

We decided to stay in Adelaide and prepare for the water speed record. This had been announced in a very matter-of-fact way by Donald. After a

long search the team had found a suitable location for the attempt –
Lake Dumbleyung near Perth in Western Australia. Donald's dream was
to break both the land and water speed records in the same year. No one
in the sporting world had ever achieved this, not even the great Sir
Malcolm Campbell, and so it was in November 1964 that we packed our
bags and left Adelaide for Perth. Before we left Adelaide to my joy a
doctor had confirmed that I was pregnant again. I was two months gone
when we left. I decided to keep this to myself and try once again to give
Donald his son. But the secret was not to be kept for long because my
morning sickness was difficult to hide. Donald had already asked
me repeatedly if I felt all right. I knew he was always worried about my
heart condition because the doctors had said the first sign of danger with
this particular defect was nausea. However, for the time being he didn't
guess.

The flight in our Aero Commander was anything but pleasant. The air
turbulence made me feel worse, but as Donald was flying I was able to
pull all the faces I wanted. We arrived in Perth in the late afternoon and
my first impression of the town was its green and delicate beauty. It would
have remained for me one of the most beautiful spots if it hadn't been for
the fact that every person we met insisted on telling us of its beauty time
and again. After our arrival a press reception was given for Donald. He
answered a number of questions and I saw him chatting with several
people. He finally came over to me, took my arm and whispered quietly in
my ear.

'If I hear once more how beautiful Perth is I shall tell them to fuck it!'
Of course he didn't and was charm itself.

The next day we flew over Lake Dumbleyung. It was only a thirty-
minute flight. At first sight it looked more like a sea than a lake. We
landed and Leo came to meet us on the small airfield. He didn't look too
happy when he greeted us.

'Stormy weather on the way, Skipper. It's not so good. People here call it
the mountain wind. It can last for weeks.'

Donald sighed. 'Trust us to get the rain on land, and the wind on water.
Will anything ever go smoothly?'

'Record attempts never do,' said Leo resignedly.

'Bloody understatement of the year,' mumbled Donald.

We set off in the Land Rover and after a short drive arrived at the lake where a caravan had been prepared for us. The place was windy all right with dust everywhere. The lake itself looked wild. Christel and Ricky, who now were part of the gang and loving it, had made the caravan as comfortable as possible. They were very happy to have come on the water speed record attempt with us. Graham Ferrett walked over with a smile on his jovial face.

'Hiya Skipper, Hiya Fred. Don't worry about this wind. It'll be good as gold when we're ready.' Donald smiled. Graham had a good influence on him and we were grateful to have him there.

A second caravan adjacent to ours was the team's daytime accommodation. At night they would be staying at a very primitive hotel in a small town nearby. It had forty rooms but only two bathrooms and was run by a husband and wife who were great characters – from what we heard they were drunk from morning until night. Donald went straight into the team caravan for a meeting. I went to ours to unpack and once this was done I stretched out on my bunk and found myself staring at yet another caravan ceiling.

We were three weeks by the lake not daring to leave, but the wind kept blowing it up like an ocean. Donald was getting very worried but he and Ferrett tried to be as cheerful as possible. As the team was much smaller this time, Ricky and Christel could cope without help and the men also had much less work than with the land speed record attempt. The boat was ready. Donald, Graham and I played cards, dominoes and whatever else we could think of to pass the time. The water might suddenly become calm and we couldn't risk taking a break to fly into Perth.

Occasionally we would go swimming in the lake which was covered with dead flies and other bugs. Whenever someone swam out further than usual we all knew to what purpose and very quickly headed in the opposite direction. The lake where we swam was the lake where we did everything!

At night Donald and I made love more as a remedy for insomnia than out of passion. Ferrett used to greet us in the morning with the usual crack of 'Caravan been rocking again last night?' and Donald's retort of

'What else old boy? Didn't you notice how it has moved ten inches?' We all laughed. No secrets in this place.

One afternoon we received a cable from the Governor of Western Australia. It turned out that he had been at the same English public school as Donald, Uppingham, and he wanted to visit the lake the very next day. Donald was happy about this. Getting the camp shipshape would keep the team busy. *Bluebird* got an extra special polish and so did our caravan. I broke some branches from the tired, dried out trees, stuck them in an empty beer jug, cut off some ribbons from my underwear and tied them here and there on the branches in tiny bows. The effect wasn't bad at all. I then took one of my silk Dior scarves, draped it over the table, and put my feathered branch arrangement on it. When Donald and Graham came in there were exclamations of delight.

'You can't beat these frustrated artistes, can you, Donald?' joked Graham.

'Artistic frustration only, Graham?' said Donald, grinning at me.

'All right you two – don't rub it in. Remember, I'm turning into a monk!' grumbled Graham.

The mood was good. It was strange how the interest of one governor could lift the morale of the whole camp. He arrived at 4 o'clock with quite a motorcade of elegant cars, all covered in dust from the journey. Everyone was given a tour of the camp and then had a beer with the team, while the governor accompanied Donald and Graham to our caravan where I was introduced. The governor smiled as we shook hands.

'Glamour on Lake Dumbleyung as well,' he said. 'I used to hear you on the *Tonight* show, Miss Bern, with Cliff Michelmore. How nice to meet you personally.'

'Thank you, Your Excellency,' I said deferentially. 'But I assure you, the pleasure is all ours. It is so good of you to visit us and your interest has given the whole team a big boost.'

Standing behind the governor, Donald winked proudly at Graham. The three of them sat for a while and drank white wine. I had been asked to join them but politely refused, saying I didn't drink. Donald and Graham were completely amazed at this false admission but realised I must have had my reasons for refusing. I had two: we only had three glasses and I was pregnant. We had a pleasant chat and then the governor got up to leave. As they were leaving the caravan I overheard the Governor say to Donald, 'This wind really is a menace at times. I bet your caravan does some rocking at night.'

Graham, who was the last one to leave the caravan, answered softly, 'It sure does, your Excellency – in more ways than one.' I hoped that this risqué comment had somehow not been heard!

The next day bad luck struck. I awoke in the early hours of the morning and although I'd felt no pain I knew by the sticky feeling beneath me that I was haemorrhaging again. I switched on the bedside light, looked, and sighed. I was lying in blood. *Here we go again*, I thought. Donald turned over and asked me what was the matter. With a sob I couldn't repress, I blurted 'I'm sorry, Skipper. I'm afraid I'm going to be a terrible nuisance.'

Donald sat up, saw the blood and gasped with horror. 'Good God, what's happened? You were pregnant?' He jumped out of bed and pulled on his trousers. 'Why the hell didn't you tell me?'

By now I was near to tears. 'I didn't want to worry you,' I cried. 'I hoped it would be fine this time.' But Donald didn't notice my tears. He was running out to call Graham. I heard him giving orders while Graham came into the caravan with a big grey blanket. Looking very serious and not at all the comedian he usually was, he told me to lie still.

'Don't you move, Fred. We'll get you safe, don't worry.' Donald came back and together they rolled me in the blanket and Graham carried me to the Land Rover.

I can't begin to describe the drive to the airfield. I was convinced I was dying – I felt weaker and weaker by the minute. When I was lifted into the plane not one word was spoken except for Donald's voice loud and clear on the radio, explaining the nature of the emergency to the authorities. We flew all the way to Melbourne where the hospital was the best equipped. I felt weaker with each movement, drifting in and out of consciousness. The flight was just a blur and I cannot recall the drive from the airfield to the hospital. I only remember waking up in a clean and comfortable hospital bed, still feeling weak and thinking how very pleasant dying was, but also thinking what a dreadful shame it was that

I wouldn't see the water speed record. I felt Donald's hand holding mine tightly and with the little strength I had left and keeping my eyes closed, I whispered to him.

'Hello, Skipper, please don't give up. Get that record for me, whatever happens. Don't let this spoil it. Please get the record.'

'Quiet, darling. You mustn't think of that now. You know I wouldn't leave you. No record is worth it, not one.'

I felt the determination in his voice and I knew he would not go. Gathering some strength, I said feebly, 'Donald, I so wanted to give you a son. Please forgive me. I tried so hard.'

Once more I heard Donald's voice speak, but it seemed very distant and faint. 'Relax, my love. You are all I need, you silly, lovable woman.' He said more, but I could hear no longer. The injection I'd been given had done its job.

I woke up what seemed like weeks later, but apparently it was only twenty-four hours. I ran my hands over my belly and I knew at once that it was all over – the empty feeling made me want to cry. *Failure, failure*, a voice kept saying in my heart. The most natural thing in the world, childbirth, and I couldn't make it. A man like Campbell would not have a son. I turned my head on the pillow. I couldn't cry and my eyes hurt from dryness. *God, why couldn't anything be just a little normal in this life of mine?* Even my heart, which was supposed to have given in years ago, was still beating strongly, so why couldn't I have the joy of a normal woman giving a son to her man?

I was willing myself into the depths of depression, imagining the thrill of holding a newborn boy in my arms when, after a gentle knock on the door, Donald's face appeared. Seeing that I was awake, he opened the door wider and there he was holding a giant fluffy toy dog in his arms. Donald looked pale and tired, but his voice was cheerful as he spoke, nodding towards the dog. 'His name is Bobs and it's a boy!' He placed the dog by my side and kissed my hair softly as if I were porcelain. Suddenly the waterworks broke – tears like rain fell from my eyes. Donald sat down on the bed and took my hands in his.

'Now, now, my love, all is well,' he whispered. 'You're safe and that is all I have ever wanted.'

I couldn't stop crying. He kissed my hand and tried to console me but it was no good, and through my tears I sobbed, 'It's my fault. I'm being punished. I'll never be allowed to give you a son because of what I did.'

Gently, Donald brushed back the hair that had fallen in my eyes. 'Tut, tut, Tonia. What could you ever have done that makes you think this?'

Still sobbing, I told him about the whole would-be abortion business in New York and how I hated that pregnancy and didn't want to give up my dreams, but instead of anger or even being amazed he came near and took me in his arms. Holding me tenderly he murmured, 'Hush, hush, my love. Poor Bobo. I really shattered your dreams, didn't I? But you didn't go through with the abortion and that's the most beautiful sacrifice anyone ever made for me. You should be applauded, not punished.'

Little by little I calmed down, not just because of his words but because the secret was a secret no more.

'You know you want a son, and I would do anything to give you one now. If I can't I would even go away so another woman could give you one.'

'Stop it, Tonia!' Donald's voice was stern now. He took me by the shoulders, shook me lightly, then said, 'Now you listen, and listen very carefully. If you want to go I couldn't stop you. God knows I'm a difficult bastard to live with, but as God is my witness I would want no other wife. You are something I never knew existed. You, woman, have become part of me. A record attempt without you there wouldn't be worth the trouble. I know you love Gina, she's our child, and I'm more than happy with her alone. Giving birth to a son who would endanger your health wouldn't be worth it. So forget all that nonsense. It's about time you knew what you mean to me. Do you realise that after the Utah mess you gave me back my own life? What's more, I will not return to the lake without you.' Then, softly, he added, 'You, Bobo, have become my only true mascot.' Years later I would remember those words with a huge feeling of guilt.

Three days passed and I felt much stronger. Although the doctors had said I should stay two more weeks to recuperate, I decided that I could do that just as well by the lake. Time was running short and we were now well into December. We didn't want to risk being away if the lake decided to become calm and conditions were right for a record attempt. So under doctors' protests we flew off, one week from the day we had flown in, and were told not to have sex for at least a month. We picked up Graham in Adelaide. He had gone to visit his family and for some necessary 'shafting' as he called it. He boarded the plane, his usual jovial self, grinned and shouted.

'Hiya, Fred! This week did me the world of good. Got all my pimples to disappear!' Then he looked at the back seat where my new toy dog sat, safely strapped in by Donald. 'Bunny boy, I always knew you two were dogs at heart!'

I smiled back at him, determined not to be gloomy and trying to give Donald all that I humanly could to compensate for what I was unable to give him. 'Well, one of those dogs is a bitch for a start,' I said, trying to joke. General laughter.

And so we flew on, with Donald and Graham madly discussing plans in the front seat, and me in the back next to Bobs the toy dog, a rather sad symbol of my achievements as a woman.

The sun came up on 31 December and still the lake was furious – at this moment Dumbleyung was a very depressing place to be. Not once had we enjoyed a calm spell on the water and the mood in the team was irritable. They had lost hope and knew failure was knocking at the door. Breaking the record on 1 January 1965 would be a complete disappointment, so today was our last hope.

I stepped out of my bunk to make Donald's coffee and heard his words as he walked to the shaving mirror. 'Well, Tonia, I'm afraid we've had it and I suppose I'll be attacked again by the Alfred Owens of this world. Ah well, I suppose it's all in the game.'

Seeing Donald's depression I told him that I thought we should perhaps just pack up and leave. He was adamant: 'I can't do that, Bobo, the skipper stays with his craft whatever the conditions. I can't leave *Bluebird*. It would not be fair.'

'Well, we still have the whole day, Skipper,' I said optimistically. 'It could still happen, you know.'

Donald sighed and continued shaving. I fell silent. Graham, Donald and I spent the morning playing cards and dominoes. Our appetite was nil. In the early afternoon Donald could stand it no longer.

'Come on gang,' he said. 'Let's take the plane for a flip. That lake is not going to be calm and I can't watch it any longer. I'm getting cross-eyed.'

'Good idea,' said Graham, 'let's go!'

We told Leo, got into the Land Rover and drove to the small airfield. The crosswind made the take-off rather difficult, but Donald had become such an accomplished pilot that it didn't matter and within a few seconds we were in sight of the bad-tempered lake. From up there looking down it appeared rather calm and strangely flat. Graham had noticed this too and mentioned it to us. Donald looked down, then pushed the stick forward and shouted excitedly.

'Fat Ferret, that lake's as smooth as a bloody mirror!'

Donald banked the plane into a turn so tightly that I thought I'd left my stomach behind. No landing has ever been faster or rougher. As we ran from the plane not a word was spoken. We jumped into the Land Rover and broke all records on that dusty road. Leo was waiting for us and the team were all shouting and crying at the same time.

'Thank God you saw the lake had gone flat, Skipper, ' Leo shouted.

'It was Fat Ferret, Leo. He saw it,' replied Donald.

From the water's edge, Maurice Parfitt called that all was ready. Donald ran to the jetty and jumped into the cockpit – no helmet, no mascot. I had rushed to get them but had arrived back too late. The cockpit was closed now, the power was on, the countdown had started and in an instant *Bluebird* was off, leaving me shaking on the jetty, clutching his helmet and Mr Whoppit. Yet, through all my fears, I had to admit that the excitement came first – the beauty of the *Bluebird* and her skipper.

At low speed the powerful engine created a giant wave that turned into a majestic swell across the lake. Then suddenly the boat's nose lifted and like a royal bird she flew over the lake, just skimming the surface.

'First run 290mph,' screeched a radio operator, then very excitedly added, 'He's turning immediately, he's not refuelling. He says he's going to take a chance. The wind is coming up again, no time to wait. There he goes.'

And yes, there he was coming right towards the jetty where I was standing trembling, holding on to his helmet and expecting the *Bluebird* to explode under my very eyes. I couldn't even pray – I stood there paralysed.

I don't remember whether it was because of the thrill of it all or just because I was scared. Then, as if in a dream, I heard screams of hysteria and joy. The engine power was suddenly cut and about 20 yards away from the jetty *Bluebird*'s cockpit opened. A very handsome, very young-looking Donald stood upright and turned his head to the sky. I knew he was saying his thanks not only to the universal God, but also to his own private god, his father, Sir Malcolm Campbell – the man I had never known, the man whom I thought had been cruel and cold, the man who still made a young boy of Donald. At that moment he was looking up at his father and saying, 'Didn't I do well, Dad?'

I could contain myself no longer. I threw off my coat and jumped into the oil-covered lake, swimming happily towards my hero. Donald was shouting 'Silly girl!' at me, but as I swam alongside the *Bluebird* he grabbed me and pulled me up next to him. And so as the boat was towed in by the expert team we were gliding gloriously to the shore where the photographers and reporters were impatiently awaiting their very own thrill.

The news was already over the radio and we heard the announcer shouting excitedly, 'Donald Campbell, son of Sir Malcolm, today made history on Lake Dumbleyung in Western Australia. He broke his own water speed record which is now 276.30mph.' This was the first time in sporting history that one man had broken both land and water speed records within the same year, and within the Commonwealth. Hearing this announcement, our excitement grew. We finally climbed off the *Bluebird* and walked on to the jetty. We were grabbed and hugged and congratulated and among all this fever and joy Donald turned to me.

'Go and change, Bobo, you're wet through. With this nasty wind coming back you'll catch pneumonia. You're not as strong as you think you are.'

The crowd grew quiet and I caught a few glances of envy and admiration. Some of those who overheard his words were surprised that Donald could worry about this during his great moment of glory. But the astonishment came only from those who didn't know Donald Campbell. It was the greatest New Year's Eve I had ever known, or am ever likely to know. The news had travelled fast and cars loaded with champagne streamed into our camp. Telegrams and radio messages came through, too. It seemed as though the whole of Australia was celebrating the Campbell victory. Hundreds of telegrams were flown in, among them congratulations from prime ministers, sportsmen, and the Duke of Edinburgh. Everyone rejoiced with the handsome Scottish daredevil. The only person who was rather quiet was Leo and I asked him what was on his mind.

'He was a naughty boy, you know, not waiting for a conditions check before doing his return run. That wind was already coming up again. He took one hell of a risk and he knows it.' Limping away he added, 'These Campbells will be the death of me.'

That evening I mentioned Leo's words to Donald and he frowned a little.

'The truth is, Bobo,' he explained, 'I wanted that record. It was my last chance.'

'Did you know the return run was dangerous with no helmet and no mascot either?'

'I not only knew, I was sure of it. *Bluebird* was thumping like mad but somehow I felt that I could get away with it. You have to take a risk sometimes. But it was a calculated one. Don't worry.'

'What if you hadn't got away with it, Donald?' I asked.

He looked at me very seriously. 'You love me more than life, don't you, Vixen?'

I nodded, but couldn't speak. He came and sat next to me on the bunk, took my hand and brought it to his lips. Looking at my hand he once again said words I will never forget.

'If ever I don't get away with it, Bobo, I'll have to leave you alone on that jetty, and you'll have to walk away, and I don't mean crawl away. I would want you to walk away, back into life, and I would want you to eventually have that lovely smile of yours again. You and I alone know how much we've already been given, and destiny is written my love. There could only be one worse thing than me not getting away with it, and that's me having to lose you, like I nearly did some weeks back. You see, my pet, I'm a skipper, and without a harbour a skipper roves around, absolutely lost. You, Bobo, are my harbour.' He kissed my forehead and then in a lighter mood he added, standing up, 'Come on. Let's enjoy our success, because this time we did get away with it!'

He winked at me and once again he was the mischievous daredevil. I smiled as I joined him. A little voice within told me that he'd got away with it this time, but what about next time?

Back in Adelaide, we were once more the toast of the town. I had learned to love the place because it had always believed in Donald and had given him his glorious parade after the land speed record. We were staying with the Swains again. Although I was longing to go home to England and to visit my father, Donald had suddenly decided to make a documentary film about Lake Eyre and the Aboriginal curse. This would take months and somehow I felt we should return home now, while the excitement about the two records was still alive. There had even been headlines in the papers saying 'Why not Sir Donald Campbell now?' This was so near to Donald's dream that I mentioned it to him.

'I don't think we'll ever get that knighthood, Bobo,' he said, smiling sadly. 'I don't think my achievements and my involvement with charities are high enough yet to make them forget the fact that I've been divorced twice. You see, I'm a naughty boy! I don't know whether it's the Queen herself, or the British establishment, but somehow divorce is a dirty word and it takes a lot of achievement to make them forget that.' Then jokingly he added, 'I'd have much more chance of an honour if I was slightly homosexual!'

'Well, the hell with that!' I exclaimed. 'I'd much rather have a naughty boy, as long as he is a boy!'

This made Donald laugh. 'Don't worry, chérie, you've certainly got that!'

And so we stayed and we made the documentary film. We called it *How Long A Mile* and once again it proved that Donald was a man of many talents. His artistry as director and producer of the documentary won him the British Lion prize for the best documentary at the Venice Film Festival in 1965. The six months we spent making it were not wasted because we learned so much about the outback, the Aboriginal race, and the mysteries of the rainmaker. In fact we could have written a book about this fascinating and enjoyable time. We finally left Australia in the midsummer of 1965 and flew straight to Hawaii where we decided to stay for a rest and some fun.

Chapter 13

TIME TO PLAY

We stayed in the beautiful Kahala Hilton Hotel just outside Honolulu town and away from all the hustle and bustle. Its fantastic ocean front setting meant it was a favourite playground for international royalty and Hollywood stars. In fact when we were there the place was packed out with tinsel town's finest – Kirk Douglas and family, James Garner and Henry Fonda, to name but a few. Otto Preminger's war epic *In Harm's Way* was being shot in Hawaii at this time so most of the cast could be seen in and around Honolulu. We met up with the great John Wayne and an old friend of Donald's, the legendary boozer Bruce Cabott, whom we had met a few years before in Palm Springs with Ray Ryan. Donald didn't care too much for the 'film set'. He was humble about his own achievements and their attitude intimidated him. Bruce was different, though, and we immediately got in touch with him. The conversation on the phone went something like this.

Donald: Hello, Bruce old boy, how are you?

Bruce: D.C. Son of a bitch! Where the fucking hell are you?

Donald: Kahala Hilton old man.

Bruce: Your woman with you?

Donald: Can't get rid of the bitch.

Bruce: What are you up to tonight?

Donald: Nothing in particular.

Bruce: Meet me at the Royal Hawaiian Bar, 8.30. I may still be sober at that hour.

Donald: Doubt it, but we'll meet you. Ciao.

I smiled at Donald. 'I think you two boys should have a real bachelor night out,' I said.

'Nonsense! Bruce loves you,' answered Donald, 'and he would be disappointed if I left you at home!'

I didn't insist as this was our first night at the Kahala and so we met Bruce, who was still half-sober, at the said bar. He had an invitation to an art exhibition. The artist was his friend, or at least the friend of a friend of his. He was insistent that we should accompany him and so off we all went. I omit the name of the artist because all three of us found his work a complete waste of paint and canvas. Slightly ill at ease, we stood in front of one huge mixture of brown, yellow and green paint trying to guess at its meaning, when the artist joined us. After the necessary introductions he asked Bruce what he thought of his master tableau. I saw Donald raise his eyebrows in embarrassment and I hoped diplomacy was on Bruce Cabott's lips. And then it came. Bruce, with his whisky glass in one hand and cigar in the other, greeted the artist with a broad smile and launched forth in a loud, clear voice. 'Well, friend, I reckon that's how it looks when the shit hits the fan.'

I could see Donald needed all his self-control not to burst out laughing. Instead he turned away, pretending to study another painting, but it was no use. The whole room had heard Bruce's remark and was softly chuckling away – Bruce had only put into words what most of them were thinking. The artist soon recovered his composure; he smiled and slapped Bruce gently on the shoulder. 'I can always trust you to bring a laugh into my circle.' Then, as if the rude remark had been completely forgotten, he added, 'I'm having a luncheon tomorrow at my house, Bruce. I'll expect you.'

Later, Donald remarked that the artist was either a conceited fool or a very clever man, taking the whole art world for one big ride.

The days in Hawaii were passed in sunning, swimming and dining. We should have enjoyed it, but didn't. One evening after Bruce had stumbled back to his hotel to sleep it off, Donald suggested a nightcap at the Royal Hawaiian Beach Bar. It was a very romantic little place, a beautiful hut right on the beach with soft background music. When we arrived we sat at the bar and Donald ordered us Cointreau. No words were spoken between us but as I began sipping my drink I took a sideways glance at him. He was staring out to sea, an expression of boredom and intense loneliness written across his face. I looked away knowing there was nothing I could do. This was Donald. He was lonely and he was bored. The anticlimax after a record attempt and the success of it – I knew it too well. So here I was, sitting next to this man who seemed obviously tired of my company. I don't know how other wives feel about this, but I just couldn't sit back and let it happen. I had to do something to get him alive again, with or without me.

For weeks now, regardless of whether he was dining me, buying something for me, or making love to me, it always had the whiff of being done out of duty, and frankly I was getting bored. Suddenly I found myself thinking out loud and I could hardly believe it when I heard my voice saying, 'We're bored with each other aren't we, Donald? I'd find it funny if it wasn't so sad.'

Donald's expression changed to one of complete amazement. 'Bobo! How can you say such a dreadful thing? You can't be bored with your old man!'

'Can't I?' I said. 'I like that. Typical of a man. You boys have the right to be bored with us, but oh, we couldn't feel that way about our lord and master.' Now I really was getting heated and the nasty side of my character was strengthening by the second. 'Honestly Donald, in these two weeks I've been bored stiff. I know you love me but that doesn't stop *you* from being bored. I want a man to sleep with me because he wants to and not because he has to.' I stopped, out of breath, and looked at Donald. He appeared terribly handsome in the candlelight and suddenly he started chuckling to himself.

'My Vixen, of course you're bored. How insensitive of me not to have noticed. You're right, my love, in all respects except for one: I am not and never have been bored with you. You're one hell of a girl in every way and never have I made love to a woman so long, so often and so agreeably! Bored isn't the word, but I'm restless. Bear with me, Bobo, I know I'm difficult. There's such a damned anticlimax when it's all over – the car and boat engines have stopped but mine's still running and it's physically painful. I don't know what to do about it.'

He fell silent. Calm now, I asked him what it was that made him want to break those records again and again. He smiled proudly.

'It's a good question and one that's been asked many times, but the truth is I don't know myself. Sometimes it's curiosity. How will a car or boat behave at that speed? Or the challenge to prove that it can be done, or that I want Britain to stay on top. Queen and country, you know. Maybe it's to please my father, or maybe it's simply in my blood. I don't know, Bobo. All I do know is that I simply have to do it.'

Both of us were quiet for a while until I told him that he should have a boys' night out. He'd often said that the best times he'd had in the past were when he went out with the boys and I suggested that's what he should do with Bruce, John Wayne and some of the other guys from the *In Harm's Way* cast.

'But what will you do?' he asked, feigning concern.

'Don't worry, Donald. This is Hawaii, the elegant Kahala Hilton, swimming all day, dancing at night. I think I can suffer alone for a while!'

So it was decided, and that night Donald had what he called 'a pink ticket and a splash' with the boys. He tiptoed back at three in the morning and went straight to the bathroom where I heard him shower at length, then gargle out loud. When at last he crept into the king-size bed he whispered, 'Are you asleep, Bobo?'

'Donald, what a stupid question! For the last 15 minutes it has sounded like being next to the zoo while you disinfected yourself.'

He laughed, then started to tell me about their visit to a massage parlour and ended the story by saying that when it came to the nitty-gritty the girl wasn't half as good as me and charged him $150. It was not long after this bizarre conversation that Donald became amorous. I put on my sweetest smile and told him I would not charge him $300 dollars but would demand 100 instead. He told me he would give me the 100 later. I said I wanted it right now.

'Bobo, I've got no cash left!' he exclaimed.

I told him a traveller's cheque would do nicely, so in haste he got the cheque and then we made love to the full. And when it was over I told him that as long as we were in Hawaii he would have to pay $100 each time he wanted to make love to me. He laughed nervously but did as he was told. We stayed four more weeks, I acquired a complete new wardrobe and Donald had no more nights out with the boys.

To my embarrassment this episode became Donald's favourite after-dinner story. He even told it to the Duke of Richmond. I wanted to hide under the table when he began to recite it but the Duke found it highly amusing and asked Donald not to tell the tale to his wife Betty because it might give her ideas!

Donald never asked me about the time that I'd spent with the Hollywood actors in Hawaii. These encounters were a revelation to me. James Garner was fun, devoted to his wife and children, but included me in the evening's entertainment if he noticed I was on my own. Kirk Douglas was the complete opposite and seemed to me a self-centred bore. Henry Fonda had his nose constantly in some book and his air-hostess girlfriend, later to become his wife, just adored him. So there was really only Jimmy Garner who made a good impression on me.

On the plane from Honolulu to L.A., Donald again mentioned how much I had helped him with both record attempts and he wanted to give me a special gift. I reminded him that he'd already bought me a beautiful diamond pendant on our last day in Hawaii, but he insisted that I tell him what I really wanted. I thought for a while then said, 'Yes, actually there is something I want. I would like to go and spend some time in Vegas. I never did it properly. Lorrea Desmond is at the Tropicana. I had a letter from her before we left Australia. I can stay with her there – she's got a double room and Alec isn't with her. I can see seven shows a day if I want to. Do you know how long it is since I've seen a good show? I'd just like one week of nothing but showbiz!'

At this Donald smiled. 'Okay, Bobo, but my woman doesn't share rooms. I'll call my friend Stan Irwin at the Sahara Hotel. I want the penthouse suite for you. He can introduce you to his gang so you're not alone, in case you need anything.' He stopped. I waited. He continued. 'In Los Angeles I'll organise your visit to Las Vegas. We could stay in Beverly Hills for a couple of days then I'll take you to the airport and I'll fly to New York to try to sell our film. Later on you can join me, after a week or two.'

I remained silent. He looked at me and asked what the matter was. Didn't I like his plans for me? I leant over and kissed his cheek.

'I love your plans, Donald, and I love you.'

He messed up my hair and said he knew that. Donald was Donald once again: the jet-set dining and the aimless outings were over. He had things to do. More importantly, he had regained his sense of freedom. He knew he could fly away for a week, maybe more, without worrying about hurting my feelings. He also knew that in the end he would want me back and I knew this too. What I didn't know was that I wouldn't want to go back that soon – but then, that's show business.

I had the penthouse suite at the Sahara Hotel, Las Vegas. Lorrea was happy to see me and decided to spend some nights in my suite which was actually big enough for six. Within a few days I had met dozens of stars – Frank Fontaine, the very exciting Juliet Prowse (who was a great joke-teller), the suave Dean Martin, Al Martino, Guy Lombardo, Don Cornell and so many others. We were a great group and usually sat around the Sahara pool. There was also an acrobatic couple called The Agostinos, a husband and wife team. Frank Agostino was one of the most handsome men I had ever seen and a fantastic clown, too. With his larking around beside the pool all was joy and laughter. In no time Lake Eyre was forgotten.

One night the showbiz gang made me get up on stage and sing. It was sheer heaven. One of the producers of the *Frank Fontaine Show*, a man called Tom Illius, raved about my singing and assured me that if ever I wanted to return to my work I should let him know and he'd do everything possible to give me the right breaks. I didn't take this seriously at the time because Tom was a good-looking man with a roving eye, but in later years he proved that he was as good as his word and meant what he had said.

This was my kind of life. Lorrea had moved virtually all her gear into my suite. She was terrific company. Laughing and joking like two silly young girls, we gave very little thought to our respective spouses, so much so that when Donald called from New York after five days I realised with a shock that I was not particularly excited to hear his voice. Donald sensed it, of course, and his voice did take on some humour.

Stepping off the plane in Sydney, 1963. The press were always waiting for us, eager to quiz Donald about his latest plans for record-breaking.

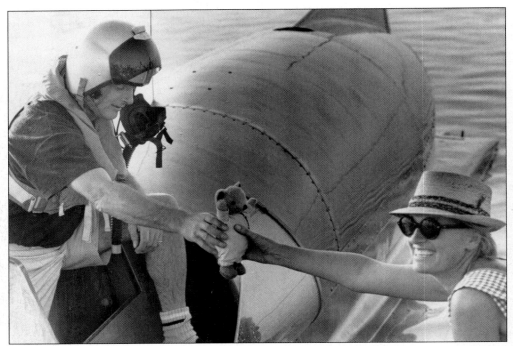

Donald hands Mr Whoppit to me after a trial run on Lake Dumbleyung, Western Australia, late in 1964.

Donald's birthday in Adelaide. The team and I gave him his own aeroplane! From left to right, Maurice Parfitt, Leo Villa, 'Fred', David Johnson, Donald and David Wynne-Morgan.

Doing the team's laundry in the outback was quite a challenge. I would be soaked through by the end of it! *News Ltd/Adelaide Advertiser*

The greatest world record attempt ever, took place in Australia in 1964. Donald broke the world land and water speed records in the same year. *Getty Images*

The victory parade through Adelaide that followed the successful record attempt – it pulled a bigger crowd than The Beatles.

With our dear
friend Maurice
Chevalier, whom
we saw as often as
we could.

Hawaii, 1965. From left to right, James Garner's wife and daughter, James himself, Henry Fonda
and wife Shirley, and yours truly, pictured at a fire-eating show.

PO ✱ GREETINGS TELEGRAM ✱

⊅ 3074 AP8 12.3 CONNISTON MR 18
ALLPURPOSE

TONIA BERN WESTCOKER HOTEL WESTCOKER YEOVIL

= HAPPY ANNIVERSARY DARLING HERES TO THE NEXT 50
FONDEST LOVE = DONALD +

The memorial to Donald in Coniston. *Westmorland Gazette*

Opposite, inset: The telegram Donald sent to me on our eighth – and final – wedding anniversary. Eleven days later he was dead.

Opposite, main picture: *Bluebird* racing to its end on Coniston Water. *Paul Allonby*

On our yacht *Fuchimi* in 1966. I will never love like that again – I wouldn't dare . . .

'Hey there, you do still remember your old man, don't you?'

I was honest when I answered. 'Donald, it's great to hear you, but you don't want me to come back yet, do you?'

'Well, I suppose we can squeeze out another few days. Having a good time there, then?' he probed.

'Yes, darling,' I said, 'a great time. Swimming, sunbathing and loads of shows. How are things in New York?'

'Hectic,' he said, quietly now. 'Met some people who may sell the film to Paramount, but I don't think we'll get our money back. Seems we should have sold it before making it. Strange business this film world. Trust me to do it the wrong way round.'

My feelings began to sink. I was being dragged back into a world of problems.

'I hope you're having some fun too, Donald. Don't want to find a grumble box on my return. Remember why we took this break?'

'Sure I remember, darling,' Donald laughed, 'and don't worry! I'm spending the weekend in New Jersey. One of these men I met, a chap called Donald Flamm, has a lovely big house there with a swimming pool and all that goes with it. He's having a big house party, should be nice. Bags of crumpet of course. He's a bachelor. Still, I would be happier if I could sell the film. Mind you, I still miss my old girl!'

He stopped there and I felt I had to say something quick, but all I could manage was a rather meek 'That's nice to hear.'

'Aha,' he said, 'I don't think this feeling's very mutual.'

I moved quickly to repair the damage. 'You're already too sure of me as it is, so I'm not going to add to it. I'm having a wonderful time, a complete "me" time – you know what I mean?'

'Yes, Bobo,' he replied, 'you deserve it.'

'You'll see,' I added, 'I'll be a new woman when I come back.'

'I don't want a new woman,' he answered. 'The old one suits me fine. I'll ring you after the weekend and we can discuss travel dates then. God bless for now.'

Lorrea looked at me quietly. She said nothing, but I knew what she was thinking. 'Okay, don't give me that look. All I want right now is just what I've got – the sun, the shows and the freedom.'

Lorrea's expression didn't change one little bit when she finished the sentence for me: '. . . and a couple of famous men chasing after you.'

Wrong-footed by this, I looked up at her and said, 'Yes, I admit I like that too. Anyway I think I'd like a drink. Frank brought some bubbly the other day. It's in the fridge. I'll get it.'

'Frank Sinatra?' asked Lorrea, her eyes wide with surprise.

'No, ninny, Frank Agostino the acrobat!' I answered. I fetched the champagne while Lorrea got the glasses and we settled ourselves nicely on the big balcony of our suite overlooking Las Vegas. After a while she asked, 'Did you have an affair with Frank?'

I laughed. 'I wouldn't call it an affair, more like a flirtation.'

'Is Donald very jealous when you misbehave?'

'Hey, wait a minute Lorrea. I don't make a habit of it and he's no angel either,' I replied.

'That doesn't mean he can't be jealous,' Lorrea said.

I thought for a moment and then remembered a couple of incidents. I told her about one evening in the South of France when a very beautiful lesbian had paid me flamboyant compliments and invited me to visit her yacht. Donald was leaving the next day for Montreal. On the plane he wrote a letter which the captain brought to me on the return flight. It was four pages long and in it Donald asked me not to accept the lady's advances. He said such a liaison could be dangerous and could spark changes within me that would sadden him. He said that if I was tempted, I should stick to 'the natural'. The other incident I recounted to Lorrea took place in Courchevel when a rich jet-setter who was reputed to hold sex parties began dancing with me a little too closely. Donald walked up to us and said, 'Excuse me, but the lady belongs to me – completely'; and with those words he took me off the dance floor mumbling 'Sorry, Bobo, but I couldn't stand his filthy hands on you.'

When I'd finished telling her about these two incidents Lorrea persisted with her line of questioning. 'Are you jealous or don't you know?'

I laughed and told her that Donald often said, 'My old girl knows what I'm going to do before I think of it.' Yes, I said, I was jealous but I was able to handle it because he was worth it.

'Women throw themselves at him. I saw that in Australia,' Lorrea added.

I agreed. 'Sometimes it's even worse. Some even ask me whether they have a chance.'

Lorrea's thoughts moved on.

'I didn't really love Alec deeply when I married him,' she said, 'not like you loved Donald, and yet with all this separation I still haven't been with another man. Tonia, if you were in my shoes, would you?'

I thought for a minute then admitted that I would. 'I'm afraid I've got to say I haven't your character. I'm not strong like you and I really like men. I know their failings – some are liars or cheats, but they're handsome devils and I love the feeling of a man near me. I don't have to love him to enjoy his nearness. You know Donald never ever lied to me.'

'I think, Tonia, my love, you should go back to New York soon,' said Lorrea. I didn't get angry, because she was right. I said nothing. She continued. 'You love all this because you know it's temporary, but if you were back in the business just being a singer you'd be constantly looking for a man to love. It's an empty life, Ton, because there are not many men worth loving. Hold on to Donald. Be proud that he's your man.'

I knew she was right and staying on in Vegas was getting dangerous. When Donald called the following Tuesday we agreed that I would fly back to join him on the Friday, and he would arrange our return tickets to London one week later. He sounded happy that I was coming back and said two weeks' rest from each other had been quite enough. So, with a heavy heart I said goodbye to my new-found friends. They gave me an all-night party and accompanied me to the airport in the morning for my 6 o'clock flight. Fortunately, my deep golden tan hid my pallor when I took a last look at my beloved Las Vegas. I knew it wasn't saying goodbye to Vegas that made me sad; it was 'Goodbye Tonia Bern – Hello Mrs Campbell'. But I remembered what Lorrea had pointed out: Donald could have married any woman but he chose me; I was Mrs Campbell.

Donald was staying at the St Regis in New York, the very hotel where years ago I had ended my career. He'd booked a lovely suite and received me royally. A bunch of beautiful roses lay on the table and a bottle of my favourite perfume, Casaque, with a handwritten card addressed to 'the most wonderful girl in the world – fondest love from your grumble box'. His kiss of welcome was real and wonderful and to my relief I felt that I was back in my niche. He had organised dinner at a restaurant called The Boat and invited all his New York friends. When one of the guests blurted in a moment of drunken indiscretion, 'Well, Donald, I've seen you with lots of girls but this one towers above them all,' Donald laughed back at him. 'This one's personal property!'

Yes, I thought, *he was right*. Within hours of leaving Vegas I had forgotten the glamour, the handsome men and all the thrills. There really was only Donald, and whether I was with him or separated from him, his power would hold me. As our wonderful friends Millie and Lou Robbins drove us back to the hotel, Millie said, 'You two really complement each other.' Donald squeezed my hand. Once again we were together, really together.

Donald never ceased to amaze me. During my stay in Vegas, he had inquired about finding a top heart specialist for me. Millie told him that a Professor Chassis was one of the best and arranged a consultation for me. After two days of tests and cardiograms we were told that so far my heart was doing its job, but the problem was that some of the blood vessels were not functioning properly and this was affecting my circulation. He advised me to hang on for as long as I could since the techniques for carrying out this particular procedure were improving by the day. Many years later I was successfully operated on at the New York University Hospital, but Donald never knew.

The flight back to England was uneventful. As usual, Donald spent most of it on the flight deck with the pilot, showing that flying was his true love. I slept part of the way and read for the remainder. At Heathrow we were greeted by everybody – family and friends, the Bluebird team, as well as the usual barrage of cameras and reporters. Gina, now a lovely young girl, handed us some flowers.

It was two weeks later, driving into London for a luncheon, that Donald told me he'd sold Roundwood. He waited for a reaction but it was one of the rare times in my life that I had none. Before leaving for Australia I'd actually seen it advertised in a magazine at my hairdresser's. When I'd questioned him about it then he'd simply answered, 'The way to make a good sale is to be in no hurry.' Surprised at my silence, he added, 'A lawyer bought it, for £36,000 – not bad is it? We bought it for £10,000 only seven years ago.'

'That's nice,' I said without feeling.

'Is that all you have to say when I tell you I've sold our house?' asked Donald curtly.

'Our house?' I exploded. 'It was never mine. And today proves that. What should I say? It belonged to you and now it belongs to this lawyer. What difference does it really make to me except that I'm going to live somewhere else?' I really struck a nerve.

Donald's voice had a gentler timbre when he answered. 'Sorry, Bobo, I should have told you. But you're just so wonderful about these things and it kept slipping my mind. I really would hate it if you had never considered Roundwood yours. You always said it was too big, and what with staff getting harder to find and then this good offer, well I thought it was the right thing to do. It only came through this morning.'

I now felt guilty for my explosion. I put my hand on his knee and smiled. 'It was just the shock of it that made me say it. Don't worry. When do we move?'

'We have six months to find another house,' he replied, 'and you, Bobo, must choose it. It has to be your house even more than mine.'

Chapter 14

FAREWELL TO ROUNDWOOD

oon after our return from America, a dinner was organised at the RAC Club in Pall Mall to celebrate Donald's double record achievement. It was for gentlemen only but for some odd reason the invitation included me. I think Donald had something to do with it because when we arrived and were shown to our places the name cards on the table read 'Donald Campbell CBE' and next to it 'Fred Campbell'. Donald whispered to me, 'If you're a boy then I'm queer!' I was honoured and very touched.

House-hunting was awful. Every time I found what Donald wanted, he decided he wanted something different. First it was a house in Surrey, preferably modern, then he decided on a big old pile that we could restore as we did Roundwood. I found a property like this in Tunbridge Wells, only for Donald to decide he wanted to live in Brighton and start a marina. After I'd found some beautiful apartments facing the sea he changed his mind yet again, and decided he wanted an old castle so he could build a motor museum and a playground for children in the grounds.

We'd already wasted four months and Donald was forced to ask for an extension of another six before we had to move out of Roundwood. The new owner agreed to three and at least that bought us some breathing space. I was now getting panicky, but not the old boy. He seemed quite sure we would find the right thing. He was terribly busy of course and had experienced a lot of problems since our return. He was also working on advertisements and product promotion. Then, to top it all, we learned that Gina's mother (Donald's first wife, Daphne) had tried to see Gina during our stay in Australia. Gina, loyal to her father, had told her mother it would have to wait until our return.

One night I could feel Donald couldn't sleep. He was trying hard not to twist and turn so as not to disturb me. I asked him if I could help. He told me how Daphne kept calling him, insisting on seeing Gina. I knew that he had loved his first wife deeply, but now disliked her intensely and rarely talked about her. (His second wife, Dorothy, was in his own words, 'a very nice girl who didn't know what hit her' when they married.) We discussed the problem at length in the darkness of our bedroom. In my opinion, to refuse to allow mother and daughter to meet would make it more tempting for Gina, and I told Donald so. He agreed, but still felt Daphne would be a bad influence on Gina. Nevertheless the next day it was decided mother and daughter could meet the following Sunday afternoon and they could go for tea together.

I remember how Donald and I sat in his study, depressed and anxious, wondering if we would lose the harmony that had grown between the three of us. Gina returned and although she was impressed by her mother's house, she didn't seem impressed by Daphne. We hoped it would remain that way.

Some time later we heard that Gina was seeing quite a bit of the son of one of our neighbours. Donald told her she could bring him home to lunch or tea, but when she absolutely refused he asked me to talk to her. 'You girls talk the same language,' he told me. I did speak to her but it had the same result and in the end she admitted that she didn't want him to come to the house as he'd take one look at me and wouldn't want to see her any more. I was horrified and wondered what on earth had given her this impression. I told her that when I was her age I was not nearly as pretty or as much fun as she was, nor as clever. She took a lot of convincing but finally gave in. When she eventually brought the young man to meet us he had eyes only for Gina and was obviously smitten by her. She soon got bored with her suitor – and many more as the years went by. Donald would be amused by it and say his little minx believed in loving and leaving them. I told him she was a true Campbell. He laughed, assuring me his own roving days were over.

In the long run Daphne didn't influence Gina. Years later Gina wrote me a letter in which she said her mother had finally admitted her jealousy towards me because I had not only Donald's love but Gina's too. In her letter Gina said she had told her mother that she loved me because I showed her what love was all about. I treasured that letter and decided to keep it always.

Donald became involved in sorting out several commercial propositions. He told me that he had to strike while the iron was hot. We had lost the support of British Petroleum, despite the best efforts of David Wynne-Morgan who was still Donald's public relations adviser. The fact that the record attempts were slowly slipping into the past didn't help either. Another setback was that Donald had no competition. There was only Craig Breedlove and although he was very talented he failed to capture the imagination of the world and lacked Donald Campbell's charisma. Without competition Donald knew the record-breaking challenge would fade. As a result he was very preoccupied with trying to find another aim, and this was not easy. If only the speed bug had left him alone he could have chosen another career – anything from top photographer to insurance broker, feature writer or film producer. This man had many talents but none of them overpowered his love of speed. To find words to describe this would be impossible. It was many different loves in one: achievement, recognition, ambition, challenge, duty. I never really knew what was the main attraction, and neither did he.

During the house-hunting period our handsome ski instructor, Pierre Grunberg, came to stay for a few days. Craig Douglas had become a regular house guest too and they were both in the house for a quiet weekend. Donald was finishing work in the office with Rosie while we were having morning coffee on my own little terrace outside my den. The jokes came easily and the laughter was loud. This didn't help Donald's concentration in the office beneath us so he joined us and we started discussing the house situation. We all had some fantastic ideas for the old castle, motor museum, playground, shooting range and God knows what else, then Donald came up with the mad idea of making a flight over Surrey and Sussex during which the three of us, armed with binoculars, would scan the countryside for any noticeable castles. I put in a few objections that were completely ignored, of course, and exactly two hours later we were flying dangerously low in Donald's new plane searching for the elusive castle.

We flew all over Surrey and Sussex, up to Brighton and back, saw a lot of houses and apartment blocks, but alas no castles. After two hours even the boys were tired and giddy from looking through binoculars. We'd flown back to Brighton along a different route when we unanimously decided to return home for a rest and a cup of tea. The castle was forgotten and the boys were now back to their favourite topic of conversation, crumpet. I was continuing the search when suddenly I saw it. It was certainly some kind of castle – there was the tower and the old walls.

'I've found one, I've found one!' I screamed excitedly.

Donald jumped and so did our plane. 'For God's sake, Bobo, don't do that!'

I ignored his remark and still shouting I asked him to turn back. 'Donald, please, I saw a castle!'

Now my excitement was shared. The plane was turned about and all eyes followed my directions. Yes, there it was, in all its glory – a dream castle standing among trees and lush greenery. I had previously pointed out Windsor Castle, but Donald had remarked he knew the place and that the owners wouldn't sell. From what we could see, this castle was more of a ruin than a stately home. The boys were excited now and had completely forgotten me. Donald circled around to pinpoint the exact location. We decided to go back home and then drive there.

We flew back to Redhill where we landed hastily and then scrambled into the car. Racing through the countryside we made it to the castle in less than two hours from the moment of my discovery. The entrance drive was actually on the main Brighton road and it led to a ghostly old building. There was no one about so we climbed over the gate and crept about the grounds like thieves, peering through the windows, which was easy as most of them were broken. We eventually found one window through which we could enter. Naturally Donald was in charge of the expedition. He cautioned us about loose stair treads and falling ceilings, of which there were plenty. The staircase was of carved wood and still looked very beautiful, despite the filth and cobwebs. The rooms were large and high, but it was clear the whole place would cost an absolute fortune to restore. At that moment Donald was not thinking of money – he, Craig and Pierre were planning the whole restoration. They could have stayed for hours in the old castle, but I was getting cold and tired and once I'd seen the place I longed to go home. I walked away into the garden and left them to play.

Within three weeks the castle became only a dream. It was owned by two old Scottish girls who didn't want to sell, but agreed to rent it to us for £1,500 a month. Donald made a business plan, calculation after calculation, benefit after benefit, and in the end had to admit that at such a high price it would just be a complete waste of money. In the meantime, house-hunting had stopped and we would soon have to vacate Roundwood with nowhere to go. As so often before, Donald found the solution.

He decided we should go for a drive around his favourite villages. It was a lovely day and bursts of sunshine broke through the clouds as we drove around Reigate and Dorking. But there was no success. Most 'for sale' signs were on dull houses. Then on the Dorking road, just before Leatherhead, we came across another 'for sale' board but could only see the property's driveway. The house was hidden behind trees and other greenery. Donald slowed down and asked me whether we should simply drive in. I said yes. I instantly fell in love with the house. It was a Spanish-style villa, with lovely arcades that were overgrown with roses. Donald stopped the car and, looking at my face, he smiled.

'Don't get too excited, chérie. There's a reason for it not being sold yet.' The house was built halfway up a hill. At the top was the Dorking road and at the bottom the River Mole. There were five acres of lovely gardens, with a neglected swimming pool. It was known as Prior's Ford and was owned by a middle-aged couple called the Josephs. The inside of the house reflected their personalities, but the actual construction and planning of the rooms were perfect. Big windows looked out on to a perfect view. Donald also liked the house and before we left he made an offer to which the owners agreed. They shook on it.

Driving away he said, 'Bobo, that's a lovely place. Now we had better give a goodbye party to Roundwood and let's make it a truly grand one! Roundwood has served us well so let's give it a corking send-off!'

Typical of Donald, I thought, not to forget the old for the new. What I couldn't guess at that moment was that my goodbye to Roundwood would also be my goodbye to happiness, and that the end of my life with Donald was near.

We were to give our party on 16 December, then afterwards travel to Courchevel for Christmas and the New Year, before moving from Roundwood to Prior's Ford in January. The new owner of Roundwood had been very patient, but we had to vacate the property before 15 January.

Julia, Louis and I were doing all the preparations for the party and things were hectic. Donald dealt with the invitations and our guest list came to 160 people. A few days before the big event, the whole place was transformed. Donald hired a huge marquee that was erected at the front of the house, taking in the front door, so that none of our guests would have to walk the length of the driveway and would be sheltered in case of rain. Into this marquee were squeezed the *Bluebird* boat and car, as well as a life-size model of Donald's new project, a jet car designed to do more than 800mph.

For a midnight thrill, a giant cracker was being made by the Bluebird team. It would take half a dozen men to pull it from each end. At the witching hour a gun would go off, balloons and snowballs would tumble down from the ceiling, and to cap it all a completely naked girl would jump out of the cracker. (Later on, 'completely naked' was changed to 'practically naked'.) Needless to say auditions for this role were held by Donald, and as usual he came up with what he called 'a corker'.

The party was a tremendous success. Not 160 but 300 people arrived and Donald remembered all their names. He was a magnificent host, devoting his evening to the success of the party and the enjoyment of his guests. Once again, democracy was the key theme: the Marchioness of Reading danced with Donald's flying instructor, and the lovely cracker girl with Sir William Pickett-Brown who, I was told, was very rich (just as well, for in my view he had very little else). He was among the friends who accompanied Sir Max and Lady Aitken's party. There were a lot of people present who I loved and admired, but I must admit there were some for whom I had very little time. Looking around the room at the people dancing to the music of the hired discotheque, I couldn't help wondering how many were true friends. I was sure I could pick them out there and then. Max Aitken, I thought, would be a friend. He was a beautiful man, but I was not so sure about his wife Vi. I smiled at the thought and guessed the feeling was mutual. I had heard she had quite a brain and knew all about boats, guns, horses and politics.

I wondered if Donald realised how often I'd been bored by some of these people, a handful of them his close friends. Roy Page and his Spanish countess wife were both superficial and materialistic; then there was Sir George Dowty and his young wife Marguerite, whom we had often invited to dinner but whose presence made me yawn, although Marguerite on her own was very pleasant. But then there were the exciting ones like Margot and Michael Reading who were funny and vivacious; the Coleys – now they were always interesting and warm; Peter and Cherry Barker, fun-loving and genuine; and of course Donald's cousin, the lovely Lady Joan Shawcross.

The whole evening was spent in seeing that everyone had enough food and drink, but I needn't have worried – the Campbell party was the talk of London for many weeks to come. The naked girl who jumped out of the cracker was a real show-stopper and Donald was as happy as a lord.

When we arrived at Courchevel on 21 December the weather and the snow were beautiful and skiing down the slopes was sheer heaven. Gina had come with us and we had booked ourselves into the five-star Carlina Hotel again, leaving our faithful Louis and Julia behind to pack up Roundwood. We were due to stay until 9 January, but fate had an ugly surprise in store. On 27 December Victor Mishcon telephoned us to say that Mr Joseph, the owner of Prior's Ford, had changed his mind and wanted £2,000 more on top of the given price. I hit the roof and told Donald we should move into an apartment until we found something else. I was adamant that we should not agree with this man out of principle. In the end Donald decided to return to London to see what could be done. Gina and I stayed on in Courchevel as we could do nothing to help, he said, until we heard from him one way or another. We heard soon enough. Not in a fighting mood, Donald gave in and Gina and I flew home on 4 January 1966 to help with the final preparations for the move.

Chapter 15

A FAILED RECORD ATTEMPT

A surprise awaited me on the plane home from Geneva to London. I happened to pick up an English newspaper and there in ugly black letters I read: 'Donald Campbell announces new record bid. This time the aim will be 300mph. The record attempt will be held in Coniston.' It went on to explain that Donald had been to visit Norman Buckley in Windermere, a man who had achieved a classified speed record himself. After all the celebrations that followed Norman's success, Donald had explained to the press that a new boat called *Hustler* was being designed in America and that it had a good chance of snatching the world water speed record from Britain. Therefore he wanted to push the record up to 300mph and, as he put it, 'Give the Americans a run for their money'.

I let the paper drop into my lap and stared out of the cabin window. *So, here we go again*, I thought. I'd vainly hoped that he wouldn't try for any more records and would concentrate instead on writing his life story. I had a terrible foreboding, a strong feeling of danger. Years earlier I'd promised myself never to interfere with the attempts, but this time my whole being rebelled. I felt I had to stop him. I lay back in my seat and closed my eyes. *A record attempt takes time and money. Let's hope there won't be enough of either.* For the first time since my marriage to Donald I prayed that he would not get the backing, that he would not get the right conditions, that he would not go for that record. I didn't tell Gina and I didn't show her the paper. There was no need for us both to worry.

Back in England, I found Donald in a very low mood. After one day with Gina and me he had gone up to London to stay at Dolphin Square where we kept a small flat for overnight use. He rarely phoned. The move had started and I was grateful for his absence because I could get on with the job much better without him. Gina was now a fully-fledged secretary and had left to work as a receptionist at a hotel in the Lake District. Louis, Julia and I could get on with all we had to do. Within a week the new house took shape. Multi-coloured carpet had been replaced by a plain dark blue one, the walls had been freshly painted, the furniture was more or less in place and the telephone was installed. My first call was to Donald in Dolphin Square. It was about 8.30 in the morning and I was just about to lift the receiver when the phone rang. I picked it up, thinking it would be the telephone engineers checking the new line.

'Hello?' I said and to my amazement Donald's voice replied.

'Hello, darling. How's everything at the Ford?'

'Fine,' I answered with complete surprise, 'fine! But how did you get the number? No one knows it yet.'

'I called the phone people two days ago to chivvy them up so I could talk to my old girl!'

'And there was I thinking how clever I was to get it so soon,' I said with dismay. Then in a lighter tone I added, 'I must say that wherever you are and whoever you're with, you can't help calling me, can you?'

Donald continued, laughing, 'That's right and most of my girlfriends are very jealous of my wife. Hey, now to business, Bobo! Is it all right for me to come home tonight?'

'Of course, darling,' I laughed. 'The house is practically in order and the heating's working well.'

'I'll be there by eight,' he said. 'Ciao, ciao, for now.'

As I hung up, I wondered whose breakfast he had interrupted to call me, then shrugged off the idea. I loved him as he was and he never pretended to be anything he wasn't. In any case, there hadn't been any girlfriends for years. I smiled and got on with my work.

John Pearson's book about the record attempt on Lake Eyre had now been published. Donald had wanted the title to be *The Lonely Mile* but instead the publishers, Collins, had chosen to call it *Bluebird and the Dead*

Lake. I received the first copy and opened it to see Donald's handwriting on the endpaper. It read:

> *Tonia my Darling*
> *In deep appreciation*
> *of the agony you*
> *suffered so unflinchingly*
> *to give me strength*
> *with this record attempt.*
>
> *With all my love and Gratitude.*
> *From*
> *Donald*

And in the years that followed, whenever I wondered whether I could have done more, I opened the book and re-read his dedication.

Donald liked Prior's Ford, but I knew he'd never love it as he did Roundwood. It didn't have the atmosphere of the English country estate that Roundwood had. In other words, it was more me and less him. He was now concentrating on his insurance business again and had turned the whole upstairs of the house into an office. We had not discussed the new record attempt and I was just beginning to hope that he had changed his mind about it when one morning he called me to his office. It was a beautiful attic room that ran the length of the house.

'Sit down, Bobo,' he said. 'Have some coffee with me.'

Louis had already brought coffee and I was rather surprised.

'What's the big occasion?' I asked.

Donald leant back in his white leather office chair and began to speak. 'As you know, I've announced a new record attempt. Of course it's going to take some money to get the old boat in order. We need a new engine to begin with. I'd love to go back to Australia where the conditions and weather are better, but the cost of fares and accommodation would be much too high, so it will have to be Coniston. Beggars can't be choosers.'

'Are we beggars?' I asked him.

'No dear, not yet,' he said. 'We have some money in the kitty. The insurance broking is doing fine and I've taken out a £15,000 mortgage on Prior's Ford.' He stopped and looked at me, an intense expression in his eyes. Taking a cigarette and lighting it, he asked me what I thought.

Slowly I shook my head, put down the now empty coffee cup and said resignedly, 'What difference does it make what I say, Donald?'

Donald flashed back, 'I still like to hear your opinion.'

'What about?' I asked. 'Mortgage or record attempt?'

'Both,' said Donald eagerly.

'All right,' I answered. 'The mortgage doesn't matter to me. You must know by now you're the one who likes the trimmings of life, the butler, the cook, the beautiful house. You're also the one who finds the money for these things, so in that direction whatever you do is fine with me. You've made and spent and remade several fortunes.'

Donald interrupted me. 'That's true, but if anything should happen to me, Bobo, you won't be a rich lady, you know that?'

'If anything happens to you I won't last too long myself,' I replied. 'That's one good thing about heart defects, so I won't need to be rich! And Gina, as you told me, has been provided for by the family trust funds, so there's no problem there.' I assumed a lighter tone. 'Don't worry, Skipper. I'll manage. I can always sing for my supper!'

I paused for a moment. Donald remained silent so I took a deep breath and spoke again, trying to sound casual. 'I promised never to interfere with your attempts and I never have, not even after the Utah crash. I don't have much merit in this because I've always felt quite confident about things. During these last seven years of our marriage I've never felt any anxiety about record attempts. But from the moment I read about this new one I've had the strangest feeling of insecurity, even premonition, Donald. For the first time I truly don't want you to do it. Every time I think of it my stomach turns over and now I'm asking you not to do it.'

I stopped. I'd said my bit. He was looking out of the window opposite his desk and said nothing, so I added, 'Well, now you know how I feel. When are you leaving for Coniston?'

Donald stood up and came over to me. Taking my head between his hands he kissed my forehead. 'You become more beautiful each day, Bobo.

Don't worry, I'll take great care.' Then going back to his desk he continued. 'You and I are going to Coniston around September or October, but there's plenty of time to discuss that. Now, I must get back to work. Tell Rosie to come up as soon as she arrives.'

I got up, put the coffee cups on the tray and walked away. As I reached the small stairway down from the attic into the house below, Donald called after me warmly.

'And Bobo, thank you!'

I smiled back at him over my shoulder, but didn't speak. I was afraid this could be Donald's death sentence and I was completely powerless to prevent it.

A few days after this conversation Donald told me he was going to Megève in the French Alps with a group of friends. His holiday in Courchevel had been cut short and he felt justified in taking another one. He said he was only going for about two weeks and did I mind? My first reaction was to explode, but then the thought of the record attempt returned.

'I always mind,' I said simply, 'but I also know it'll do you good. Anyway, there's plenty of work to occupy me here. When are you leaving?'

'At the weekend,' he said, walking away and looking much more miserable than I did. He left two days later, bad-tempered and irritable, and I didn't envy the lady who was to be his companion on this trip. That lady was Vi Aitken. He called on Friday evening to say he'd arrived in Megève and didn't like the place at all. Before hanging up he told me to look under my pillow before I went to sleep. I hurried to our room, looked under my pillow and found an envelope addressed to Tonia Bern-Campbell, my surname hyphenated. I opened it. Inside was a note and a cheque. The note read: 'To my lovely wife for her patience and understanding. From her old grumble box. Please bear with me once again. Fondest love, Donald.'

True to form, Donald found it difficult to spend money if he didn't give me the same opportunity. I knew at once what I had to do. This cheque would buy orchestrations, clothes and rehearsals. I wondered why I felt so strongly that I had to go back to my work. The answer would come to me within a year of that day, but at the time all I knew was that I had decided to return to showbiz. He had promised not to get back in the boat and I had promised not to go back on stage. We had both broken our promises.

Two days later I received a telegram: 'Tried to call you unsuccessfully. Am now in Courchevel. Hope you are well. Fondest love – Donald.' As I read it my anger nearly choked me. How could he take someone else to the place where we took our holidays and moreover where we had our honeymoon? I sent a telegram to Courchevel. It read: 'Happy second honeymoon and the best of British luck – Tonia.' The reply from Donald was swift and was delivered to me the very next morning. 'There was only ever one honeymoon. There was only ever one woman – You. All my love. Donald.' Donald returned home four days earlier than planned. After this escapade he constantly demanded my presence, but my days were full as I had already started rehearsals.

Vera Freedman had introduced me to a very charming young agent called Mel Collins who lived next door to her. Mel was positively bubbling with enthusiasm since he specialised in grooming and managing new artistes. His attractive and witty wife Jill helped him with the admini-strative work. Before long, publicity photos and brochures were under way and I had designed two new costumes, both of which were cat-suits and completely novel at this time. Orchestrations were being penned and I was rehearsing practically every afternoon at the Astor Club in Berkeley Square which we hired by the hour. Mel was simply wonderful at producing and directing. He thought of everything. It was good to be singing on stage again and into a mike, even without an audience.

I hadn't spoken to Donald about my plans. There'd be time enough, I thought, when I secured my first contract. Donald's mother, Lady Dorothy Campbell, came along to rehearsals one afternoon. She was excited about what I was doing but kept her word and said nothing to her son. She told me that I should never have given up my career and that it was a good thing for me to start again. 'No woman should have just a Campbell to think about,' she said. 'They are far too complicated and difficult.'

I decided I needed a break and flew to Knokke. Donald would have said it was to recharge my batteries so that I could cope with 'the impossible grumble box', as he called himself. My cousin Maurice told me about the 21 Club which Franz Jacob had just opened in Brussels and I decided to pay it a visit. Franz had been friends with Maurice since their childhood and was flamboyant to say the least. He was also a close friend of the famous Belgian entertainer Jacques Brel. I had met the enormously talented Brel when I was fifteen and he had become my tutor for a little while. I was a devoted disciple, studying fanatically to be able to do justice to his magnificent songs.

Franz received us with open arms and proceeded to introduce everyone at the club to Maurice and me, whom he kept calling 'la belle chanteuse'. In no time I was being asked to sing and did so willingly. The pianist was familiar with Brel's material and we chose the ballad 'Ne me quitte pas'. I sang more to myself than to anyone else and closed my eyes to savour the joy of the music.

Towards the end I opened them to see a dark, handsome man looking up at me from the crowd. His name was Aldo Vastapane, a member of the incredibly wealthy Martini family. Aldo was freshly divorced, full of fun and could charm the birds from the trees. From the moment we met he hardly left my side and when he invited me to stay the night at his house, stipulating that I would have a guestroom and we would drive to Knokke the next morning, I accepted. I told Maurice of my plans and he surprised me by insisting we leave together without Vastapane. On the way back he explained that he admired Donald very much and as a result he felt he had to protect me. Marcel Arnault was one thing but Vastapane was quite another. He was important, powerful and not to be played with. I told him that Donald himself was playing a dangerous game at that moment. Maurice replied curtly, 'That doesn't mean you should too.'

Nevertheless, when Aldo arrived the following day I was truly pleased to see him. We wined and dined, walked hand in hand on the beach, sometimes silently, sometimes talking about anything and everything, but Donald was never mentioned. Aldo assured me there would be no sex between us unless we both knew it was right. This was certainly tempting, especially as he put no pressure on me, but I knew Maurice was right: this was serious stuff and I could get burnt.

Before I left, Aldo asked me whether I would consider a trip to Africa with him. I told him I needed to think about it. He took me to the airport and gave me a huge toy rabbit (named Harvey, of course) for which he had booked a seat next to me on the plane. He said the rabbit was to be my companion until he himself could sit next to me again. Some days later when I was back at home he called early in the morning to speak to me. We were still in the bedroom and Donald picked up the phone. When Aldo asked to speak to me he said, somewhat pompously, 'May I ask what this is about?'

Aldo replied, 'No, you may not.'

Without another word Donald handed the phone to me and left the room. Before I had found time to tell Aldo that I could not go to Africa he had already guessed what I was going to say. His final words to me were: 'Je suis très jaloux de ton mari. Adieu, tendre Tonia.' ('I am very jealous of your husband. Adieu, gentle Tonia.')

Donald continued to spend a lot of time with a new group of friends but I was rarely asked to join them. The frosty atmosphere between them and me was palpable. One afternoon as I arrived home late from rehearsals in London Louis met me in the driveway. He looked irritable and I wondered if he was going to complain about our new house. Julia and Louis did not share my love for the new place. Their rooms were very small and we were hoping for planning permission to enlarge them.

'Mrs Campbell, may I speak with you?' This was his usual opening.

'What is it, Louis?' I asked.

'Mr Campbell called to say that he's bringing six people home to dinner. The shops are closed and we're stuck for food.'

Oh dear, I thought, *not that group of county snobs again.* But turning to Louis I said reassuringly, 'Don't worry, we'll manage. Have you got any eggs?'

'Yes, madam, plenty of those,' he said.

'All right,' I answered, 'that's the problem solved. Eggs and bacon it is!'

'Not very chic, is it, madam?' said Louis, somewhat nonplussed.

'Not chic, Louis, but good enough for the mood I'm in!'

There was very little to do in the way of preparation. I dressed to kill then waited until Donald arrived. Of course, he was accompanied by Vi Aitken and her entourage. He sauntered in, all smiles, and kissed me.

'Hello, darling, I believe you know everyone.'

'Yes,' I said, wearing a false smile, 'I do. Hello everyone, do come in.' I was going to add 'and make yourselves at home' but they had already done so.

I stayed until the drinks were served then went to pick up my coat and the small overnight case I had already packed. I returned to the living room where my appearance caused an abrupt silence.

'Please don't let me disturb you,' I said apologetically, 'I just wanted to say goodnight to you all. Not knowing you were coming I accepted a dinner invitation up in town. Oh, and by the way Donald, I hope eggs and bacon will be fine. You see, the shops were closed when you called. Well, have fun. Goodbye.'

And with that I left the perplexed group. As I backed my car out of the garage, Donald came walking out to me.

'Tonia, wait a moment, my dear!' he shouted. I stopped the car and asked him if anything was wrong.

'I should say so!' he blurted. 'Where do you think you're going? We have guests.'

'Correction. *You* have guests,' I reminded him. Then, forgetting all the English reserve I had ever learned, I added, 'Donald, I've always left you your freedom and I've tried not to question you because I know that's what you want, but I'll be blowed if I'm going to entertain that phoney crowd.'

'What phoney crowd?' he exclaimed.

'The phoney crowd in there,' I said, wagging my finger at the house. 'Anyway, I must go, I'm late already.'

Donald looked puzzled. Lowering his voice he quietly asked me where I was going.

'Ask no questions and you'll be told no lies,' I said defiantly and drove off. I cried all the way to London and slept at a Kensington hotel. It was a nightmare. The next morning I rang Donald and told him I was coming home and that I wanted a long talk. He answered with a weary voice but agreed.

When I arrived home I noticed a car parked in our driveway and realised Donald had a visitor. I was putting my car in the garage some

50 yards away from the house when I saw Louis running towards me. Taking my overnight case he told me that Lady Aitken was having coffee with Donald. At once my mood changed to one of bad temper. I had looked forward to a day alone with Donald.

Recently, Vi Aitken had become a more than frequent visitor. As I entered the living room Donald embraced me warmly and Vi gave me a very friendly hello. I was offered a coffee but refused, saying I was tired from the drive and wanted to freshen up. When I returned Vi had gone. Relieved, I said, 'Oh good, she's gone.'

Donald smiled. 'Of course darling, you didn't exactly make her welcome.' His manner wasn't angry, just matter of fact. Walking over to the mantelpiece he reached for his tobacco and began to fill his pipe.

'You don't like Vi much, do you?' Donald's tone remained quite friendly so I decided to do the same and laughed provocatively.

'The only thing I like about Vi Aitken is her husband Max!'

Donald joined in my laughter and the rest of the day was quite pleasant. Nevertheless, I'd had quite enough of the Vi Aitken visits. I didn't know whether there was an affair going on between her and Donald, and they certainly weren't intimate when I was around. Although I wanted to believe there was nothing between them I knew Donald too well not to realise that this liaison, whatever form it took, was not healthy. I decided to do something about it.

During one of my recent shows, Mel had brought an American record producer to see me. His name was Jerry Shifrin and he told me I could make it in the States with a good gimmick. So far I hadn't given this any serious thought because of Donald's plans for the coming record attempt, but the following morning I broached the subject by telling Donald that I'd like to go to New York to continue my career. I had a recording offer, I told him, and had earned enough to stay there for a while.

'When did you decide this?' he asked with a look of surprise.

'Last night, Donald. Look, don't be angry with me but I'm sick of this thing between you and Vi Aitken. I've always accepted girls chasing you but now it seems the chase is constant and mutual. You're free to do it but I don't want to stay here and watch it in our home. I think you're infatuated and that's when I take a bow.'

He didn't answer for quite a while and I remained silent. I'd said what I had to say. Finally he spoke.

'First, if you go to New York, by hook or by crook I'll pay for it, but I've one question to ask: what will it take for you not to go?'

My answer was direct. 'Stop seeing Vi.'

He laughed. 'Easier said than done. I told her last night I might join her in the South of France. She has a place there, you know.'

'I bet I wasn't invited,' I said cattily.

'Well, considering your obvious dislike for her, are you surprised?' he answered.

More seriously, I asked him why he didn't go somewhere else with someone else, instead of joining Vi: 'She might then realise you choose your own trips.' It couldn't be with me because that would seem like the fulfilment of duty. Donald was amused by my proposal and we made plans for him to go to the Italian island of Capri with Wendy Mitchell. She was a lovely young woman whom we often engaged as a secretary when Rosie was on holiday. The plan was that Donald would endeavour to work on his book while he was there.

In no time at all the Capri trip appeared in the gossip columns as well as a full description of the mysterious young woman. Donald was supposed to stay for three weeks but after ten days he called asking if he could come home. He said I'd been right all the time. Innocently I asked what he meant.

'Well, Bobo,' he began, in contrite mood, 'it was an infatuation as you pointed out, but it wasn't love and I'd like to point that out.' Donald returned two days later and harmony was restored. Prior's Ford became my home at last.

The following week a present arrived at our home to celebrate my return to show business. Donald had given me a very sleek, pale blue E-Type Jaguar, so now my songs and I were floating on cloud nine. If only there hadn't been another record attempt on the horizon.

My opening night at The Pigalle, a London supperclub, was a triumph. Donald made it a glittering evening and brought along a whole bunch of people to see me. He appeared much more nervous than I was and told the press that he found *Bluebird* cockpits much easier. 'This,' he said, 'was murder!' His comments made headlines in the *Daily Express*.

The show went well and when I closed with a song called 'He Touched Me', which I dedicated to Donald, the crowd stood and cheered. Later, Vera Freedman told me that she'd looked more at Donald than at me.

'You should never again doubt his love,' she told me. 'My God, it was showing all over.'

I knew it was. He fussed around me like a new bridegroom. When the show was over the champagne flowed and my dressing room looked like a florist's shop. From Donald I received my favourite, birds of paradise. Mel and Jill stayed with me while Donald was held back, hosting his thirty guests.

'I must say, for a man who does such important things he certainly hasn't lost interest in others,' observed Jill.

'Interest!' laughed Mel. 'Seems like sheer fanaticism to me! Tonia, he was so proud of you.'

'I know,' I said, almost embarrassed.

Mel added, 'I do have one sad thought. I'm afraid Tonia's fee for the week won't cover Donald's expenses for tonight!'

There was a knock on the door and in came Donald with the press and camp followers, including Rocky Marciano, the famous boxer. Compliments and flattery followed. Eventually Donald came and stood next to me with his arm around my shoulders, leaving no doubt as to whom I belonged. When the press asked him how he felt about me working he laughed.

'Well, old boy, someone in the family has to keep me in the manner to which I've become accustomed!' Donald had suggested I should take over our London flat for the month so that I didn't have to drive back and forth to Prior's Ford in the dark when I was tired. Then quietly, he whispered in my ear.

'Do you think that I may take the star home and maybe if she isn't too tired, I might have the pleasure of . . .'

I whispered back. 'Only if you promise you won't tell your wife.'

'That,' and he spoke a little louder now, 'is a definite promise, but only if you don't tell your husband.' Then softly he added, 'Now enough of this joking. Let's go home and perform together. I promise you a great duet!'

And once again Donald and Tonia entered a lovely phase in their relationship.

We now heard that Gina had become engaged to the German head waiter at the hotel near Coniston where she was working. Donald decided at once that we should go to visit her and I agreed.

We arrived in Windermere after a short visit to Coniston to see Connie Morrison, proprietress of the Sun Hotel, and her son Robbie. Gina came to visit us at the Buckleys' house where we were staying. During the evening it was arranged between father and daughter that Donald would visit Gina the next morning to meet her fiancé. He went quite early while I enjoyed breakfast with Betty Buckley. When Donald eventually returned we both asked for his opinion.

'Well,' he said, 'I don't mind that he's a head waiter and I don't mind that he's German – but a German head waiter? Oh dear, oh dear!' He said it with humour and it made us laugh.

'Did he click his heels when you were introduced?' I teased. Donald laughed now.

'No, not quite, but hey, knowing my little minx she'll get bored with him soon enough.'

Gina broke off the engagement a year later, but sadly Donald was never to know this.

Before the end of the summer we decided to take a trip to the French Riviera that we loved so much. Earlier that year Donald had acquired a 74-foot yacht called *The Earl David*. It was a bit tatty and needed a lot of money to be spent on it, but once the work was done it would easily double its value. Bill and Betty Coley were with us and we worked on the boat all day and every day. At night we dined out. On one such evening we went to a lovely restaurant up in the hills called Chez Joseph, where an accordion player and a guitarist serenaded the diners. It was at the time that the 'Zorba' dance was in fashion. With dinner nearly over, the music changed tempo and launched into a popular tune Zorba style. The entire crowd were clapping hands to the rhythm of the music when suddenly Donald cleared our table and shouted, 'Come on, Bobo, give us a demonstration, I dare you!'

I told him I was a singer and not a dancer, and that Aunty Betty, as we called her, wouldn't approve. But I got an 'Oh yes I do!' from Betty, so with that I climbed on to the table and performed an improvised dance, more amusing than professional, to the delight of the customers. When the music stopped and we were having coffee, a gentleman stopped at our table on his way out of the restaurant.

'We enjoyed your dance immensely,' he said. 'It was the hit of the evening!' I looked up and stared with horror into the face of the magnificent entertainer Danny Kaye.

'Oh Mr Kaye,' I said with huge embarrassment. 'If I'd known you were here I would never have done it.'

He laughed. 'Not only did I enjoy it,' he said, 'but so did my friend.' I looked at the friend who had now joined him; he was none other than the world-famous ballet dancer Rudolf Nureyev. I could take no more and crawled under the table!

The following day we lunched with Aristotle Onassis to discuss Donald's idea for a marina and to talk about building a small pleasure boat we had called *Jet-Star*. The idea was to create a vessel with an inboard motor – much safer for waterskiers and swimmers who were often cut by propellers. When I first met Onassis I was amazed at how his charm turned him into someone quite handsome. Like Donald, he was serious about this new venture and when Donald suggested adding a French-style bistro with music, which I could manage, he agreed wholeheartedly. I was beaming from ear to ear.

Chapter 16

FINANCIAL STRUGGLES

utumn was in the air, but no date had yet been fixed for the record attempt at Coniston. When we arrived back in London the press met us at the airport and Donald's words suddenly shattered the beautiful world in which I'd been living.

'Yes, old boy,' he said to a reporter, 'we're leaving for Coniston next week to start preparations.'

'Are you accompanying him, Mrs Campbell?' the reporter asked, but Donald replied for me.

'That will depend on Miss Bern's engagements. She'll be talking to her manager Mel Collins today, but I hope she'll be able to be there.'

Then the reporter smiled and bowled Donald a leg spinner. 'There's a rumour that your marriage is on the rocks. Is that true, Donald?'

Donald laughed and skilfully blocked the ball. 'Certainly old boy, it's on the rock of Gibraltar. She and Mr Whoppit are my mascots, you know.'

He was full of confidence and smiling; I was plunged into misery. Later on in the car he noticed my silence and told me to stop worrying, saying it would 'come right directly', as Elliot would have put it. I smiled at him, but I wondered if it really would be all right again.

Mel had kept most of October and November free of engagements for me, but from 8 December onwards we were heavily booked until close to the New Year. To my delight I was asked to do a royal charity show for the Not Forgotten (Army pensioners) at Buckingham Palace. This pleased

Donald enormously. He said by then the record attempt would be over and we could make a night of it.

We left for the Lake District in different cars because we would need them both. We'd rented a lovely cottage in Coniston that belonged to Connie Robinson, proprietress of the Sun Hotel. Connie had witnessed most of Donald's record attempts and had known him through good times and bad. Remembering my earlier visits to the Lake District, I knew the locals considered me to be 'a bit of a madam', as they put it, and except for Donald's friends Norman and Betty Buckley I had no fans there.

I left Prior's Ford one week ahead of Donald to get the cottage ready. Louis and Julia, Donald's dog Whoppit and Coco, my newly acquired poodle, would follow on. I stopped over in Manchester to spend the night and to see Craig who was doing a season at one of the clubs there. His show was terrific. Later, in my hotel we drank a bottle of champagne with some of his friends and Craig asked me how I felt about Coniston. I decided to be truthful and told him I hated the whole thing and that I truly wished Donald wouldn't go through with it.

'I nearly hope for bad weather,' I told him.

'Come on, Tonge,' said Craig, using the nickname that Lorrea had coined for me, 'don't be like that. The whole of England is rooting for him.'

'Some are,' I answered. 'Monty Berman gave a thousand pounds in one go and just because I told him at a cocktail party that no one seemed to support Donald. The very next day he sent the cheque for a new engine. Donald was terribly touched by this act of generosity. After all, Monty Berman is a theatrical costumier and has very little to do with the world of sport. But I suppose he shares this love of British prestige. Anyway,' I said, 'let's have some more bubbly and change the subject.'

Craig's friends left, but we continued talking into the early hours of the morning. When we finally said goodnight, Craig looked me straight in the eye.

'Tonge, I'll be there if you need me,' he said with sincerity. 'You know that, don't you?'

I knew what he meant. 'Thanks, Craig. Yes, I know.'

The next day I drove to Coniston and went straight to the Sun Hotel where I met Connie. She gave me a surprisingly warm welcome and asked if I'd like some tea and scones. Her son, a tall youngster, hugged me and made me feel very welcome too. After tea, the three of us went to the cottage. Donald had been absolutely right; it was lovely and had two double rooms and one single. The double beds were small compared with our eight-footer at home, so I decided to move the single bed into the room with the double so we could spend more comfortable nights.

I spent the following day in domestic mood, reorganising the cottage and going shopping to stock the larders and fridge. Louis and Julia arrived two days later and completed the work. The dogs felt happy at once in their new home and by the time Donald arrived in his Ferrari all was ready. He was very pleased.

Bedtime came and I hadn't yet moved the beds, so I suggested I should sleep in the single room but Donald strongly refused. Later, he held me tightly and for no apparent reason said, 'Goodnight my love, and don't worry. I'll take care.' In the warm darkness of our cottage bedroom I smiled contentedly to myself. Right there with his arms around me I felt safe.

The days passed slowly and Coniston Water became my dreary companion. This time I made no special effort to be friendly to the townspeople, although strangely enough they seemed a much friendlier bunch than before. Donald was always busy, if not with *Bluebird* then with *Jet-Star*. Almost every day the team would end up at the bar of the Sun Hotel with a drink to warm them up after the cold day beside the lake. Mel had called several times and had warned me that it would all be happening in December, so I thought I'd take the opportunity of learning some new material. I made arrangements to hire the town hall where occasionally, on a rather badly tuned piano, I learnt my new songs.

We'd been in Coniston for four weeks and the *Bluebird* was not behaving well. The new engine was lighter than the old one, which meant that the weight distribution was now wrong. At least, this is what Donald thought and he decided to prove his point. He got hold of several small sacks of cement and attached them securely to the *Bluebird*. When he made the next run along the lake it was obvious from the perfect behaviour of the boat that the Skipper had been right.

Phone calls were made to the Norris brothers that evening and Ken Norris soon called back with a solution. The extra weight could be added by fabricating some special sections to fit into the *Bluebird*. Donald told Ken how pressed they were for time and after some negotiation he was told the new sections would be ready for collection in one week. As nothing could be done at Coniston, Donald decided we should go south and spend the week at Prior's Ford. It would be nice in the house without any staff, he said, and winked. 'All alone, just you and me!'

Next day we drove to London and he was partly right. I was alone in the house, while Donald went to visit his friend Ralph Loosemore in Brighton. He was only meant to stay for one day, but they got very excited about *Jet-Star* and a possible marina in Brighton and I received daily phone calls with commentary on the search for a suitable site. When Donald finally returned at the end of the week he'd collected the new pieces for *Bluebird* from the Norris brothers at Burgess Hill and was in great spirits. The Campbell enthusiasm was sparkling as he told me the news over tea.

'After the record attempt is over we could have this marina in Brighton and really work on *Jet-Star*, get it to perfection. The Norris Brothers would build it and then with some good publicity and demonstrations we'd have a good business going, and it would be fun as well. How would you like to live in Brighton?' Donald didn't wait for my answer, but continued. 'I saw a great property for a possible marina. Well, what do you say, Bobo?'

'It would be terrific, Donald,' I said with genuine enthusiasm. 'I'd love it. I've always felt you should get into the boat business.'

'Yes, you're probably right. The only snag again is money. It costs a lot to get a boat business going and the return from it is slow and very often small.'

'Well, we can sell the house to start it,' I chipped in quickly, 'and for the rest we must just think positive. Onassis will be a big help, I'm sure.'

He smiled, cheerful again. 'That's right, Bobo, it might just work. Now, what mischief have you been up to this week?'

I poured another cup of tea and began to tell him. 'Well, for a start I had a sing-song with myself on my birthday.' Although this was meant as a joke, as soon as I saw his face I regretted saying it.

'Bobo!' he exclaimed. 'Oh, Bobo! Of course, 8 November. What a forgetful bastard I am. Why didn't you go to London, or call me and come down to Brighton?'

'Come on darling,' I laughed, 'it's not a major drama, it's only a birthday. Anyway you had my car, and I hate trains as you know. What's more, it's about time I forgot my birthdays.'

But Donald had got up and called back over his shoulder as he left the room, 'I'll be back in a tick.' He came back within the hour carrying a pink box. The only shop still open had been a toyshop. Inside the box was a lovely little pink toy dog and attached to his collar was a cheque for £50. Donald's face was a picture of affection as he apologised and said it was all he could think of. I kissed him, hugged the little toy dog and told him he might be a rotten husband, but he was a beautiful man and I loved him.

Later that night, Donald said with a sigh, 'I wish I could get half as excited over *Bluebird* and the record attempt as I am over *Jet-Star* and the marina.' I quietly crossed my fingers.

On the way back to Coniston we stopped at Donald's favourite pub just outside Manchester for lunch. I had never been there, but the manager and waiters all welcomed Donald. I was dressed in navy blue bell-bottomed trousers and tight blue sweater with a white fur kangaroo jacket. We went to the bar and on the way I excused myself to go to the cloakroom. As I returned, Donald was laughing out loud.

'Bobo, the barman just told me you were the most attractive bird I've ever brought here. How do you feel about that, eh?'

'Attractive bird.' I smiled, looked at the barman and said, 'Thank you for the compliment, but you see he *bought* this one!' to which Donald laughingly added, 'And she even sings like a bird!'

He was in a good mood. While we were drinking our coffee he leant over, took my hand in his and asked if I was jealous of the others he'd taken there.

'Of course I am, Donald,' I answered. 'I'm a Scorpio, remember?'

At that he frowned. 'I'm sorry, I didn't think you were. You know I could never belong to anyone else. You and me, partners in crime, that's where it's at.'

The smile returned to his lips and lifting his cup as if it were a glass of champagne he said, 'Here's to Tonia Bern-Campbell. My own woman who still amuses me!'

'I'll drink to that!' I responded, making a mental note to tell Mel that my professional name in future would be just that – Tonia Bern-Campbell. It had never sounded better.

The new pieces were fitted to *Bluebird* and all was ready now except for the weather. We all sat around waiting, but Donald was madly working away with Leo on *Jet-Star*. He finally decided to do a dry run with *Bluebird* to make sure the new engine was still in good shape after the additions. The whole team was present and I was now officially a member. Donald had the *Bluebird* chained solidly to the ground and had taken all necessary precautions to prevent anyone from coming near her during the test. When I asked him why, he patiently explained that the immense thrust and power of the new engine might cause something to go flying.

'In the water she shoots forward, but chained down she may just spit with rage,' he said. 'Can't blame the old girl,' and he walked away to give the starting orders.

It was fantastic. First came that deep slow roar that grew by the second into a strong high-pitched whistling sound. Then earth and dust flew everywhere. I looked at Donald and even from several yards' distance I could see the excitement on his face. I was thankful when the screeching subsided to a low roar again, and then suddenly there was silence, beautiful silence.

Standing near me I noticed a beautiful girl. She looked like a model except for the animated face and the pale vivid eyes that were looking straight at Donald. As he approached she went to meet him, and with both hands grabbed him. She spoke to Donald in a lovely warm voice.

'Excuse me being so forward, Mr Campbell. I've travelled all the way from New York to meet you and wish you the very best.'

Donald, obviously flattered, murmured, 'I do hope you won't be disappointed Miss . . .'

'Miss Rowen, Leonora Rowen. My friends call me Mara.'

'May I call you that?'

'If I may call you Donald,' she answered cutely.

'It's a deal, but if you'll excuse me, I must get back to the *Bluebird*. She's very jealous you know.'

With that he left, forgetting that he'd been on his way to speak to me when the girl had stopped him. I looked at her and had to admit that it would be difficult for any man to resist that kind of beauty. Now noticing me she spoke.

'I think he's as handsome as he is courageous. I do hope my enthusiasm didn't shock him.'

I smiled at her and answered, 'I don't think so.' With my fur coat and cap, and the dark glasses covering my eyes, she had no reason to recognise me and had probably never seen a picture of me.

'Do you know him?' she asked.

'Yes, I know him.' Later on in the pub she found out who I was. She came over to me and asked me why I hadn't told her that I was Donald's wife.

'Would that make any difference?' I asked.

'None whatever,' she answered frankly.

'Then,' I said, lifting my glass, 'may the best woman win!'

A few days later she gave up the battle and, I guess, returned to the USA. When I asked Donald how he could resist that kind of beauty he laughed. 'That girl was after a dashing hero. Better not spoil her illusions, what?'

December arrived and still no record attempt. I had to decide whether to pick up my work or ask Mel to cancel the lot. I had one more week and decided to go ahead. My pianist Tommy Harrison was arriving the following day to rehearse. I had met Tommy years before my first encounter with Donald during several TV appearances in London. He was then in his forties and completely grey haired, had a great sense of humour and I loved him like a brother. He was a much better pianist than he ever gave himself credit for and could play any song in any key. As soon as he'd settled in at a bed and breakfast we went to the town hall to rehearse.

One of the press photographers had asked if he could take a few shots while I sang. Publicity being good for a singer, I said yes to his request, but during the intervals between songs the man started coming on to me with compliments in very poor taste. At first I was polite, but eventually I told him to get on with the job in hand as that was all I had given permission for. Before he could answer Donald entered the hall. He'd been standing outside the door to hear me sing and had overheard my remark. His voice was friendly but firm as he turned to address the photographer.

'I would listen to my wife if I were you, but don't be too vexed. She's often turned down better men.' Needless to say the photo session was cut short.

The very next day I had to make up my mind whether to cancel some of my engagements. I asked Donald for advice and reminded him I had the show for the Army pensioners at Buckingham Palace as well.

'Well,' he said, 'you can't cancel Buck House, that's for certain. How many other shows have you booked?'

I looked in my diary. 'I start on 8 December with BBC Television and then I'm practically booked through until New Year's Eve. But in January I'm free again.'

Donald thought for a while. 'I'll miss you, but you must do those jobs. If you start cancelling, Mel and the agents will not believe you're serious about your work. You've made a great return to showbiz. You must keep it going. I won't hurt you that way again.'

I interrupted him. 'You are still my first priority, Donald.'

'I know,' he answered. Then in a lighter tone he added, 'Tell Mel to keep January free. That's for you and me in Courchevel.'

This conversation took place on Thursday 1 December 1966, the day on which Donald chose my fate.

Outside, it had not stopped raining and blowing. I was packed to leave by train for London. Donald wanted to keep my E-Type in Coniston because he was not happy with his Ferrari and I would go to my gigs in Tommy's car. I was giving last-minute instructions to Louis and Julia when Donald came in from the lake, announcing that he would drive me to London himself and I needn't take the train.

'What about the record attempt?' I asked.

'The weather isn't likely to settle. There's nothing I can do here. Anyway, I need a break myself.'

We drove off at noon and the mood inside the E-Type was one of mutual light-heartedness. Donald put the radio on and occasionally joined in with the music.

'Either your singing has improved or I must be getting used to it,' I joked.

'Not improved,' he laughed. 'You're getting more tolerant of your old grumble box as the years go by,' and with that he gave me one of his winks.

I looked out of the window and hoped the rain and wind would last forever. As if he had guessed my thoughts Donald added, 'I do want to get that bloody record, Bobo, but by Jove I'm so glad to have a rest away from the tense atmosphere, and those bloody reporters just waiting for me to make a mess of it.'

'I think some of them wish you well, though,' I said.

'Very few. Still, it's their job.' He was silent for a moment then added, 'I wish I'd listened to you and never started this bloody record attempt.'

I didn't answer and Donald changed the subject. 'Let's have a slap-up dinner tonight then go to some nightclub. What do you say, woman?'

'Woman says, "Yes please!" Last time we had dinner was at the Wild Boar in Windermere with Norman and Betty Buckley. It seems ages ago, before Gina left to work in Switzerland *avec le fiancé*.'

'It wasn't so long ago,' Donald remarked. 'It just seems that way because the days drag by when you're sitting around waiting.'

And so our journey to London continued pleasantly. We arrived at Dolphin Square at around 6 o'clock. Our flat looked comfortable and inviting after the poor heating in the cottage at Coniston. We looked at each other and I knew at once what we were both thinking and hoping: that we would soon return to London for good. I went to the bedroom where Donald had put the suitcases and started to unpack. Donald shouted to me from the kitchen.

'How about a drink, darling? There's a small bottle of bubbly here.'

'I'd love it,' I shouted back. Just as Donald brought in the glasses of champagne the phone rang and he went to answer it. I picked up my glass and followed him, thinking it might be Mel. Instead it was Leo Villa. I overheard Donald's conversation.

'Hello, Unc! Nice to hear you. Is everything under control?' Then Leo spoke for quite a while. Finally Donald answered, 'No, no Unc, you were quite right to call me. I'll have a snack and drive back tonight. Maybe I'll have an hour's lie-down before starting. In any case, I'll see you in the morning.' He put down the phone and placed his hand over it. Donald had his back to me and I knew he couldn't turn and look at me. Both of us had been called back to reality.

I went to the bedroom, put down my champagne and sat on the bed. I felt like death. My hands were in my lap and I felt as if all the sadness and loneliness of the world were resting on my shoulders. Donald came in and sat down next to me. He put his arm around my shoulders.

'My poor girl. Are you really that miserable without me?' I nodded. 'I hoped show business would take a little place in your heart and make things easier for you.' I shook my head, not able to speak. 'Leo phoned because the wind has dropped and the weather report is hopeful for the morning. I can't let the boys down. You do understand if there is a chance of the right weather conditions I must be there.' He paused, sighed and continued. 'It would make me a good husband if I stayed, but I would not be much of a skipper. Don't make it difficult, Bobo.'

I looked up. 'Sorry, it's just that I'd looked forward to a few hours alone with you.'

'Now wait a minute, Bobo. I intended to get that record sooner.' Then he kissed me. It was a tender kiss filled with emotion and all at once we were making love. It was to be the last time we would be together and subconsciously I think we both knew it.

As I closed the apartment door behind him I suddenly felt the need to see him once more and I shouted his name out loud. I opened the front door just as he was going to knock. He looked like that small boy again.

'I wanted another kiss to keep me going, Bobo. Do you mind?'

I ran to his arms and he held me so tightly I could hardly breathe. Then suddenly he let go and walked purposefully to the lift. The door opened and he disappeared inside. I closed the door of the flat, leant against it and sobbed my heart out. Hours later when preparing miserably for bed, I removed the bedspread and there upon my pillow was an envelope. A few words were scribbled on it in Donald's hand: 'Would have loved to stay in your arms and kiss you to sleep but that will have to wait. In the meantime take this one, with my fondest love Bobo – Donald.' Inside the envelope was one of Donald's sleeping pills. I took it gratefully.

The next day the newsreels announced that Donald had made a record bid, but the wind had come up too strong for the return run. My loneliness had been in vain. So we talked on the phone. On 13 December I did the show for the disabled pensioners with Russ Conway, Joe Brown and Fenella Fielding among others. It was fun and we were royally treated.

I received a telegram from Donald with the words: 'Merde, for the show, and if they ask after me tell them I'm doing it for Great Britain – especially when misbehaving. D.C.'

I sent him the royal programme with my name on it. At the top I wrote in red lettering: 'Her Royal Highness did ask how you were and I told her you did it all for Great Britain.' I knew he would laugh and I wanted to imagine him doing just that. I closed the envelope and looked in the mirror. I wanted to be with him, especially now that he needed and wanted me. I desperately hoped he wouldn't find an understudy and I said to myself, 'You seem jealous Miss Bern?' Then I answered, 'You bet I am. Now tell me something new!'

The other shows were fun that December too and Mel Collins was terrific. We travelled everywhere by car, Mel and my pianist Tommy Harrison. I enjoyed it, but my feelings of guilt were rarely absent and when speaking to Donald I tried not to be too enthusiastic about my work. He had made many unsuccessful runs and was feeling low. In nearly every conversation he asked when my last show would be and the answer was always the same: 'I'm free in January.' New Year's Eve was my last booking.

His answer was always the same too: 'You will come back then, won't you?'

One day he asked me how the car was behaving. I was driving the Fiat 800 that was usually driven by Louis. I told him I had no problems with it.

'It will have to be serviced before you drive all the way here in it,' he said. 'Take it to the Fiat dealers in Epsom. They'll do it quickly for you.'

'Don't worry, darling. I'll see to the Fiat. How's my E-Type behaving?'

Donald answered in a lighter mood. 'Waiting for you, of course. And so am I. Suppose I'll see you in the New Year then?'

'Or before, if you break the record.'

'Yes,' he said. 'Yes dear. Well, ciao for now.'

I kept abreast of events on Coniston by phone and through listening to the news reports about *Bluebird* on the radio. Then suddenly it was Christmas Eve, our eighth wedding anniversary. When Donald and I spoke on the phone the previous evening he told me he had been worried about the press. Because he was in a troubled mood I hadn't reminded him of our anniversary. He missed me a lot, I could tell, but there was nothing I could do. We had both decided that this was the way it had to be. Now the Buckingham Palace show was over Donald seemed to change his mind about the importance of my other bookings, and somehow I agreed with him.

Vi Aitken was still a frequent visitor and although their friendship had cooled off somewhat since Capri – at least on Donald's side – he still had great respect for her and didn't quite know how to tell her not to come up to Coniston. She was most enthusiastic about Donald breaking the record before the London Boat Show opened, so that *Bluebird* could be displayed there in all its glory. This would be great, of course, but somehow he wished she would stick to communicating by telephone and not visiting him in person.

Years later I became good friends with Max Aitken and was often among the guests at his lovely home on the Isle of Wight. One weekend Max took me to a cocktail party and Vi, who had her own place across the bay, was present. She came over to greet her husband, making a point of ignoring me, to which Max said, 'You remember Tonia Campbell, don't you?' She pretended not to have heard him and walked away. Max made me smile as he said, 'Actually, you're the one who should be ignoring her.'

I laughed. 'Frankly, Max, I think your wife just paid me an enormous compliment.' I could not help thinking that it had been all right for Vi to flirt with my husband but now that he was gone, God forbid I should flirt with hers. I never did.

The West Coker Hotel near Yeovil in Somerset, where I was doing three Christmas shows, was warm and pleasant. They had given me a lovely room and everyone there was most considerate. It was 10 o'clock in the morning when I was woken by a knock on my door. I put on my dressing gown and went to open it. No one was there, but on the floor outside stood a huge basket of my favourite flowers, birds of paradise. Next to it on a tray I found a telegram. I took the flowers in and placed them on the desk, then picked up the telegram. It read: 'Happy anniversary darling. Here's to the next fifty. Fondest love, Donald.'

I smiled, as it was so obviously an answer to my own telegram: 'Happy eighth anniversary skipper. It only feels like fifty. Love Tonia.'

The next day, Christmas Day, I received yet another telegram from Donald: 'Fondest love darling for every success. Happy Christmas, but I miss you. Love D.C. P.S. Remember, I'm only doing it for England.'

I threw myself on the bed in desperation. I wanted him so badly that it hurt. I did the Christmas show and fortunately had a great audience. The next day at noon the hotel management invited me for drinks and Christmas lunch. I went down into the lounge next to the ballroom. The Christmas decorations were lovely and the blazing fire so welcoming. Champagne was being served and the conversation flowed freely. Suddenly one of the Italian waiters burst in shouting, 'He did it! He did it! Signor Campbell, he did it!'

I dropped my glass and yelled, 'The record?'

'Yes,' answered the excited waiter, '305mph! Fantastico, veramente fantastico!'

I didn't know what to do first, run to the phone or kiss everyone. All my terrible premonitions had been wrong after all. He had done it and all was well, thank God.

'Thank you, thank you,' was all I could think of saying. Somehow in all the chatter they got me to the phone and I called the Sun Hotel in Coniston as I was sure the team would be celebrating by now. It seemed like forever before they got Donald and I heard his cheerful voice.

'Hello, Donald Campbell here.'

I answered, equally cheerfully, 'It's me, darling! Did you really do it?'

'Ah, Bobo, how's my favourite girl?'

I became impatient with him and asked, 'Please, Donald, don't tease. Is it really over?'

'No, not over,' he answered gaily, 'but we did do an average of 302mph and the boat behaved beautifully. Unfortunately the timekeepers had gone home for Christmas. Some of the team have also gone home. There was only

Leo and a couple of press boys, bachelors, who got it all going, and Norman Buckley timed it.' He went on, 'Shows you what one can do with a small bunch of men, as long as they're enthusiastic. Just five men and a boat, and we did the job of twenty. Of course it can't be official because we have to have it officially timed. The great thing about it is that we're now pretty certain of success. All we need is one more calm morning and it's in the bag. There have been quite a few good mornings. The thing is to do the first run just before sun-up, because the wind seems to come up with the sun.'

During this conversation my spirits sank at a rate of knots, but I said as cheerfully as I could, 'Congratulations anyway, Skipper. That was a great effort.'

After I hung up I went to my room because I was no longer in a party mood. I could not face the crowds and questions.

New Year's Eve 1966 and my last show at Harvey's Restaurant in Bristol was finally over. Because of the festive season, Mel was not with me. I had decided to return to London during the night but I'd not told Donald because he hated the thought of me driving on icy roads in the dark. We'd spoken twice that day. The first call was depressing because of the dreadful weather and gloomy atmosphere in Coniston. Anticlimax had followed their success of Christmas Day. Everyone seemed to want to go home now and even our good-tempered Louis and Julia were longing for Prior's Ford.

Because of his depressed mood, Donald had called again just before midnight. He sounded in a better frame of mind, or at least pretended to be.

'How did you like Bristol?' he asked

'Very much. Ted and Sheila Leather sent me a lovely bouquet of roses. [Our friend Ted Leather was then the MP for Bath.] I had tea with them in the afternoon. Ted admires you very much, you know. The people here and the management are very nice and terribly keen you should make it. Everyone is on your side, darling.'

'That's nice to know,' he said. 'Do give Ted and Sheila my very best. I only wish more members of parliament were as genuine as Ted. He's a great character. One hell of a sense of humour. Are you going to see them again?'

'No,' I said. 'I'm leaving for London first thing tomorrow. The sooner I get the car serviced, the sooner I'll be with you.'

'That, darling, will be wonderful. And by the way, with all the waiting around and long evenings I've started to write again as you wanted me to. I've got quite a manuscript for you to read when you get here. You'll be very pleased. I haven't exactly wasted my time.'

'That's great, Donald. Is it a continuation of the one you wrote in Palm Springs?'

'No, it's a completely new one. You'll see it soon enough. Anyway Vixen, have a very happy New Year. I miss you.'

'I miss you, too. Happy New Year, Skipper!' I said. Although the call was supposed to cheer me up, it actually depressed me. The show had gone well for a New Year's Eve when everyone is usually drunk and beyond caring. I had a quick glass of champagne and was given two bottles to take home because I could not stay to celebrate. My drive to London was fast because there was no traffic on the roads and I sighed with relief when I entered our flat in Dolphin Square.

I looked at the time. It was 5.30 a.m. Donald would now just be getting ready to go to the lake, so I decided to ring him. He answered the phone himself.

'May 1967 bring you everything!' I wished him cheerfully.

'Bobo? What the hell are you doing up at this time of night . . . or morning?'

When I told him I'd driven back to London he was angry but on hearing my reason about getting the car collected for servicing he calmed down, especially as Epsom Garage had promised to start work on it on the first day of the New Year, which in 1967 was a Sunday. We finished our conversation, promising to speak again later that day.

I'd been promised the Fiat back on the evening of 2 January but it transpired that, because of some extra work on the brakes, it wouldn't be back until midday on the 3rd. Donald had been fed up about this but there was very little we could do. We both realised the garage were doing their utmost and brakes had to work perfectly. The car was safely back with me at 12 noon on Tuesday the 3rd. I called Donald and told him I was all packed and ready to go. 'If you start the trip now it means you'll hit the difficult part of the road in the dark,' he said, 'and with your sense of direction that worries me Bobo.'

I laughed. 'I know my sense of direction is not my greatest asset but I'll just have to watch it, Skipper!'

'I don't like it, Bobo. The roads up here are very icy. I'd rather you waited and started the trip in the morning. I could call you when I wake up, and though it will still be dark when you start you'd hit the tricky part of the drive in daylight.'

I was disappointed. 'I wanted to be with you tonight. It seems ages since I've seen you.'

'I know, darling, and I've missed you more than I can say. Remember the song, "You never miss the water till the well runs dry"? Well, this well is very dry without you!'

'I believe you, and I didn't really want to do those shows. I hope you know that.'

'Oh I know that, darling,' he said, 'but I wanted you to do it. It makes me feel good that you have something going for you.' He continued in better humour. 'Still, better to be safe than sorry. You start the trip tomorrow morning when I wake you up. And be very careful because I want you here in good condition. You know a woman is like a car; if she isn't used regularly, she gets rusty.'

'Well, the car's been thoroughly serviced, but I must be very rusty by now.'

'Don't worry,' he laughed, then added, 'when you get here I'll give you the servicing of your life!'

I decided to write some letters and spend a quiet evening so I'd be well rested to start the trip in the morning. It was 9 o'clock and I was watching TV when the phone rang. It was Vera. We chatted about mundane matters then she asked casually, 'How are things up in Coniston?'

'Still waiting for the right conditions, I'm afraid.'

'Do you still have your horrid premonition?' she asked.

'Yes, I have, but maybe it's just because of my dislike for Coniston and all the setbacks weatherwise.'

'What would you do, Tonia, if things did go wrong?'

'I don't know, Vera, but I have thought of it. I think my own life would stop if he went. Somehow I sleep, eat and breathe Donald, whether away from him or not, whether in show business or not.'

'So, showbiz didn't really help then?' asked Vera.

'It helped, but only superficially. Deep down, all I want is to be with him. But I also know that Donald needs to feel free. It's good for him to know that I have another interest apart from him.'

'I'm glad you took my advice,' said Vera. 'You stick to it now! Although I bet you'll give it up again if he wants you to.'

I laughed. 'You'll lose your bet, my friend! This time part of my life will remain in showbiz. It has to for all our sakes.'

These words were spoken lightly, but sadly my entire future life would only ever be showbiz.

Chapter 17

THE CRASH – 4 JANUARY 1967

I returned to my TV viewing but couldn't concentrate any more. I was in bed by 10.30 and must have been asleep soon after. The next thing I knew was the shrill of the phone. Drowsily, I picked it up and said a feeble ''Allo?'

It was Donald's voice at the other end. 'Hello darling, had a good sleep?'

'Lovely,' I said, stifling a yawn. 'What time is it?'

'4.15 a.m.' I sat up in bed and having collected my thoughts I asked him about his plans.

'Well, darling, just keep your little fingers crossed. The lake's like a mirror so we'll have a go as soon as daylight breaks.'

'Shall I start the trip now?' I asked.

'No, love, hold on a while. The whole thing may be over in a couple of hours and as soon as it is, I'm driving to London and so is *Bluebird*, in time for the Boat Show. Wouldn't that be nice?'

'Yes, Donald, but please don't get impatient. That kind of talk is too pushy for my liking. Please be careful.'

'Hey there old girl, don't you worry. I know the boat and I know the dangers, and nothing will make me forget them. We've still got a lot of living to do, and speaking of that, you be careful yourself! When I was playing cards last night I drew the Queen of Spades and that means the chopper. I immediately thought of you and little Gina. In any case, I'd prefer you not to drive today. Just pack a suitcase. We'll go to Courchevel or Jamaica after the 7th. I must go now, Poppet. Try to get some more sleep. Ciao for now.'

The phone clicked as Donald hung up and although I was still tired I couldn't go back to sleep. I made some tea and read the paper to kill time, but couldn't concentrate. I kept thinking of Vi Aitken's pressure. All the exciting boat talk had months ago reawakened Donald's desire to make this latest attempt, a decision he had come to regret of late.

In a nervous mood I started tidying the flat and was almost finished when the phone rang again. I picked it up to hear Donald at the other end.

'Hello love!' His voice came over the line through lots of background crackle. 'I'm at the lakeside and all is ready for the first run. I really think it's in the bag. Stay close to the phone 'cos as soon as the return run is over Andrew Brown has orders to ring you from the caravan. That's where I'm calling you from now. I want you to be the first to hear it so you can start packing for Courchevel.'

'Donald, please be careful. I'll keep my fingers very crossed.' I didn't dare say any more.

'It'll be all right, old girl. The conditions are fine and little Whoppit is taking your place as my mascot. He'll do a double job!' he said cheerfully.

'I do wish I was there,' I said, holding back my emotion.

'So do I, Bobo, so do I. This is the first one I've done without you since we were married, but it can't be helped. We'll soon be together again, must go now, so pucker up!'

I thought he was hanging up and quickly sent a good luck kiss. 'Merde, Skipper!'

He was still there. 'Thanks, Bobo.' Then he seemed to hesitate and after a pause added, 'God bless you darling and take good care.'

We hung up but I was puzzled. Why the last words? Why should I take care when he was the one who was going into the cockpit?

Approximately one hour later I received the phone call from Andrew Brown that I will never be able to forget. Andrew was usually a cheerful team member, but this morning he didn't sound himself.

'Hello, Tonia, this is Andrew. Are you alone?'

'Why?' I asked, thinking this was an odd thing to say. 'Tell me Andrew, how did it go?'

'Tonia,' this time his voice seemed to shake, 'you'd better sit down. There's been an accident.'

'Accident?' I said, my heart tearing up through my chest. 'Andrew, it's not serious. Please tell me it's not serious. Donald is all right isn't he?' I was nearly yelling this down the phone.

Andrew, his voice trembling, said, 'I'm sorry Tonia, it's very serious. We haven't found Donald yet. The boat has crashed.'

I screamed. 'No, no, no! Not my Donald, please find him Andrew, please find my Donald!'

'We're doing all we can, Tonia. Please ring a friend. You shouldn't be alone. I must hang up now. I must go and help.'

The phone clicked. I was in a state of complete hysteria but I thought of ringing Mel. Having heard the news on the radio, Jill told me he was already on his way. I flew into his arms when he arrived, sobbing.

'Mel, I wasn't there. It was my fault. I wasn't there!'

Mel helped me to some brandy and told me he had accepted an offer of help from the *Daily Mirror* to fly me out to the lake. He would come with me.

'Yes,' I said. 'Yes,' with new hope in my voice, 'they will have found him by now. He'll only be hurt and I can nurse him again.'

I was rattling on like a maniac when Mel shook me gently by the shoulders and said, 'Tonia, Donald is gone. It's going to hurt, Ton, an awful lot.'

I stared at Mel then slowly shook my head and cried, 'No Mel, no, not gone.'

Donald had tried too hard to take *Bluebird* to the Boat Show. When we reached Coniston they still hadn't found him. The photographers and reporters were cruelly doing their job and I, like a zombie, tried desperately to be dignified and still make my big man proud of me. I sat beside the lake for two days in case they found him.

The boat was broken in half, lying at the bottom of the lake and contrary to the press reports it had not disintegrated. The Royal Navy was conducting the underwater search with patriotic fervour. Donald seemed to have been their hero, too.

The photographers clung to me and the reporters constantly pestered me for comment – anything that would give them a sensational headline or a picture that showed me on the verge of cracking up. But I wasn't going to give it to them. They even recorded Andrew Brown's call to me and replayed my pain-filled voice shrieking over the radio, 'Not my man, not my Donald.' I never believed that the British press could stoop so low.

But beautiful things happened too. I was asked to give my permission to haul up the *Bluebird* boat as Donald might possibly be underneath it. By then I was hoping Donald would never be found so I refused to move the *Bluebird*. If Donald was buried underneath he would not wish for another grave. I remembered what he told me on Lake Dumbleyung: the skipper stays with his craft and the craft stays with the skipper. Bill Coley, his loyal friend, was with me on this and explained that unless Lloyd's Insurance could inspect the boat they might refuse to pay out the insurance Donald had arranged. I was amazed there was insurance, but I was determined to refuse permission to bring the boat up. I could not show a mutilated Donald to the world. I would rather lose the insurance.

The press photographers were furious and called me all sorts of names. They asked questions like, 'Are you afraid of the truth, Mrs Campbell?' or 'Maybe the truth is suicide and the proof is down there!' I didn't respond to any of them. No words could hurt me now, nothing could any more. I didn't think them worthy of an answer.

Bill called Lloyd's Insurance and the answer was loud and clear and truly British. Part of the insurance would be paid, although Donald had omitted to pay the recent premiums. Study of the *Bluebird* wreck was not necessary, they said, because belief in Donald Campbell was complete. I cried softly when I heard the news.

While the search was going on I stayed with Norman and Betty Buckley in their house, Cragwood. I knew I would never be able to repay their help and devotion. My old friend Wendy Kidd had flown out to be with me and Sir Norman Joseph, my dear friend from years back, had sent his chauffeured car to be at my disposal. Everyone was fighting to keep the press from upsetting me and everyone was frightened of my deadly, white face and red eyes.

The only press who seemed kind and human at this time were those from the *Daily Mirror*. They had many opportunities to photograph my breakdowns during the flight from London to Coniston, but Mel had asked them not to. He knew how desperate I was to walk tall and be worthy of

Donald's own pride and dignity. They purposely looked the other way whenever things got rough.

I knew that I was surrounded by friends, but nothing seemed to ease the pain. I didn't want to sleep because I was afraid of waking up and facing reality all over again. I was a complete mess. I knew it and I didn't care. I made one big effort when I called my father. Now, I just wanted to die and not feel this immense burden of guilt.

Why was I not with him?

After a few terrible days beside the lake I was finally persuaded by Bill and Norman to return to London, as there was now very little hope that Donald's body would be found. The search would continue for another week and I would be kept informed by phone. I agreed to leave but wanted to visit the bungalow where Donald had spent his last night. After some protest, I was allowed to do so. I went alone to the room where Donald had slept only a few days earlier, but I couldn't feel his presence. Everything was empty. My telegrams and Buckingham Palace programme were still standing on the chest. Next to it was a pile of typewritten papers – Donald's new manuscript. I gathered it up and left the room.

We passed the lake where Leo was waiting to say goodbye. Poor Leo looked grey and crumpled. He handed me a parcel with the words, 'I think you should have these.' I gave my thanks to the divers, the Royal Navy and all those who'd helped in the search. As the car drove away I looked at the parcel Leo had given me. It contained one battered helmet and one mascot called Whoppit, the only remains of Donald to be found in 1967.

Back at Dolphin Square I would not leave the phone, still afraid they would find something. I didn't eat or speak, I drank a lot of brandy and unlike some people who can't cry, I simply couldn't stop. My eyes were constantly tearful and if I had spoken about Donald I would have sobbed uncontrollably. Wendy, who was staying with me, became an emotional mess and had to be relieved first by Cherry Barker, then Vera Freedman. Sir Norman Joseph was sending me daily food parcels from the Cumberland Hotel, and everyone was worried about my health and state of mind. Craig Douglas had spent several nights just holding me while I sobbed. All these wonderful friends were helplessly watching me slip away into an abyss of despair. Strangely enough the thought of suicide never entered my mind. I was simply hoping that not eating, and drinking a lot of brandy, would eventually put me to sleep.

The sympathy notes came from all over the world – sent by everyone from Prince Philip to a humble bricklayer, hundreds and hundreds of messages. Rosie wrote replies and I signed them. When I was finally told that the search was being called off because it was costing around £5,000 a week, I got in touch with the holiday king Billy Butlin. He immediately offered to pay for one more week, but the Royal Navy commander in charge of the search operation came to see me and explained that Donald would never be found. They had searched everywhere and nothing more could be done. I accepted the mystery and called Billy Butlin. He told me the £5,000 would be used to endow a memorial seat at London University that Victor Mishcon and Sir Max Aitken, together with other friends of Donald, had already started to perpetuate his name.

Now letters began to arrive from all kinds of cranks telling me where I could find Donald's body. The cruelty of some of them didn't help ease my constant fear that Donald might have been trapped in the cockpit while still alive. My friends stood by me at this time, but many others who had never meant that much to me also came forward. The feelings between Janique's husband Bunny Lewis and me had never been very harmonious, but he was the first person to offer financial help. He explained to me the difficulties of English death duties and the lengthy legal process, and he wanted me to know that he had the money if I needed it. Hélène Cordet, cabaret singer and discotheque proprietress, offered me the running of her exclusive discotheque in Mayfair. My friends were anxious that I should accept this offer. I didn't know why Miss Cordet wanted to help me because I had only met her once. Cherry Barker gave me the answer when she told me a woman like Hélène Cordet would know and understand me. The offer was to remind me that I had to go on, and the sooner the better.

'She's lovely to worry about me, Cherry, but I just can't do it. I just can't.' Cherry didn't answer.

Within two weeks I had found jobs for the whole Bluebird team, mostly through the Norris brothers. I did all this by phone. I also called a meeting with the brothers to discuss Donald's last venture, the little pleasure boat *Jet-Star*. I couldn't continue this by myself but I still didn't want all Donald's work to be wasted. We held the meeting at the flat and a decision was taken. *Jet-Star* would be put into production by a new company called Bluebird Marine and of course it would be backed and directed by the Norris brothers. They would own most shares. The other shares were to be divided between Leo Villa and myself. I was happier when this was settled and I knew *Jet-Star* would not sink without trace.

Gina, in Switzerland, was still engaged. She had called several times. I didn't want to upset her young life more than necessary. She was shattered by her father's crash, and seeing me would only have made things worse. I told her not to worry and that I was well. She seemed to relax and we left it at that. Nevertheless, one week later she came back to England and gave me all the help, affection and care possible. She couldn't have done more had she been my own flesh and blood.

Chapter 18

THE MEMORIAL SERVICE

Then came the call from Downing Street. Donald had been given the honour of the Queen's Commendation for Brave Conduct. My first impulse was to tell them to stuff it: if they couldn't honour him in life, then why bother now? Instead I said a quiet 'Thank you, he would have liked that.' Then I added, 'Donald is no more, but Leo Villa is. Donald always felt Leo deserved some recognition as Chief Engineer of so many speed records for Great Britain.' There was a short silence at the other end of the phone, then the Prime Minister's secretary came back on the line. 'Could you send us all the details, Mrs Campbell, such as Mr Villa's date of birth, and the dates of all the record attempts. I will then submit them to the committee. That's all I can promise you.' There ended our conversation. I did as I was asked and later that year Leo was made an OBE.

The news of Donald's honour revived the curiosity of the press and back they came in their droves. Cherry tried to talk with them on the phone but we finally cancelled all calls. The Dolphin Square telephone operators were helpful, but although one can stop all press calls one can't stop the press themselves. Within fifteen minutes they were ringing and knocking at my door and we eventually had to call the police. An officer arrived almost immediately and although they stopped knocking and ringing, the reporters settled themselves in the corridor until the small hours of the morning. I rang Victor Mishcon the next day to ask his advice.

'Tonia, my dear, you have been hiding behind a locked door and you are becoming a curiosity. They will only give you peace if you give one newspaper a full feature. Only then will you stop being news,' he explained.

'How can I give them a feature on my own feelings? They're mine and very personal, and anyway I'm still far too emotional at this moment.'

'If you want to be left alone you must give them their feast,' he answered. He eventually convinced me and I chose the *Daily Sketch*, which was the only paper to have backed Donald's final attempt. The interview was arranged by Victor, with an agreement that it would appear in one issue only and exactly as I had told it, with each page initialled by me. For this they were to pay me £1,000.

They didn't keep their word. Not only did the article appear on two consecutive days, but they also took the liberty of changing the tense of the second part. Influenced by the bills I was receiving from the record attempt, I decided to hit the *Daily Sketch* for damages. They agreed to pay but I still regretted not having given the interview to the *Daily Mirror* whose reporters had been so good to me on the day of the crash.

A few days after this I received a visit from a feature reporter called Rex North, who had been a friend of Donald's. He told me I was being offered £24,000 by a Sunday newspaper for the Donald Campbell story and that Donald had once told him that I kept a diary. If that was the case, then sight of the diary would be highly appreciated. I explained that the diary in question was actually just some loose pages in which I occasionally wrote about my life with Donald, and that I was not willing to share them with anybody. I could remember Donald reading some of them. He always complimented and encouraged me, but I was not yet ready to publicise them and I was in no mood to write my memoirs. At that time I didn't know my financial position and was petrified of comments in the press such as 'Donald Campbell's widow, destitute'. Even so, I didn't accept the offer. I resolved that the Donald Campbell story should be properly written at a later date when I was no longer emotional or in need of money. My Belgian optimism must have been at the back of my mind.

David Benson, sports reporter of the *Daily Express*, had been at Coniston during the last few weeks of Donald's record attempt and soon became one of his closest supporters and friends. In later years the *Mail on Sunday* implied there had been a liaison between David and me, which is an absolute fiction. If there had been an attraction, which there wasn't, his friendship and loyalty to Donald would have prevented such an affair. Of course, they waited until after David Benson had died to print this. Still, they say that yesterday's newspaper is tomorrow's fish and chip wrapping. In this case I felt sorry for the fish.

I couldn't help but tell David how disgusted I was with the press. He tried to calm me.

'After all, they have a job to do,' he explained.

'They're not doing it too well, are they? They printed "*Bluebird* disintegrated" and that was false for a start. They also said that Donald, after drawing the Queen of Spades in a card game, had remarked that it meant someone in his family was going to get the chop, and he hoped it wouldn't be him. As if Donald would say such a thing. Then they said I had a heart attack while in Coniston, simply because Betty Buckley wanted me to take one of her sleeping pills and called the doctor to check with him first.'

David defended the integrity of the press. 'Isn't some of that your own fault for not wanting to speak to them?'

'We saw what happened with the *Sketch* when I did speak to them,' I answered testily.

David smiled. 'Don't be angry, Tonia. I came to see you because I wanted to see for myself if the rumours were true.'

'What rumours?'

'That you're not eating, not taking any fresh air, thinking too much and just sitting here.'

The tears were back in my eyes. 'I'm sorry, David, but right now it's all I can manage,' I answered feebly.

'Tonia, you must get out! Donald believed in your strength; you were very much his woman and you know that. The one and only.'

'Yes, I was his woman,' I said sadly, 'but not his one and only.'

'Oh well,' said David, slightly wrong-footed by my revelation, 'boys will be boys and the others were just passing ships.'

'Wrong again, David,' I said. 'You didn't know him at all if you think that. Donald was never the animal type. In different ways he loved every woman he was ever close to. They were like champagne to him and, frankly, with his power and fame he wasn't half as wild as he could have been.' I stopped. David didn't speak. 'Don't worry, David. Believe me, I'd like to give one of Donald's trophies to every woman who gave him joy. If his life had to be so short, my one consolation now is that it was a full and exciting one. He always did what he wanted to do and the only people I despise are those who hurt him.'

'I believe that,' said David, 'and I can see why the others were temporary but you stayed on.'

Now I smiled when answering. 'I stayed! He was exciting and alive and, yes, infuriating, but during the eight years I lived with him he gave me more happiness and pleasure than I thought possible.'

When we finally said goodbye, I closed the front door and leant against it with my forehead. More pleasure, I thought, but now there's only pain. I had to hear the echo of Donald's last words repeatedly on radio, television and in my nightmares.

'I can't see much and water's very bad indeed . . . I can't get over the top . . . I'm getting a lot of bloody row in here . . . I can't see anything . . . I've got the bows up . . . I'm gone . . . oh . . .'

It was now 2 February 1967, one month since doomsday, and I hadn't left the flat since my return from Coniston. My friends were no longer staying overnight but occasionally visited to check that I was all right. Whenever Craig Douglas was not singing his way around the clubs he would stay with me. Louis and Julia were still living in Prior's Ford. I had given them until the end of February to look for another position, and although Louis was looking around they both still worked hard to get the house empty of all personal effects so I could eventually let it to pay the mortgage. Together with Betty Coley they had disposed of Donald's clothes.

Bill Coley had been chosen by Donald as an executor of his estate, together with Victor Mishcon, Leo Villa and me. Donald had added that he also wanted me as legal guardian for Gina. To quote him, he said this was in Gina's best interests, but it was one wish of Donald's that didn't come true. Gina and I drifted apart.

During those miserable days my anxiety about dishonourable comments in the press was beginning to lessen. I realised that to live I would have to borrow from my father. I also sold my beloved E-Type along with some of my personal jewellery. I knew this would keep me going for some months. My only expense in those days was my constant companion – brandy.

I received the most beautiful letters from Maurice Chevalier who had been part of my family ever since I was six. He advised me to start work again and offered me his help. In one of his letters he wrote: 'You were married to a great man and he was proud of you, now you must safeguard that pride. Stop crying for him and start singing for him. I'll be applauding you and so will the whole world.' The letter continued, telling me loud and clear to stop hiding in a bottle. Although I was touched I still had no desire to think of the future. All I could think of was the past – Donald, his dreams and his final disappearance. What if Donald's remains were to wash up on Coniston's shore? This was my constant nightmare.

The people of the Lake District had started a collection to build a memorial to Donald. I wished they hadn't because to me it would seem like a grave. But a close friend of ours, Grevelle Howard, advised me to agree to the idea. He said I had to let people honour Donald. Grevelle had been tremendous and written beautiful letters to all who had helped during this tragedy – from the Royal Navy commander to the Dolphin Square telephone operators.

Slowly I began to realise that I had to pull myself together, but then I received another shock which pulled me back down again. I was starting on my first glass of the day, listening to the midday news, and Julia had come to do some cleaning. The newsreader's voice said that a body had been found in Coniston Water. He went on to say that the authorities thought it might be the remains of Donald. Having heard this, Julia came into the room shaking her head in disbelief.

'Yes, Julia, will it ever stop? I wish I were dead.'

'Madam, that's a terrible thing to wish for. What would Mr Campbell say?' She didn't have time to continue because the phone started ringing and once again the press were on the warpath. I didn't answer the phone and in no time at all they were hammering at my door. It remained firmly closed and they shouted their questions from the corridor.

Did I think it was Donald's corpse?

Would I go and identify it?

Did I know how many pieces of his body they had found?

And so it went on. Fortunately, Grevelle had heard the newsflash and arrived within thirty minutes. With relief I heard his lovely warm voice taking control of the reporters.

'Please, gentlemen, do give the poor girl some peace. There is no further need to harass her. The remains found in Coniston have been identified as belonging to a man who drowned there several months ago. Nothing to do with Donald Campbell!'

To my amazement the reporters and photographers left and Grevelle came in.

'Is it true, Grevelle? It's not Donald?'

'It is quite true, dear. Identification is official.'

He looked at me and frowned. I had lost a stone in one month, my eyes were blurred with tears and brandy and surrounded by dark circles. I was in no way the woman he had once described to Donald as 'one hell of a healthy beautifully shaped female'.

I lowered my gaze and sat down in my armchair. Then leaning my head on my hands I pleaded with Grevelle. 'Please don't look at me like that. I'm so terribly empty. I had so much and now I have nothing.'

'You're so wrong, my girl. You have more than you deserve,' he answered with conviction.

'What do you mean?' I asked, looking up through my fatigue-rimmed eyes.

Having taken off his coat he sat down opposite me and began to talk. 'There are many widows in this world, Tonia, who are left all alone. But you have the whole nation by your side. Naturally there is a nasty side to this like the crank letters and press hammerings, but that's only because Donald was famous and loved by his people. I think you should start honouring him yourself by eating instead of drinking, by making plans for your future and by starting to think about a memorial service for him.'

'Memorial service?' I asked. 'Why?'

'Because England wants a chance to give him honour and recognition.'

'A bit late, isn't it?'

'Donald wouldn't think so.'

'Donald's gone!' I said, sighing. 'And if there was a spiritual life by now he would have given me a sign. I would have felt something. You know he believed in spiritualism. If there was anything in it he would be the first to help me or guide me, but I feel nothing. I search for him at night. I call his name but there is no nearness, only a cold feeling. He has completely deserted me. Maybe he didn't love me after all?'

Grevelle's voice was stern when he answered. 'Tonia, my dear, you disappoint me terribly. Donald and I believed you were beautiful and strong and would be able to cope. You're letting the side down.'

I knew he was right and excusing myself I apologised. 'I'm sorry, Grevelle, but he made all these plans. He said we still had so much living to do and now there's just me and I suppose I was not ready for the shock.'

'Well, my dear, promise me you'll at least think about what I said regarding a memorial service.'

He left just as Craig arrived. I was happy to see Craig because he was the only one who never made any demands on me. He didn't even try to stop me from drinking. I immediately asked his opinion about the memorial service.

'You'll have to do something,' he said. 'Mr Howard is right. The people of England will want to honour Donald.'

'People? Who cares? I don't need a grave or a memorial to remember him. It would be an admission that he's really dead.'

Craig poured himself a drink and looked at me.

'He'll never be dead, Tonge. You and me and all those who have ever been in close contact with Donald will remember him and keep him alive. I myself love and admire him as much today as I ever have. He knew that I loved you, but he respected and trusted that love. Tonge, we who have been privileged to enjoy his electrifying personality should be big enough to allow others to come and give him a last salute.'

I looked at this young man, a man of depth who showed the true class of an Englishman. 'Craig, you are beautiful music!'

He looked embarrassed, then changed the subject. 'Didn't you say Maurice Chevalier wrote you a long letter?'

'Yes, it's in my desk, top drawer.'

He went to the desk and opened it. Out came the letter but as it was in French he asked me to translate it out loud. I did as he asked and somehow Chevalier's words gained a new meaning and as I read I knew I had to pull myself together.

YES, I'LL SMILE AGAIN
FOR DONALD

After I'd read the letter to Craig, I became slightly dreamy. He stayed until Julia had done all the housework, then at around 5 o'clock he offered to drive her to Victoria station to catch her train. Before leaving he asked me if I'd be all right. I nodded and said I had a lot of thinking to do. After they'd left I made some strong coffee, poured away the rest of the brandy and called Grevelle Howard to tell him that I agreed to a memorial service.

Grevelle and Victor went to work. It was to be held at St Martin-in-the-Fields in London's Trafalgar Square. To this day I don't know who paid for it. I have a big suspicion that Victor Mishcon and Grevelle Howard picked up the tab, although neither has ever admitted this to me.

No grave, no funeral, just a beautiful memorial service – something Donald would have chosen. He was always so depressed when visiting his father's grave. He once told me that Leo Villa believed in cremation. I had said I agreed with that solution and Donald in a lighter mood had answered, 'Well, Bobo, if I get shot in the back by a jealous husband – and hopefully after 'le moment critique' – have me cremated and throw my ashes over the hills. But make sure I've got the wind behind me!'

My beloved Donald – I can still hear his laughter and his jokes. I can see the pride in his eyes when speaking of his country and its people, and the glow of pleasure that came upon him when he watched Gina's magnificent show-jumping. I melt when I remember his kindness to animals and I hurt when I think of the small boy in him still trying to please his father, and how I adored that naughty grin when he winked at me. I never felt more at home than when I was in his arms and, oh yes, I admired his determination to bring glory to Britain. He never thought that he would become a legendary hero and there are many other things he never knew, but he did know that I loved him, of that I am sure and proud – even though he left me behind.

And now it was over. It was strange how during a short car drive from St Martin-in-the-Fields to Dolphin Square I could see my whole life rushing by. I'd heard people say this usually happens in moments of danger, but I was no longer in danger and I knew this now. I had found my aim. I would keep his name up there and carry it with pride, because after all I was a very lucky woman. I had nothing to cry about. Quite the contrary. In those precious eight years I had received more and felt more than most women feel in a lifetime. The girl from Knokke-le-Zoute had shared the life of the most exciting, fun-loving, daring speed king and had received a beautiful love, a sensational outlook on life. No, I had no right to cry any more or to hide in a brandy bottle.

The car stopped at the entrance of Keyes House, Dolphin Square. Louis was waiting for my return and opened the door.

'I'll take you upstairs, Mrs Campbell.'

'No thank you, Louis,' I smiled. 'I'm going for a walk. Tell Julia I'll be very hungry when I come back.'

His face lit up. 'That's very good news, madam. I'll tell Julia right away!'

The Embankment was so near and I walked towards it. I looked down at the River Thames rolling along before me and all at once I stopped, thinking there was someone beside me. I turned around and although I saw no one I continued to feel this acute presence. Then, all at once I knew that Donald had come back. I stopped and put both hands on the iron railings that bordered the riverbank, closed my eyes and enjoyed the ecstasy of the moment.

With this feeling of nearness I could live again, I could do all the things my friends wanted of me. With Donald guiding me I would be all right.

I could almost hear him saying, 'That's the spirit, my girl. Get in there and fight and, Bobo, keep smiling for me!' I opened my eyes and I did smile, not just with my lips but with my whole being.

Less than two years later I sang at Carnegie Hall in New York. I sang for Donald – and I still do.

THE FUNERAL

C an a funeral ever be called beautiful? If so, then Donald Campbell's was. For thirty-four years Donald and *Bluebird* lay in peace at the bottom of Coniston Water. I, and many British people, hoped they would remain there. They didn't. After he was found and recovered I personally wished for a very private cremation ceremony and for his ashes to be scattered on the lake. Donald's daughter Gina was adamant: she wanted a funeral that everyone would remember. I didn't know whether she was right or whether I was, but I did know that Donald, now in the spirit world, wouldn't care whether his remains were in the lake or in the ground. All he would care about was that those he loved were at peace with each other. I gave my blessing to his daughter who took on all the responsibility for the event. Gina went to great trouble and expense. The ceremony at St Andrew's Church, Coniston, was touching and dignified.

On 12 September 2001, hundreds, young and old, stood in the pouring rain to see the coffin pass by on its open carriage. Later there was a reception and yes, it was nice to see so many old friends. To many it was a great event worthy of a great man. The new generation was there too – young boys, some in wheelchairs. It made me realise Gina may have been right and once again I faced the fact that Donald did not belong to me. In 2001 he gained a new following who very much wanted to be at his funeral to honour him and his achievements. His daughter and I held hands and that was great too. But in spite of all this I could not subdue all the agony I felt. It's impossible to describe the pain, the sense of loss that hit me just as it had thirty-four years earlier. It hurt. It hurt an awful lot.

I will never forget standing next to Gina at the graveside watching the coffin being lowered. I cringed when I heard the sound of earth being thrown down upon it. Eventually I turned and noticed Lou Norris (of Norris brothers, designers of *Bluebird*) watching me. There was so much compassion in his eyes that it gave me the strength to remain calm and not to run for shelter out of the rain, out of the misery.

I had ordered yellow and blue flowers which arrived in the form of a wreath. With a shock I remembered that Donald didn't like wreaths, but then he liked funerals and graves even less. The only reason I was there was for Gina, Donald's only child. She can now visit her father's grave. I know she will do this as often as she can, and talk to him there. I hear that's what people do. I loved my own father very much but to this day I have never visited his grave although I talk to him often. I talk to Donald too. I can do that right here in my villa by Lake Gregory where nothing is gruesome and the memories are beautiful.